BECAUSE INTERNET

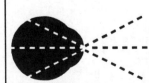

This Large Print Book carries the
Seal of Approval of N.A.V.H.

BECAUSE INTERNET

UNDERSTANDING THE NEW RULES OF LANGUAGE

GRETCHEN McCULLOCH

THORNDIKE PRESS
A part of Gale, a Cengage Company

Copyright © 2019 by Gretchen McCulloch.

Thorndike Press, a part of Gale, a Cengage Company.

Thorndike Press® Large Print Nonfiction.

The text of this Large Print edition is unabridged.

Other aspects of the book may vary from the original edition.

Set in 16 pt. Plantin.

LIBRARY OF CONGRESS CIP DATA ON FILE.
CATALOGUING IN PUBLICATION FOR THIS BOOK
IS AVAILABLE FROM THE LIBRARY OF CONGRESS

ISBN-13: 978-1-4328-7307-3 (hardcover alk. paper)

Published in 2020 by arrangement with Riverhead Books, an imprint of Penguin Publishing Group, a division of Penguin Random House, LLC

Printed in Mexico
Print Number: 01   Print Year: 2020

To the people who make internet language.
You are the territory, this is merely a map.

CONTENTS

CONTENTS

CHAPTER 1:
INFORMAL WRITING

Imagine learning to talk from recordings rather than people. If you learned how to have a conversation from movies, you might think that people regularly hang up the phone without saying goodbye and no one ever interrupts anyone else. If you learned to think out loud from news programs, you might believe that no one ever "ums" or waves their hands while searching for an idea, and that people swear rarely and never before ten p.m. If you learned to tell stories from audiobooks, you might think that nothing much new had happened with the English language in the past couple hundred years. If you only ever talked when you were public speaking, you'd expect that talking always involves anxious butterflies in your stomach and hours of preparation before facing an audience.

Of course, you did none of these things. You learned to speak English domestically, conversationally, and informally long before you could sit through an entire news report or deliver a speech. You might never be wholly comfortable with public speaking, but of course you can complain about the weather to a friend. Sure, they both involve moving the same body parts, but they're hardly the same task at all.

And yet this is exactly how we all learned to read and write.

When we think about writing, we think about books and newspapers, magazines and academic articles — and the school essays in which we tried (and mostly failed) to emulate them. We learned to read a formal kind of language which pretends that the past century or two of English hasn't really happened, which presents words and books to us cut off from the living people who created them, which downplays the alchemy of two people tossing thoughts back and forth in perfect balance. We learned to write with a paralyzing fear of red ink and were taught to worry about form before we even got to consider what we wanted to say, as if good writing were a thing of mechanistic rule-picking rather than of grace and verve. Naturally, we're as intimidated by the blank page as we are by public speaking.

That is, we were until very recently. The

internet and mobile devices have brought us an explosion of writing by normal people. Writing has become a vital, conversational part of our ordinary lives. In the year 800, Charlemagne managed to get himself crowned as Holy Roman Emperor without being able to sign his own name. Sure, he had scribes to write up his charters, but illiterately running an empire? Today it's hard to imagine even organizing a birthday party without writing. One type of writing hasn't replaced the other: the "Happy Birthday" text message hasn't killed the diplomatic treaty. What's changed is that writing now comes in both formal and informal versions, just as speaking has for so long.

We write all the time now, and most of what we're writing is informal: our texts and chats and posts are quick, they're conversational, they're untouched by the hands of an editor. If you define a "published" writer as someone who's had something they've written reach over a hundred people, practically everyone who uses social media qualifies — just make an announcement post about a new job or a new baby. It's not that edited, formal writing has disappeared online (there are plenty of business and news sites that still write much like we did in print), it's that it's now surrounded by a vast sea of unedited, unfiltered words that once might have only been spoken.

I'm a linguist, and I live on the internet. When I see the boundless creativity of internet language flowing past me online, I can't help but want to understand how it works. Why did emoji become so popular so quickly? What's the deal with how people of different ages punctuate their emails and text messages so differently? Why does the language in memes often look so wonderfully strange?

I'm not alone in wondering about these things. When I started writing about internet linguistics online, I quickly ran into more follow-up questions from readers than just another article could answer. I went to conferences and dived into research papers and ran a few of my own queries. I realized that in many cases there were answers, just not from an internet native speaker, not all together in one place, not in a form that's fun to read regardless of how much you already know about linguistics. So I wrote this book.

Linguists are interested in the subconscious patterns behind the language we produce every day. But traditionally, linguistics doesn't analyze writing very much, unless it's a question about the history of a language and written records are all we have. The problem is that writing is too premeditated, too likely to have gotten filtered through multiple hands, too hard to attribute to a single person's linguistic intuitions at a specific moment. But internet writing is different. It's unedited, it's unfiltered, and it's so beautifully mundane. And, as I've continued rediscovering with every chapter of this book, when we analyze the hidden patterns of written internet language, we can understand more about our language in general.

Internet writing is also useful because speech is an absolute nightmare to analyze. First of all, speech vanishes as soon as it's said, and if you're just taking notes, you might be misremembering things or not noticing everything. So you want to record the audio, but that's your second problem: now you need to physically transport people into a recording lab or travel around with a recorder. Once you've got recordings, you've got a third problem: processing. It takes about an hour of skilled human work per minute of audio recording to get speech into a transcript usable for linguistic analysis: to transcribe the overall gist, to go back and add detailed phonetic information, to extract parts and analyze their acoustic frequencies or sentence structure. Many a beleaguered linguistics grad student has spent years of their life doing precisely this, in search of the answers to just a handful of specific questions. It's hard to do at a massive scale. All the while, there's a fourth challenge: your participants probably won't talk to an academic interviewer the same way they'd talk to a friend. Want to analyze a signed language instead? Instead of analyzing audio in just one dimension, now you're facing video in two. Want to skip a step and use preexisting recordings? Good luck: most of that is news, acting, and other formal varieties.

There were difficulties in studying informal writing before the internet, too. It existed, in forms like letters, diaries, and postcards, but by the time a collection of papers is donated to an archive, they've generally been moldering in boxes for decades, and of course they also need to be processed in order to be analyzed. Deciphering old-timey handwriting on fragile paper is only marginally easier than transcribing audio. Studies of Victorian letters and medieval manuscripts can tell us that a particular word is older than we thought, or provide evidence of changing pronunciations through idiosyncratic

14

spelling, but we don't want to limit our studies of present-day English to a fifty-year time delay, based solely on the highly biased sample of the kinds of famous people whose papers get donated to archives. But if we wanted more recent stuff, we'd again face the logistical challenges of getting people to write, for instance, sample postcards for our study and hoping that they're not too self-conscious about researchers reading their words.

Lucky for us, internet language is both easier to work with, since the text is already digital, and less likely to get distorted because someone's observing it, since much of it is already public as tweets and blogs and videos. (Although the would-be internet researcher must also consider the ethics of working with linguistic data that is functionally public but would embarrass or harm the people that made it if distributed out of context.) Even the logistics of distributing fun language surveys or asking people to donate archives of their private messages has gotten easier online. Internet linguistics isn't just a study of the latest cool memes (though we'll get to memes in a later chapter): it's a deeper look into day-to-day language than we've ever been able to see. It brings new insight to classic linguistic questions like, How do new words catch on? When did people start saying this? Where do people say that?

Now, I like me a good book. I've watched a few TED Talks in my time. I'm very aware of the hours of craftwork that go into making ideas flow gracefully through formal language, and there's much to be admired there. But there's already plenty of admiration for literature and oratory. As a linguist, what compels me are the parts of language that we don't even know we're so good at, the patterns that emerge spontaneously, when we aren't really thinking about them.

Even keysmash, that haphazard mashing of fingers against keyboard to signal a feeling so intense that you can't possibly type real words, has patterns. A typical keysmash might look like "asdljklgafdljk" or "asdfkfjas;dfI" — quite distinct from, say, a cat walking across the keyboard, which might look like "tfggggggggggggggggggggsx dzzzzzzzz."* Here's a few patterns we can observe in keysmash:

- Almost always begins with "a"
- Often begins with "asdf"

*With thanks to Eliza, the Very Good Cat of A.E. Prevost.

- Other common subsequent characters are g, h, j, k, l, and ;, but less often in that order, and often alternating or repeating within this second group
- Frequently occurring characters are the "home row" of keys that the fingers are on in rest position, suggesting that keysmashers are also touch typists
- If any characters appear beyond the middle row, top-row characters (qwe . . .) are more common than bottom-row characters (zxc . . .)
- Generally either all lowercase or all caps, and rarely contains numbers

Sure, a lot of these patterns relate to the fact that we're mashing on the home row of the QWERTY keyboard rather than using random-letter generators, but they're reinforced by our social expectations. I conducted an informal survey, asking if people retype their keysmash if it doesn't look, er, smashing enough. While there were a few keysmash purists, who posted whatever came out, I found that the majority of people will delete and remash if they don't like what it looks like, plus a significant minority who will adjust a few letters. I also heard from several people who use the Dvorak keyboard, where the home row begins with vowels rather than ASDF, who reported that they just don't bother keysmashing anymore at all because their layout makes it socially illegible. Keysmashing may be shifting, though: I've noticed a second kind, which looks more like "gbghvjfbfghchc" than "asa-fjlskfjlskf," from thumbs mashing against the middle of a smartphone keyboard.

It's not just that we make patterns. It's that even when we're not trying to make patterns, when we think we're just a billion monkeys mashing incoherently on a billion keyboards, we're social monkeys — we can't help but notice each other and respond to each other. Even when something looks incoherent to an outsider, even when it's intended as incoherent for an insider, we as humans are still practically incapable of doing things *without* patterns. My mission with this book is to map out what some of those patterns are, to examine why they fall into the patterns that they do, and to give you the tools to look at internet language and other cutting-edge linguistic innovation through the lens of a pattern-seeker.

As with any period of tremendous disruption, the explosion of informal writing is changing the way we communicate. The norms that we worked out for books and newspapers

18

don't work so well for texts and chats and posts. Imagine how weird you'd think ordinary conversation was if you'd only ever seen scripted TV monologues! We have a sense, more or less, of how informal speech works. We have a long history of doing it, and it's the primary thing that linguistics studies, much as literature and rhetoric study formal writing and formal speaking. But the combination of writing and informality has been neglected — and this quadrant is precisely where internet writing excels. How does it fit in among these known quantities?

	SPOKEN	WRITTEN
INFORMAL	conversations, talking to yourself 💬	texts, chat, social media, diaries, notes 📱
FORMAL	speeches, radio, television, acting 🎤	books, articles, static websites 📕

One way to think about informal writing is through the lens of efficiency. Across languages, short words tend to be more common words, which contribute a small amount of information to a sentence, while longer words occur less frequently and contribute more information. Think about the English words "of" and "rhinoceros." "Of" is clearly more common, and it's also much shorter

— a simple vowel + consonant sequence that can even be reduced into a single neutral vowel, as in "sorta" or "outta." "Rhinoceros" is longer and way more informative: if you hear "rhinoceros!" out of the blue, you can form a pretty solid hypothesis about what's going on, and if it's accidentally omitted ("I am fond of this _____"), many other words could take its place. Hearing "of!" out of the blue is pretty much meaning-less, and if it's accidentally omitted ("I am fond _____ this rhinoceros"), you can be almost certain that it was meant to be there. It would be a waste to use the short, versatile monosyllable "of" for the relatively uncom-mon concept of an odd-toed ungulate. Simi-larly, if we assigned the meaning of "of" to a sequence of sounds as long as "rhinoc-eros," it would be a clear drop in efficiency. In this chapter alone, the word "of" occurs over one hundred times, and making them all five times longer would be a lot rhinoc-eros sounds for a small amount rhinoceros meaning!

Frequency isn't completely static: the word "rhinoceros" entered English around the fourteenth century, but as the animal be-came more common in the lives of English speakers, we shortened it to "rhino" by 1884. "Rhino" splits the difference. It's not quite as short as "of," but then again, even a zookeeper still says "of" more often. Truly obscure animals, like the axolotl (a type of salamander) or the *Wunderpus photogenicus* (a type of octopus which, true to its name, is very photogenic), don't have nicknames in common use, although I expect to hear from the Association for Researchers of the Axolotl and the *Wunderpus Photogenicus* (ARAWP?) any day now informing me that they say them often enough that they've devised more efficient names for them.

Sometimes, as with "of" and "rhinoceros," efficiency in writing and speaking amounts to basically the same thing: more letters on the page equals more sounds in the mouth. Other times, they take different paths. In speech, we often make language more efficient by dropping unnecessary syllables or squishing sounds together, even if it's not writable. We truncate words without regard for spelling: you can say the first syllable of "usual" or "casual" and everyone knows what you mean, but do you write it "yooj"? "uzh"? "cazh"? "casj"? It's simply not clear, but speech proceeds merrily along anyway. An even more extreme example comes in how English speakers smooth out "I do not know." We've been saying it out loud for generations, long enough for it to have worn down to "I don't know," "I dunno," and even a simple triplet "uh-huh-uh" or "mm-hm-mm" to the low-high-low melody of "I dunno." "I dunno" is easier to articulate than "I do not know," but it's not really much shorter to write (even though we sometimes write it to evoke speech). The melodic triple hum is exceedingly easy to produce (you can even do it with a mouthful of sandwich) but not efficient at all in writing, requiring a full-on explanation. We also try to maintain a constant rate of information flow: to say predictable words more quickly and unpredictable words more slowly. One study showed that people say the word "mind" quite quickly in a sentence like "Mama, you've been on my mind," where it's very predictable thanks to a certain oft-covered Bob Dylan song, but they say it much slower in an unpredictable context, like "paid jobs degrade the mind," one of Aristotle's more obscure sayings. (Of course, if you're a big Aristotle fan who's never heard of Bob Dylan, you may find that the inverse is true for you.)

In writing, we often make language more efficient by selecting just a few important letters or squishing symbols together into a new shape, even if the resulting formations aren't pronounceable. The types of ideas that get acronyms or abbreviations have evolved along with what sorts of things people wanted to write efficiently. The Romans found it much easier to inscribe coins and statues with *SPQR* than the full *Senatus Populusque Romanus*. Medieval scribes smooshed common words together into new symbols such as & and %. When the Renaissance brought with it an increased interest in the classics and sciences, scholars abbreviated Latin phrases like *e.g.* ("for example") and *ibid.* ("in the same reference already cited"). But the true golden era of acronyms began surprisingly recently. The word "acronym" itself entered English only in 1940, and acronyms, especially the kind that are pronounced as a single word rather than a series of letters, began flourishing during World War II, when soldiers used acronyms like AWOL, snafu, WAAF, and radar.* After the war, acronyms just kept proliferating, especially for organizations, new discoveries, and other names: laser, NASA, NATO, AIDS, NAACP, codec, Eniac, UNESCO, UNICEF, OPEC, FIFA, NASDAQ, FDR, CD-ROM, MoMA, DNA, and so on. These

*Absent Without Official Leave, situation normal all fucked up, Women's Auxiliary Air Force, and RAdio Detection And Ranging.

forms are shorter in writing, but not necessarily more efficient in speech, even though we sometimes speak them aloud when we're talking about specialized topics: it takes longer to say "ampersand" or "WWF" than "and" or "World Wildlife Fund." Technical acronyms reflect writing as a formal domain, which aims to maximize efficiency on bureaucratic procedures and long-winded names.

The internet has acronym'd some technical terms as well, like url, jpeg, or html, but a lot of what we're writing is informal and conversational. A new kind of social acronym has come into use, based on common conversational phrases rather than technical jargon — less BAC (blood-alcohol content) and more btw (by the way), less OBE (Order of the British Empire) and more omg (oh my god), less LAX (the airport code for Los Angeles) and more lol (originally "laughing out loud," though now a more subtle meaning, which we'll get to in Chapter 3). I think it's disingenuous to follow formal tradition at the expense of regular usage in a book that's entirely about regular usage, so I've made the stylistic decision to write social, internet acronyms in all-lowercase, while often keeping technical acronyms in uppercase, because people on the internet primarily reserve LOL and OMG for when they're SHOUTING.

Internet acronyms are a perfect example of the intersection between writing and informality. Their form comes from the writing side: acronyms reduce the number of letters you type, although not necessarily the number of syllables you articulate. In other words, "I dunno" is efficient in speech, whereas "idk" is efficient in writing. Their function comes from the informal side: the phrases are personal expressions of our feelings and beliefs, like "I don't know," "what the fuck," "just so you know," "as far as I know," "in my opinion," "today I learned," and "that feeling when." With technical acronyms, the long version and the short version are invented at the same time, sometimes with an eye to how the initial letters of a phrase will fit together as an acronym. Social acronyms are instead made out of phrases that are already common: a sure sign of bad internet linguistics is EIAFUP (Elaborate Invented Acronyms for Uncommon Phrases). We're not pure efficiency maximizers, however; we also sometimes respell words when we want to make writing evoke speech, or speak acronyms when we want to make speech evoke writing. Efficiency simply points to where and why a particular abbreviation originated.

Another example of how the internet melds writing and informality is in how we use visuals. In casual speech, we don't generally converse in pitch-blackness, with our backs to each other, or with our hands tied behind our backs, a paper bag over our heads, and our voices in a robotic monotone. I mean, you could get a message across that way, but you'd be missing something. Often, we gesture: the next time you're in a public place, look around at groups of people and notice how you can tell who's talking by looking at who's gesturing. We use gesture and tone of voice to reinforce our message or add another layer of meaning to it: "Good job!" plus a thumbs up is sincere, while with rolled eyes it's sarcastic.

Formal speech uses fewer and more stylized gestures. Television reporters may point at a weather map or shuffle a few pieces of paper, but for the most part, their hands remain still and their faces remain in a narrow range between serious and cheerful — no waving, eye-rolling, sobbing, or uproarious laughter. Public speakers are often advised to cut down on their natural movements: a classic tip for improving your public speaking is to watch a video of your

26

performance so you can notice and reduce repetitive gestures. Both styles are often cropped just below the shoulder, by a camera or a lectern, so we can't see the speaker's hands even if they did move them. People have been prescribing formal gestures for a long time: the Roman orator Quintilian advised rhetoricians that acceptable gestures included pointing and gestures of admiration, wonder, rejection, certainty, pleading, and others which "naturally proceed from us simultaneously with our words," but that pantomime and similar attempts to act out one's actual words should be reserved for the theater rather than the law courts.

Writing is a technology. Speaking and signing require only our human bodies and the energy we infuse them with, and we've never met a society without one or both. But writing requires something external to the body: even if you write on your own arm with your own blood, you'll need to prick yourself to do so, thereby making the blood external. Writing systems, therefore, are greatly affected by the tools available to make them: it's easier to carve wood or stone in a straight line, but easier to swirl and loop with ink. The images that go along with our writing also reflect the available tools. Medieval illumination was on calfskin vellum with pigments made of ground beetles or stones; print drawings were cut into wood so the raised areas could be inked and pressed onto paper; cameras fixed a tiny pinhole of light onto a ribbon of film with silver compounds. In any circumstance, some colors and shapes were easier than others.

Formal writing is disembodied in the same way that formal speech is. Just like a news anchor is supposed to be a conduit for the news, not its maker, the images of formal writing represent the content, not the author. Sometimes formal images present information, like graphs and diagrams. Sometimes they create a record, like maps and portraits. Sometimes they're eye-catching and tell stories, like in stained glass and picture books.

What's cool about informal writing is that, once we had the technology to send any image anywhere, we used it to restore our bodies to our writing, to give a sense of who's talking and what mood we're in when we're saying things. Take emoji, those small images that enliven our digital messages. There are thousands of them, ranging from animals to foods to nature to common household and workplace objects. And yet the most commonly used sets of emoji are the faces and hands, like the smile, the face with tears of joy, the thumbs up, and the crossed fingers. We use emoji less to describe the world around us, and more to be fully ourselves in an online world.

We do the same with gifs. In theory, you can put any image in an animated eight-frame loop. (In the 1990s, people used grainy, animated "under construction" gifs, ornamented with hard hats and traffic cones, to apologize for portions of their homepages that were incomplete.) In practice, the gifs of the 2010s are reaction gifs: silent, looping animations of people, animals, or cartoon characters doing a specific, expressive gesture which you invoke as a representation of your own body under the circumstances, saying that right now you're laughing, or applauding, or looking around in bewilderment, just like the person in the gif is. Early visualizations of cyberspace thought we might want to manipulate three-dimensional figurines of ourselves in order to interact with each other in virtual space. But it turned out, what we really wanted was less about dressing up our avatars in fanciful digital clothing and more about conveying what we're thinking and feeling. We can recruit a wide range of tools, from acronyms to emoji to punctuation, in order to do so.

The first writing systems were deeply aware of their limitations. They wrote only words, a mere aid to the memory of the reader, who had to infuse them with life again on saying them. Gradually, over the centuries, we began adding punctuation and other typographical enhancements. Just as crucially, we began expecting more subtlety from the written text: we began to see writing as a thing that could represent verbatim speech and stream of consciousness, even if most of us were reading it rather than writing it. The internet was the final key in this process that had begun with medieval scribes and modernist poets — it made us all writers as well as readers. We no longer accept that writing must be lifeless, that it can only convey our tone of voice roughly and imprecisely, or that nuanced writing is the exclusive domain of professionals. We're creating new rules for typographical tone of voice. Not the kind of rules that are imposed from on high, but the kind of rules that emerge from the collective practice of a couple billion social monkeys — rules that enliven our social interactions.

Whatever else is changing for good or for bad in the world, the continued evolution of language is neither the solution to all our problems nor the cause of them. It simply is. You never truly step into the same English twice. When future historians look back on this era, they'll find our changes just as fascinating as we now find innovative words from Shakespeare or Latin or Norman French. So let's adopt the perspective of these future historians now, and explore the revolutionary period in linguistic history that we're living through from a place of excitement and curiosity.

If you're worried that this revolution is leaving you behind, or if you're so cutting-edge that it's hard to explain yourself to non-internet people, this book will help you bridge that gap. It will help you understand how we got here, why people get so passionate about a stray period or three, and how linguistic changes on the internet fit into the broader picture of the incredible capacity of human language. You'll never look at your quickly dashed-off text messages the same way again.

CHAPTER 2:
LANGUAGE AND SOCIETY

Why do you talk the way you do?

You've lived somewhere — perhaps many somewheres. Your friends or family have influenced you. You've probably even thought about how you like some linguistic features and want to avoid others. People have long been aware that these factors influence why different groups speak differently, but the systematic study of dialect began in the eighteenth and nineteenth centuries, as part of the same scientific movements that gave us the Linnaean catalogue of the living world and the periodic table of the elements. While some cataloguers set out with nets to study butterflies, or burned candles inside jars to distill gases, others pored over ancient scripts and compiled lists of verbs.

MAPS

But what kind of net can you use to capture living language? A German dialectologist named Georg Wenker thought he had an answer: he sent out a postal survey to schoolteachers across German-speaking Europe and asked them to translate forty sentences (such as "I will slap your ears with the cooking spoon, you monkey!") into the local vernacular. It was a wise enough idea: teachers would be guaranteed to be able to read and write, and even if Wenker didn't know the name of every single village teacher, surely the village post office in, say, Quedlinburg, could pass on his letter to the Quedlinburg village school. But in order to make it easy for the schoolteachers to respond, Wenker didn't provide them with any training in phonetic notation. This meant that if one teacher wrote "Affe" (monkey) and another teacher wrote "Afe" or "Aphe," it was anyone's guess whether they were trying to represent the same pronunciation.

A French linguist named Jules Gilliéron thought he had a better method. Rather than send out letters like Wenker, he'd send out a trained fieldworker to administer all the surveys. Back in Paris, Gilliéron could get a start on analyzing the results as they came in. The fieldworker he selected was a grocer named Edmond Edmont, who reportedly had a particularly astute ear (it's not clear whether this referred to the acuity of his hearing or his attention to phonetic detail, but either way, it got him the job). Gilliéron trained Edmont in phonetic notation and sent him off on a bicycle with a list of 1,500 questions, such as "What do you call a cup?" and "How do you say the number fifty?" Over the next four years Edmont cycled to 639 French villages, sending results back to Gilliéron periodically. In each village, he interviewed an older person who had lived in the region for their entire life, counting them as representative of the history of the area.

Both Wenker's and Gilliéron's dialect maps are meticulous, fascinating, and complicated, but if you know how to read them, you can trace the line between the villages in the north where French people around 1900 called Wednesday *mercredi* and those in the south where they called it *dimècres*.* Or you can read Wenker's hand-drawn map of Germany showing which regions pronounced "old" as *alt, al,* or *oll*.† If you studied French

*If you're wondering why *mercredi* won, well, the north is where Paris is. *Di* means "day," so either order is logical in principle, and indeed for *dimanche,* "Sunday," the *di*-first version won.
†If you think of English *ol'*, these latter two may not seem surprising.

or German in school, it's easy to think that they're each a single, unitary language, but that's just the formal version: the maps showcase how these languages are truly constellations of dialects, hundreds of varieties that differ slightly from village to village.

But these spectacular linguistic atlases are also limited. If Edmond Edmont, towards the end of his four-year odyssey, realized that different regions also had different words for *bicycle,* he either had to bike back through those same 639 French villages, or make a note of it and just hope that some future scholar would undertake a second linguistic Tour de France. Georg Wenker's project was almost too successful: he ended up with more than 44,000 completed surveys between 1876 and 1926, more than he could possibly analyze by hand. (His colleagues continued analyzing his results for decades after his death.)

As technology advanced, so did dialectology. In the 1960s, the *Dictionary of American Regional English* sent out fieldworkers in "Word Wagons" (green Dodge vans outfitted with a fold-out bed, an icebox, and a gas stovetop) to record locals in over a thousand communities on briefcase-sized reel-to-reel tape recorders. In the 1990s, the creators of *The Atlas of North American English* let their fingers do the biking and conducted telephone interviews with 762 random people, at least two from each major urban area. In 2002, the Harvard Dialect Survey produced a linguistic questionnaire that anyone could complete online: thanks to media coverage in *The New York Times, USA Today,* and many other outlets, over thirty thousand people did.

All of these studies have produced incredibly cool results: not only did they show that the rise of radio, television, and other mass media wasn't eradicating regional language variation, but they've also made many of their resources freely available online. You can go browse *The Atlas of North American English* yourself and see changing colors of dots midway through the United States where people switch from "pop" to "coke" to "soda," and then another line at the Canadian border where they switch back to "pop" again. On the *Dictionary of American Regional English* site, you can scroll through a "Word Wheel" of interesting vocabulary items, from "Adam's housecat" to "zydeco." The Harvard Dialect Survey results, downloadable in full, even found new life a decade later as the YouTube accent challenge, a viral video meme where thousands of people from around the world filmed themselves answering questions from the survey, and as the dataset at the base of "How Y'all, Youse and You Guys Talk," the massively popular *New York Times* dialect quiz that introduced many people to the idea of mapping out how you speak in 2013.

But if you've ever hung up on a telemarketer or fudged your answers to a "Which Disney Princess Are You" quiz, you know some of the potential problems with phone and internet surveys. On the phone, researchers could record audio, but they still had to have an individual conversation with each person they surveyed. While operating a Word Wagon or a linguistic phone bank is a fascinating job for the right type of language nerd (um, hi), such nerds still need to be paid for the massive amounts of time and labor they're putting into the interviews. Internet surveys are faster and cheaper to conduct at a huge scale, but people still don't always accurately report on their own language usage.

Running through all the surveys is a problem called the observer's paradox: when you sit someone down with a tape recorder or hand them a list of questions to check off, it tends to bring out the formal, standardized, job-interview style of language, which is the least interesting linguistically because it's already so well documented. But looking into less well-documented varieties requires researchers to seek answers that they may not know the questions for, and the people they're studying are sometimes unaware or self-conscious about some of the most interesting aspects of their speech, so they can't or won't talk about it explicitly.

It's not completely hopeless: linguists have devised several methods for getting at more natural-sounding speech. One is to ask open-ended questions ("Could you describe your family?" rather than "How do you pronounce 'aunt'?"). Another is to ask about an exciting or emotional event, to get people thinking about the content rather than the words (a popular, though perhaps rather morbid, question is "Can you tell me about a time you thought you might die?"). A third is to work with a community as an insider: many a linguist has analyzed the speech of their own children, grandparents, or extended family, or else worked with a local collaborator to conduct interviews. The Word Wagon linguists would even carry small notebooks, in case they overheard any interesting language at the grocery store, so that they'd remember to follow up on it when they got the tape recorder out.

But one particularly effective way of getting

at unselfconscious speech is on the internet. Not only can researchers look at countless examples of public, informal, unselfconscious language, from videos to blog posts, but in many cases, it's also searchable. No more hours of transcribing audio files, hoping for a few examples. Twitter is particularly valuable: even the most casual of searchers can look for a word or phrase and form an impression of how people are using it. They might notice that a lot of people who used "smol" in 2018 also appeared to be fans of anime or cute animals, or that "bae" was used primarily by African Americans until around 2014, when it started appearing in tweets by white people, only to get co-opted by brands shortly thereafter.

The presence of researchers on social sites is a still-evolving ethical domain. Regardless of who technically has access to their information, people tend to have a mental model of who they expect to read their posts, and feel that their trust is violated when someone outside that model does so. When the Library of Congress announced in 2010 that they'd be archiving every single tweet, Twitter users had to update their mental models for a previously ephemeral website. Many reacted by posting tongue-in-cheek instructions or commentary to future historians. Several people took advantage of the opportunity to make the august institution expand its holdings of choice four-letter words, while others asked, "What's up, posterity?" or noted, "Please index all my kitten pictures properly under 'kitteh' as well as 'kitten' now that you're saving my tweets." Not much came of it, in the end: the Library of Congress changed course in 2017, restricting their Twitter archive to tweets that met stricter criteria of newsworthiness. A less benign social media data controversy happened in 2018, when British political consulting firm Cambridge Analytica was discovered to have obtained personal data from millions of Facebook users in 2015 by convincing people to link a personality quiz with their Facebook account. The personal data derived from the quiz was then used to target voters and potentially sway elections. The Library of Congress and Cambridge Analytica represent two extremes, but less publicized researchers have continued mining for data on social media, restricted only by terms of service and their own senses of fair play.

In this book, I have for the most part restricted my citations to social media data in aggregate, not linked to individual users, or examples which are already cited and anonymized in research papers. But where I've needed to pull out individual examples, I've aimed for those in which the writers are already clearly having a metalinguistic discussion, like the tweets addressing the Library of Congress archivists. Quoting people's innocent chatter about their lunch or deeply personal heart-to-hearts felt to me uncomfortably like spying, but quoting comments about internet language in a book about internet language is, I hope, a way of entering into a conversation. After all, if you're going to address your tweets to posterity, perhaps you shouldn't be surprised when posterity addresses you back.

Twitter research is especially fruitful because about 1 to 2 percent of people who post on Twitter tag their tweets with their exact geographic coordinates. A reasonably competent data miner can therefore code up a county-level map of where Americans tweet "pop" versus "soda," where they switch from "y'all" to "you guys," or which states prefer which swear words — all in less time than it took Edmond Edmont to bike from Paris to Marseille. As a simple proof of concept, let's look at the work of the linguist Jacob Eisenstein, who found that geo-tagged tweets containing "hella" (as in "That movie was hella long") are most likely to occur in

Northern California, while those containing "yinz" (as in "I'll see yinz later") are clustered around Pittsburgh. Both of these findings are consistent with previous linguistic research done in the labor-intensive interview style. Other features he found on Twitter probably wouldn't have shown up in an interview: a later study by Eisenstein and colleagues found that the abbreviation "ikr" ("I know, right?") was especially popular in Detroit, the emoticon ^_^ (happy) was characteristic of Southern California, and the spelling "suttin" ("something") was popular in New York City.

Some of the linguistics research happening on Twitter wouldn't be possible at all without the internet. The linguist Jack Grieve researches constructions like "might could," "may can," and "might should" in the American South — things like "We might should close the window," where speakers of other dialects would say, "Maybe we should close the window." Grieve has pointed out that as recently as 1973, prominent linguists said that it would simply be impossible to research these constructions: they're vanishingly rare in edited text, and occur maybe once an hour, if you're lucky, in a spontaneous spoken interview. That's a heck of a lot of audio to transcribe for a tiny amount of data. But on Twitter, Grieve and his collaborators combed through nearly a billion geo-coded tweets and unearthed thousands of examples. Beyond just reinforcing the informal intuition that these constructions (known as double modals) exist, they've been able to make detailed county-level maps showing that they can actually be divided into two groups: some, like "might could" and "may can," map onto the Upper South, while others, like "might can" and "might would," are more common in the Lower South.

We may even be able to discover things about various regions that we hadn't realized before. For example, after "might could," Grieve turned his attention to swear words, finding that, while people in every state swear, their preferred swear words varied. Keeping it to the somewhat milder terms, people in the American South were especially fond of "hell," while people in the northern states preferred "asshole," the Midwest used a lot of "gosh," and the West Coast liked the Britishy "bollocks" and "bloody." The *Oxford English Dictionary* has also begun using Twitter as a source of data, especially for regional words that are less often printed in books and newspapers. The dictionary's quarterly update notes for

September 2017 gave the example of the word "mafted," a northeastern British term defined as "exhausted from heat, crowds, or exertion." The example quotations for "mafted" are a study in old-school and new-school lexicography: the oldest citation is from "a glossary compiled around the year 1800," and the newest is from someone on Twitter in 2010 saying, "Dear Lord — a fur coat on the Bakerloo line, she must have been mafted."

We can even use creative respellings on Twitter to investigate how people pronounce things differently. It's a little bit harder than just searching for words, but the linguist Rachael Tatman gave us an example using two well-studied sounds in varieties of English. The first is the pronunciation of words like "cot" and "caught" or "tock" and "talk." Some Americans (primarily in the West, Midwest, and New England) pronounce each member of the pairs the same, while others (primarily Southerners and African Americans) pronounce them differently — a trend which has been long established by the kind of linguists who make audio recordings. Tatman hypothesized that speakers who do have two distinct vowels in "sod" and "sawed" would sometimes want to call attention to one particular vowel,

44

by respelling it as "aw." Sure enough, she found that in tweets where a common word, like "on," "also," and "because," was respelled with "aw," as in "awn," "awlso," and "becawse," there also tended to be respellings for other well-documented features of Southern American English and African American English, such as deleting the "r" in words like "for" and "year" (writing "foah" and "yeah") and writing "da" and "dat" for "the" and "that."

But that could just be a coincidence. To test it, Tatman looked at a completely different sound in a completely different region: the pronunciation of words like "to" and "do" as "tae" and "dae." This sound, and this particular spelling of it, is associated with Scottish English, and has been since Robbie Burns. Here again, Tatman found that people who tweet this respelling tend to show other linguistic markers of Scottishness: they also tweet respellings like "ye" for "you" and "oan" for "on." To be sure, not all Scots, Southerners, or African Americans use these respellings, and those that do don't use them all the time. But the point is, when we respell words in casual writing, we tend to do so with a purpose — we jump in with both feet and try to represent our whole manner of speaking. Even if it's not always this clear which sounds are intended by a particular respelling, looking at which words and sounds people respell can help give linguists an idea of where to focus their audio recording energy.

The internet lets linguists do the kinds of dialect mapping and analysis of spontaneous speech that we've been trying to do for centuries, but with more data, from the comfort of a laptop, and without distorting the data by observing it. Just as the telephone study showed that people were still talking like their neighbors rather than like TV and radio broadcasters, and the bicycle peregrinations showed that regional dialects persisted even after centuries of print standardization, the internet studies show us that we often keep our local ways of speaking when we use social media. Our deep wells of enthusiasm for internet dialect quizzes give us a clue about why: talking in particular ways reinforces our networks, our sense of belonging and community.

NETWORKS

Does it ever feel like your family or friend group speaks its very own dialect? This was the premise of a book called *Kitchen Table Lingo,* which collected examples from what the linguist David Crystal called familects:

"the private and personal word-creations that are found in every household and in every social group, but which never get into the dictionary" (or onto dialect maps). The book's initial appeal for "familect" words attracted thousands of submissions from around the world, with stories of misheard song lyrics, onomatopoeia, children's coinages, and no less than fifty-seven words for the TV remote control. Dialect maps are just the beginning of our linguistic differences: every time we talk with some people more than others, we have the chance to develop a shared vocabulary, whether that's families, friends, schools, workplaces, hobbies, or other organizations. Family dialects are often inspired by a cute word that comes out of a kid's mouth (Queen Elizabeth II was apparently nicknamed "Gary" by a young Prince William, who was unable to say "Granny" yet), but the peak importance of in-group language happens at a later life stage: teenagehood.

High school is a place where people really notice small social details, whether that's the cool brand of jeans, who's now going out with who, or vowels. The linguist Penelope Eckert embedded at a high school in the Detroit suburbs in the 1980s to study the correlation between language and high school cliques. She found two main groups: jocks, who participated in the power structure of the school through activities like varsity sports and student council, and burnouts, who rejected the school's authority. In Detroit, along with many other American cities around the Great Lakes, there's a vowel change going on, where some speakers say "the busses with the antennas on top" in a way that sounds to people outside the area like "the bosses with the antennas on tap." For Eckert's students, the "bosses" pronunciation had a connotation of "street smarts," so the burnouts were more likely to use it than the jocks — despite the fact that they all lived in the same neighborhood and attended the same school, and irrespective of the social class of their parents. You could arrange the students into more subtle cliques, from "burned-out burnouts" to "jock-jocks," and their vowels would follow suit. To put it in the terms of classic high school movie characters, if Eckert's high school was Rydell High from *Grease,* we'd expect Sandy to say "bus," Rizzo to say "boss," and Frenchy to be somewhere in between.

Further studies at other high schools show other groups with other linguistic attitudes. A group of girls in California identified as nerds, and rejected the jock-burnout dichotomy altogether: linguistically, they avoided the slang and cool vowels developing among their peers (such as pronouncing the word "friend" as "frand"), because they didn't want to be heard as caring about high school popularity. Instead, they adopted linguistic features linked to intellectualism, such as hypercareful articulation, long words, and puns. A study of Latinas at another California high school found a linguistic distinction between Norteñas, who identified as American or Chicana and generally spoke English, and Sureñas, who identified as Mexicana and generally spoke Spanish. We could keep going, but let's pause and think about how we develop our senses of what's cool in the first place.

Remember how you learned about swearing? It was probably from a kid around your age, maybe an older sibling, and not from an educator or authority figure. And you were probably in early adolescence: the stage when linguistic influence tends to shift from caregivers to peers. Linguistic innovation follows a similar pattern, and the linguist who first noticed it was Henrietta Cedergren. She was doing a study in Panama City, where younger people had begun pronouncing "ch" as "sh" — saying *chica* (girl) as *shica*. When she drew a graph of which ages were using the new "sh" pronunciation, Cedergren noticed that sixteen-year-olds were the most likely to use the new version — more likely than the twelve-year-olds were. So did that mean that "sh" wasn't the trendy new linguistic innovation after all, since the youngest age group wasn't really adopting it? Cedergren returned to Panama a decade later to find out. The formerly untrendy twelve-year-olds had grown up into hyperinnovative twenty-two-year-olds. They now had the new "sh" pronunciation at even higher levels than the original trendy cohort of sixteen-year-olds, now twenty-six-year-olds, who sounded the same as they had a decade earlier. What's more, the new group of sixteen-year-olds were even further advanced, and the new twelve-year-olds still looked a bit behind. Cedergren figured out that twelve-year-olds still have some linguistic growth to do: they keep imitating and building on the linguistic habits of their slightly older, cooler peers as they go through their teens, and then plateau in their twenties.

In terms of swearing, that's like saying some twelve-year-olds swear, but a lot more sixteen-year-olds do. But swearing is very socially salient (we have laws about it!) and not really changing that much. It's been peaking in adolescence and declining through adulthood for decades. The other trendy linguistic features that we acquire in adolescence (new pronunciations like "bosses" and "shica," and innovative uses of words like "so" and "like") are a case of subtle social discernment rather than massive social taboo, and so we tend to keep them as adults.

This age curve is important when we think about when young people start using social media: age thirteen, if you believe the terms of service of most sites and apps, or slightly younger, if you assume that some users lie about their ages. This is right at the beginning of the age range when the language of teens is tremendously influenced by the slang of their peers. Sure, little kids play games and watch videos and even ask questions of voice assistants, but their social lives are still mediated by their families and their reading level. This coincidence of peer influence and social media access means that it's easy to conflate how the youth are talking now with the tools that they're using to do so. But every generation has talked slightly differently from its parents: otherwise, we'd all still be talking like Shakespeare. The question is, how much of that is influenced by technology, and how much is the linguistic evolution that would have happened regardless?

The answer seems to be that both happen simultaneously. Researchers from Georgia Tech, Columbia, and Microsoft looked at how many times a person had to see a word in order to start using it, using a group of words that were distinctively popular among Twitter users in a particular city in 2013–2014. As we'd expect, they noticed that people who follow each other on Twitter are likely to pick up words from each other. But there was an important difference in how people learned different kinds of words. People sometimes picked up words that are also found in speech — like "cookout," "hella," "jawn," and "phony" — from their internet friends, but it didn't really matter how many times they saw them. For rising words that are primarily written, not spoken — abbreviations like "tfti" (thanks for the information), "lls" (laughing like shit), and "ctfu" (cracking the fuck up) and phonetic spellings like "inna" (in a / in the) and "ard" (alright) — the number of times people saw them mattered a lot. Every additional exposure made someone twice as likely to start using them. The study pointed out that people encounter spoken slang both online and offline, so when we're only measuring exposure via Twitter, we miss half or more of the exposures and the trend looks murky.

But people mostly encounter the written slang online, so pretty much all of those exposures become measurable for a Twitter study. The researchers also found that you're more likely to start using a new word from Friendy McNetwork, who shares a lot of mutual friends with you, and less likely to pick it up from Rando McRandomFace, who doesn't share any of your friends, even if you and Rando follow each other just like you and Friendy do.

But these networks aren't formed in isolation: people tend to follow others with similar interests and demographics. One study demonstrating this looked at the geographic spread of a couple thousand words that became massively more popular on Twitter between 2009 and 2012. It found that terms tended to leapfrog from one city to another based on demographic similarity, not just geographic proximity. So slang would spread between Washington, D.C., and New Orleans (both have high proportions of black people), Los Angeles and Miami (high proportions of Hispanic people), or Boston and Seattle (high proportions of white people), but not necessarily the cities in between. For example, the abbreviation "af" for "as fuck" (as in "word maps are cool af") starts out at low levels in Los Angeles and Miami in

2009, then spreads elsewhere in California, the South, and around Chicago in 2011–2012, suggesting that it was spreading from Hispanic to African American populations. The study stops there, but we can continue: in 2014 and 2015, "af" started appearing in *BuzzFeed* headlines, a decent measure of when it came to be co-opted by mainstream brands capitalizing on its association with African American coolness.

We're especially likely to pick up new words when we're first entering a community. Linguist Dan Jurafsky and his colleagues looked at over four million posts from members of RateBeer and BeerAdvocate, two online beer communities that have been around for more than a decade. They wanted to know how people's language use changed the longer they'd been members of the forum. They found that older accounts were likely to stick to older pieces of beer jargon, such as talking about a beer's "aroma" if they joined in 2003, whereas younger accounts were quicker to adopt newer beer jargon, such as preferring "S" (for "smell") if they joined in 2005. The study provides an interesting way of teasing apart the effects of age and peer groups, suggesting that people are more open to new vocabulary during the first third of their lifespan, regardless of whether that's an eighty-year lifespan in an offline community or a three-year "lifespan" in an online one.

What's unique about adolescence, then, may not be our susceptibility to linguistic trends. Rather, it's the last time that a whole population is entering a new social group all at once. Adults periodically move to new cities and start new jobs and develop new hobbies, all of which bring us under new linguistic influences. But we don't all change careers or become parents or join beer-tasting messageboards at exactly the same age, so it's harder to study linguistic changes that happen later in life. Harder, but not impossible: it also depends on where we want to look. Researchers are part of society, and as a society, we're more likely to be worried about teen slang than about parents adding new terms to the familect or businesspeople adopting new corporate buzzwords. Perhaps we need to rethink our demographic questions to ask about dates of joining new social groups in addition to date of birth.

Finding networked language patterns on social media isn't an anomaly: people offline are generally also more similar to their friends than to the rigid, unfeeling demographic boxes of a census-taker. It's just that we had no practical way of measuring it. Doing a network analysis of people's friends and interlocutors used to be *really hard*. Like makes-biking-around-France-for-four-years-look-easy kind of hard. You could start by doing a typical language survey, but that would just be the beginning of your work. You'd also have to get people to manually make a list of all their friends, how long they've known them, and how often they talk with each one. Then, you'd have to somehow get ahold of all these friends and also survey them. But that's just a one-layer network. You'd want to repeat these steps several times so that you could make webs of connections between people. Social scientists have done this kind of research occasionally — there's a city in Massachusetts called Framingham where researchers have followed a couple thousand people, with their health and social connections, for three generations now — but understandably, they don't do it very often. Not for daily words produced by tens or hundreds of thousands of people. Even though your Twitter network doesn't represent absolutely everyone you talk to, even though not everyone is on Twitter, it makes for an intriguing new way of approaching the very old question of how new words catch on.

Analyzing language based on social

networks also complicates another traditional demographic check box: gender. The traditional finding for gender is shown in a study by the linguists Terttu Nevalainen and Helena Raumolin-Brunberg at the University of Helsinki, which looked at six thousand personal letters written in English between 1417 and 1681. Personal letters make a great corpus because, like tweets, they don't go through editorial standardization. Unfortunately, there's also a lot fewer of them, and they tend to overrepresent the leisured, educated classes. But they're still the best record we have of what day-to-day English looked like back then. The linguists examined fourteen language changes that occurred during this period, things like the eradication of "ye," the switch from "mine eyes" to "my eyes," and the replacement of -*th* with -s, making words like "hath," "doth," and "maketh" into "has," "does," and "makes." (Pretty shocking stuff.) For eleven out of the fourteen changes, Nevalainen and Raumolin-Brunberg found that female letter-writers were changing the way they wrote faster than male letter-writers. In the three exceptional cases where the men were ahead of the women, those particular changes were linked to men's greater access to education at the time. In other words, women are reliably ahead of the game when it comes to word-of-mouth linguistic changes.

Research in other centuries, languages, and regions continues to find that women lead linguistic change, in dozens of specific changes in specific cities and regions. Young women are also consistently on the bleeding edge of those linguistic changes that periodically sweep through media trend sections, from uptalk (the distinctive rising intonation at the end of sentences?) to the use of "like" to introduce a quotation ("And then I was like, 'Innovation'"). The role that young women play as language disruptors is so clearly established at this point it's practically boring to linguists who study this topic: well-known sociolinguist William Labov estimated that women lead 90 percent of linguistic change in a paper he wrote in 1990. (I've attended more than a few talks at sociolinguistics conferences about a particular change in vowels or vocabulary, and it barely gets even a full sentence of explanation: "And here, as expected, we can see that the women are more advanced on this change than the men. Next slide.") Men tend to follow a generation later: in other words, women tend to learn language from their peers; men learn it from their mothers.

What's less clear is why. Lots of reasons have been proposed, from the fact that women still dominate the caregiving of children in the societies studied, that women may pay more attention to language to compensate for relative lack of economic power or to facilitate social mobility, and that women tend to have more social ties. But in many cases, gender (like age) seems to be a proxy for other factors related to how we socialize with each other.

Several internet studies have highlighted the importance of differentiating between gender and social context. One study, by linguists Susan Herring and John Paolillo, looked at how people write blogs. At first, it seemed like there was a significant gender difference in the language of blogs. But when they looked again, the linguists found that what was really going on was a *genre* difference: men were more likely to write topic-based blogs and women more likely to write diary-style blogs. But of course, there were also many people who didn't pick the genre most typical for their gender. When the researchers compared within each genre, the original "gender" difference disappeared.

Another study, looking at a corpus of 14,000 Twitter users, and guessing their gender based on the skew of their first name in census data, appeared at first glance to show clear gender differences: people with predominantly female names were more likely to use emoticons, for example, while people with male-associated names were more likely to swear. But when the researchers looked one step further, they found that the words people most often tweeted formed natural clusters into over a dozen interest groups, such as sports fans, hip-hop fans, parents, politics buffs, TV and movie fans, techies, book fans, and so on. True, many of the groups had a gender skew, but none of them were absolute, and they also had clear associations with other demographic factors like age and race. Sometimes whole groups defied gender norms — men overall tended to swear more, but techies, a cluster that was male-dominated, didn't swear much at all, presumably because they were using Twitter as an extension of the workplace. At the individual level, people followed the norms of their clusters rather than their genders — a woman in the sports cluster or a man in the parenting cluster tweeted like their fellow sports fans or parents, rather than like an "average woman" or "average man." Moreover, restricting the analysis to accounts with names that showed a clear gender skew in census data excludes precisely those users that would complicate a binary view of gender, including nonbinary people and others who've deliberately chosen a non-census-gendered username.

Offline, ethnographic research has also pointed to the importance of network factors. Linguist Lesley Milroy was doing a pretty standard study of language change in a couple working-class neighborhoods of Belfast, Northern Ireland. As with many communities, the young women were leading a linguistic change — in this case, changing the vowel in "car" to sound more like "care." This vowel is common elsewhere in Northern Ireland, but it was new to this particular community, and it was the young women who were bringing it in. What was mystifying was *how they were getting it*. When Milroy asked the women who they were close to, they named friends, family, and coworkers, all from their neighborhood — the same neighborhood where no one else yet had this vowel change.

In a later paper with James Milroy, the two figured out why by linking linguistic change to another concept in social science: strong and weak ties. Strong ties are people you spend a lot of time with and feel close to, who you share mutual friends with; weak ties are acquaintances who you may or may not share mutual ties with. In the case of the Belfast study, the early-adopting young women all worked at the same store in the city center, where people were already using the new vowel. Although they didn't have close friends from the city center, they did have weak-tie contact with customers, which would have often exposed them to the new vowel — more than the young men of their neighborhood, who weren't employed outside it.

Milroy and Milroy figured that, just as your weak ties are a greater source of new information like gossip and employment opportunities than your close friends who already know the same things you do, more weak ties also lead to more linguistic change. To demonstrate, they compared the history of English and Icelandic. English and Icelandic have a common Germanic ancestor, and a millennium ago Old English and Old Norse (the ancestor of Old Icelandic spoken at the time) were still more or less mutually intelligible. But from there, their histories diverge. Icelandic has changed only a little: twenty-first-century Icelandic speakers can still read their Sagas from the thirteenth century, written in Old Icelandic, without much difficulty. English has changed a lot: although we can manage Shakespeare, from only four centuries ago, with the help of footnotes, even *The Canterbury Tales* (six centuries ago) requires a full translation or a course in Middle English to understand. This means that, despite the fact that it's technically written in Old English rather than Old Icelandic, Icelanders would have an easier time learning to read *Beowulf* than would modern English speakers.

Clearly, English has changed faster than Icelandic has over the same timespan. Milroy and Milroy proposed that the reason is weak ties. The thing to know about Iceland is that it's got really close-knit communities. Icelandic surnames are still based on the given name of your father (or sometimes mother), which makes a lot more sense in a society where most of the people you meet already know your family, and this tendency to introduce oneself by naming an extensive network of relatives dates all the way back to the Sagas. If everyone you know already knows each other, your only source of new linguistic forms is random variation — you don't have any weak ties to borrow from.

English, on the other hand, has had several significant sources of weak ties over its history — invasions by the Danes and the Normans, a tradition of uprooting and moving to London and later other cities to seek one's fortune, and imperial expansion of its own. True, the English-speaking world has its own small, tight-knit communities where everyone knows everyone else's relatives (I still introduce myself by referring to my parents or grandparents at family reunions), but it also has many more big cities where you can be anonymous in a crowd or have three different friend groups who never meet each other. What's more, the map studies from the beginning of this chapter tell us that within English, it's the bigger, looser-knit cities that give rise to more linguistic change.

But weak ties can't be the only factor. After all, it's also clear that we talk like people in our social circles, whether that's French villages, Detroit jocks, or familects — all examples of strong ties. How can both strong and weak ties be responsible for how we speak? And how can we map out exactly who says what to who over a large population for a couple centuries, long enough for several changes to run their course? That's not just bicycling — that's time travel.

Linguist Zsuzsanna Fagyal and colleagues solved both problems using a computer simulation. They made a network of nine hundred hypothetical people over forty thousand turns. Each person had a certain number of ties to other people in the network and started with a randomly assigned value for a hypothetical linguistic feature, like how you might call the thing you drink water from in a school a "water fountain" but your neighbor might call it a "drinking fountain." Then, at each turn, each person looked to the other people they were connected to and had a certain probability of adopting their version of the feature, like how you might start saying "drinking fountain" if you have a friend who uses the term. If you do pick it up, that word now becomes yours as well, and the people you're connected to might pick it up from you the next round. They repeated this turn process forty thousand times, with three different kinds of networks. In one version, the entire network was made up of close ties: everyone was well connected to the rest of the network. This dense network behaved like Iceland: one linguistic option caught on very quickly and stayed completely dominant for the rest of the simulation. In another version, the entire network was made up of weak ties and no one was well connected. The loose network behaved like a world of tourists: all of the options stuck around and none of them ever became dominant. But in the most interesting simulation, they made some of the nodes highly connected "leaders" and others less connected "loners." This mixed network behaved like English: one option would catch on for a while, but the other options would never totally disappear, and eventually one of them would become popular instead — a cycle that repeated several times. The researchers concluded that both strong and weak ties have an important role to play in linguistic change: the weak ties introduce the new forms in the first place, while the strong ties spread them once they're introduced.

The internet, then, makes language change faster because it leads to more weak ties: you can remain aware of people who you don't see anymore, and you can get to know people who you never would have met otherwise. The phenomenon of a hashtag or funny video going viral is an example of the power of weak ties — when the same thing is shared only through strong ties, it ends up merely as an inside joke. But the internet doesn't lead to the collapse of strong ties, either: the average person has a small handful of people who they message on a regular basis, between four and twenty-six, depending on how you count. What's more, social networking sites that prompt you to interact with denser ties — people you already know and friends of friends — tend to be less linguistically innovative. It's not an accident that Twitter, where you're encouraged to follow people you don't already know, has given rise to more linguistic innovation (not to mention memes and social movements) than Facebook, where you primarily friend people you already know offline.

But geography and demographics and even networks aren't destiny. In addition to having some amount of choice in where we live and who we associate with, we also have a certain amount of control over how much we want to be influenced by our interlocutors: who we want to project ourselves to be, linguistically speaking.

ATTITUDES

If you want to sum up Canada in a headline, you might reach for the catchphrase "from Eh to Zed." You'd be in good company: this slogan features in the titles of three books, items like t-shirts and YouTube videos, and news articles about everything from sports to the language itself. But what many people don't think about, even Canadians, is that small Canadian children often call the last letter of the alphabet "zee" instead. Normally, when linguists see a word or construction that's common among parents but not their kids, we simply conclude that there's a change going on — that in another generation it'll be a grandparent-y sort of word, and eventually pass into history. "Chesterfield" is doing exactly this in Canada: it's been receding for decades in favor of "couch."

But "zed" has been acting really weird. The linguist J. K. Chambers did a survey of Canadian twelve-year-olds in the 1970s, and found that two-thirds of them said "zee" — but when he went back and surveyed the same population in the 1990s, he found that the vast majority were now using "zed" as adults. The same shift happened with successive generations. Chambers figured that children learn "zee" from the alphabet song and American children's television programs like *Sesame Street,* but when they get older, they learn that "zed" is associated with Canadian identity and switch. Indeed, noted Chambers, "zed" is one of the first things that American immigrants to Canada change about their speech, "because calling it 'zee' unfailingly draws comments from the people they are talking to."

I first learned about this phenomenon when I was eighteen, in a linguistics class that I took about Canadian English in Kingston, Ontario. It stood out for me among the sea of dialect maps and survey methodologies because I realized that I'd done this exact thing. I was a child who sang "zee" at the end of the alphabet song in the 1990s, until some point around middle school when I switched to using "zed" consistently. What's more, I was still slightly embarrassed by this fact and had done my best to put it out of my mind, because clearly I should never have been using the un-Canadian "zee" in the first place. When I realized that I'd done this, I asked my mom what she called the last letter of the alphabet. I've only ever known her as a zed-sayer, but apparently she'd done the same shift long before I was born. My switch from "zee" to "zed" happened at about the same age that I started consistently using Canadian spellings in words like "centre" and "colour" instead of "center" and "color." I don't recall anyone telling me to do it, but I do recall it being a conscious choice, fueled by that exact sense of social identity that Chambers described. At the time, acquiring a sense of linguistic nationalism was a way of going with the flow, of following the dominant usage of my parents and teachers. In adulthood, especially on the internet, I use Canadian spellings in my posts and messages partly out of habit, but partly also because it goes *against* the flow: it's a subtle way of reclaiming space against the idea that all English speakers on the internet fit neatly into the choice I've faced in so many dropdown menus between "American" and "British."

We all make linguistic decisions like this all the time. Sometimes, we decide to align ourselves with the existing holders of power by talking like they do, so we can seem rich or educated or upwardly mobile. Sometimes, we decide to align ourselves with particular less powerful groups, to show that we belong and to seem cool, antiauthoritarian, or not stuck-up.

The most legendary study of social factors in language differences is about how much people of different social classes use the stereotypical "New Yawk" accent, with the R dropped from after the vowel. In November 1962, linguist William Labov went into various department stores in New York City and asked how to find something — the shoe section, for example — that he already knew was on the fourth floor. The salesperson would reply "fourth floor" or "fawth flaw" and then Labov would pretend not to have heard, getting the salesperson to repeat the location more carefully. After this exchange, Labov would head off in the appropriate direction, but not to buy shoes. As soon as he was out of sight, he'd pull out a notebook and record whether the salesperson pronounced the R in "fourth" and "floor." He found that, sure enough, the salespeople at the fanciest department store, Saks Fifth Avenue, said R more than those at the mid-range one (Macy's), who in turn used R more than the bargain store (the now defunct Klein's), and that people also tended to pronounce R more in careful speech, when he asked them to repeat themselves, than they had the first time around. But it's hard to shop at Saks Fifth Avenue on a retail salary: the salespeople themselves came from similar class backgrounds across all three stores. Instead, it was their perception of the kind of customer they catered to that made the difference, even though Labov took pains to report that he dressed the same in all places: "in middle-class style, with jacket, white shirt and tie, and used my normal pronunciation as a college-educated native of New Jersey (r-pronouncing)." (One assumes that the pronunciations might have varied even further if he'd dressed up or dressed down.)

But where did our ideas of what sounds upper or lower class even come from? In New York City, the R-less pronunciation is less prestigious. Although it's a feature of many American varieties, such as Boston English, African American English, and Southern American English, it's not favored in media.

When people in the United States talk about "losing an accent," they often mean gaining an R in words like "fourth floor."

If we hopped across the Atlantic and did the same study in British department stores, however — if we went to, say, Harrods and Debenhams and Poundland — we could find the inverse. Salespeople at Harrods, the poshest of the posh, would have no Rs at all, whereas staff at Poundland, where (almost) everything costs a pound, might have Rs if we picked our city carefully, such as Bristol or Southampton. R-ful varieties are found in parts of Britain, including Scotland and Northern England, but they're not favored in London or on the BBC. English speakers don't all talk like our books and media any more than actual French and German speakers talk like the model dialogues in language-learning textbooks. When people in the UK talk about "losing an accent," they often mean losing the R in words like "fourth floor."

Clearly, it's not R's fault. R is a harmless consonant that never asked to be embroiled in any of our petty human squabbles. Rather, it's what we take R to mean in different contexts. It's like how blue can signal a sports team, a cold-water setting, a hyperlink, a period in the life of Picasso, and so on. R in itself is neither good nor bad: its meaning, and the meaning of the accents that do or do not have it, is constructed by society. Like how money is just squiggles on paper or on a screen until it determines whether you can eat lunch, words are just meat twitches until they determine whether you can get a job — or whether someone will even deign to tell you where the shoe section is. If we all woke up tomorrow and decided that every single vowel sounded better with an R after it, we could make it happen. (Ermargerd, whart ar world thart wourld ber.)

But we don't generally wake up and decide to change our minds about R. Instead, we get our social linguistic cues from the people and power dynamics around us. One vivid example of this power dynamic comes via James Milroy, who we last saw comparing social networks in England and Iceland. In the story of a language, just like everywhere else, history is written by the winners: Milroy recounts a typical attitude from an influential historian of English named H. C. Wyld in 1927, who "was quite insistent that the only worthy object of our study was Received Standard English. . . . The language of 'the Oxford Common Room and the Officers' mess' is an appropriate object of study, whereas that of 'illiterate peasants' is not."

You practically want to reach back through time and punch the elitism.

Wyld wasn't the first linguistic elitist: before there was the elite Oxford Common Room, there was the Roman forum. The Romans, good at roads and aqueducts and armies, also left a legacy of writing: for over a millennium after the fall of the Roman Empire, if you were educated, you learned Latin. To be an English writer in the era when formal writing was shifting over from Latin to English was to be a self-hating English writer: anything you could do to make English more Latin-like would also make it better. Robert Lowth, who wrote a widely used English grammar in 1762, culled examples of so-called false syntax from luminaries of English writing like Shakespeare, Milton, and the King James Bible — not as hints that perhaps English grammar was actually just fine as it was, but as cautionary tales about how even the greats should have been more Latin-y.

It was like a competition to see who could be the most uptight. Lowth gave us an early suggestion against the sentence-ending preposition: "This is an Idiom which our language is strongly inclined to; it prevails in common conversation, and suits very well with the familiar style in writing; but the placing of the Preposition before the Relative is more graceful, as well as more perspicuous; and agrees much better with the solemn and elevated Style." Lowth himself wasn't completely against it (after all, he used it himself in "strongly inclined *to*"), just passing an aesthetic judgment. But later grammarians elevated this preference into a full-on ban, and by similarly specious reasoning objected to infinitive splitting and "they" as singular, despite centuries of prior English usage. The same Latin-worshipping tradition was responsible for adding superfluous silent letters to words like "dete," "samoun," and "iland," because "debt," "salmon," and "island" look more like Latin "debitum," "salmonem," and "insula." Never mind that "island" doesn't even come from Latin, or that generations of schoolchildren would now have to go to extra effort. Many languages can't have spelling bees because their spelling systems are so logical that no one would ever get knocked out. English spellers can only dream!

We could almost feel sorry for the depths of self-loathing that these grammarians must have felt, to be so determined to replace their own language's forms with that of another, if it weren't for how they infected us with it as well. While they didn't wholly succeed at the grammatical side, especially in speech and among skilled writers who trusted their own ear or felt they knew enough to break the rules, they did leave us with a vague sense of unease at the whole prospect of the written word. Even after years of writing, most of us have a hard time trusting what we naturally think sounds like a reasonable English sentence, haunted as we are by the ghosts of misguided grammarians.

But while modern linguistics has moved on, and even modern writing manuals are scraping off the heavy lacquer of Latinization with more or less enthusiasm, we've acquired a new form of linguistic authority on our digital devices. Tools like spellcheck, grammarcheck, autocomplete, and speech-to-text impose someone's ideas of the rules of English automatically — invisible authorities that we can defy but not avoid. If a writing handbook like Lowth's or Strunk and White's displeases you, you can throw it across the room or leave it to gather dust, but when you want to type a word that's not in a predictive text model, you'll fight for every letter. In her book *Fixing English,* Anne Curzan describes how Microsoft Word's grammarcheck continues to perpetuate this same kind of discredited, Latin-based style advice and how her colleagues in the English department, while considering themselves sufficiently expert in writing to ignore or turn off the green squiggles, had still never wondered where the grammar advice came from. If English professors who question the authority of texts for a living haven't thought to question the origins of their invisible electronic grammarians, what possible hope do the rest of us have?

Language features are not neutral in the way that the calculator feature is neutral. "Standard" language and "correct" spelling are collective agreements, not eternal truths, and collective agreements can change. Communication tools that expose us to more people may speed up the spread of new words, but tools that aim to help us with language can also slow down natural linguistic evolution by nudging us towards the versions that have already been programmed into the device.

I'm convinced that spellcheck is responsible for people's consistent misspelling of my surname: my spelling, "McCulloch," is never found in spellcheck by default, but the very similar name "McCullough" is always there instead, and when people misspell my name on a computer, they always pick the spellcheck version. Conversely, people occasionally misspell my first name, Gretchen, when writing by hand, but never do so when spellcheck is available. It seems that my names belong to two different classes of digital citizenship: one supported by the machine and the other rejected by it. This might seem relatively harmless given my German first name and Scottish surname, but I expect that if we looked at which names are found in autocorrect and autocomplete, we'd find that typical English names would be well represented and names from other languages less so. At a societal level, it's a case of bias-laundering through technology that serves to reinforce people and names that are already powerful.

Default computer spellings are powerful enough to have created a shift in British English since the 1990s: while American English prefers a Z in words like "organize" and "realize," British English has tradition-ally used both *-ise* and *-ize* spellings. But spellchecks have tried to prevent people from spelling the same word differently within the same document by enforcing "organise" and "realise" all the time when set to British English, leading to an upswing in *-ise* endings among the general British typing public and the perception that *-ize* is only for Americans.

In writing this book, I'm therefore very

aware that upholding the old-school Latin worship is a political decision, just as it would be if I decided to go full-on grammar anarchist. I think it's important to be upfront about such things, especially in an age when everything from books to tweets may later be mined to prove how common or acceptable a particular usage was at a particular time. Yes, I'm writing for you, the reader, but in another sense we're all writing for the unblinking eye of Data. If the most enduring legacy of this book is the slight shifting of a point on a line graph in some yet unborn person's analysis of this decade in the English language, I want to be deliberate about which direction I'm shifting that point in. What I've seen from several editors and lexicographers is the realization that we're becoming trapped in a loop: dictionaries and writing manuals refer to edited prose in order to determine what is "standard" English, but the creators of such prose refer back to the same dictionaries and manuals in their editing, each waiting for the other to move first. I've decided to play my part in correcting for this bias by opting for the more innovative direction wherever I perceive a choice: going towards where I think edited English prose will be by the end of the century, catering to the reader of the future rather than the reader of the past. As a reader and analyst of data myself, I get a joyful thrill every time I zoom out on the English language and realize that we're somewhere in the middle of its story, not at the beginning or end. I don't know how we'll be writing in the twenty-second century, but I feel a responsibility to help its linguists gain a broad cross-section of the language of the twenty-first by not lingering overlong in the twentieth.

To that end, I've chosen to lowercase "internet" and social acronyms like "lol" and "omg" and to write "email" rather than "e-mail," and when I've needed to make a decision on other spelling choices, I've looked up which ones are more common in the Corpus of Global Web-Based English and tweets by ordinary people rather than which ones are favored by usage manuals, which has led me to close many compound words. (While I was working on this book, the Associated Press switched its recommendation from "Internet" to "internet," so I have every expectation that any similar judgment call I make will seem boring within a decade.) I've adopted the retronym "networked computers" for what were formerly called small-i internets, and I talk about "websites" rather than trying to insist on a distinction between "the internet" and "the worldwide web" which is no longer active for younger and nontechnical users. (I avoid the now dated-sounding "the Web" or "the Net" entirely, and reserve "cyberspace" for jocular historical use.) I've also included a substantial proportion of absolute time references rather than relative ones, aiming to be precise about whether I think something is true of the early twenty-first century, the 2010s, a specific year, and so on, rather than saying "now" or "currently" and requiring readers to flip to the copyright page and subtract a year or two for preparation, as I've had to do many times when reading other sources. I've freely used the singular "they," and split what infinitives needed splitting, and preserved all spelling and typographical choices found in quotes from other people, but I've otherwise kept to standard bookish spelling and capitalization and punctuation, and even suffered to have my Canadian spellings changed for US audiences. But, although it's common internet usage, I have not lowercased names of internet companies and platforms like Facebook and Twitter and YouTube.

Despite my many objections, I still use spellcheck and predictive text. Most of the time, they're pretty useful! I don't have to remember the c-to-s ratio in "necessary" or the exceptions to the "i before e" rule, which surely frees up valuable brain cells, and I can simply add words like lowercase "internet" to my phone's dictionary. But I also wonder what a world would look like where none of us cared about such things in the first place. From a linguistic perspective, all varieties are equally worthy: every language and dialect is just as much a manifestation of the incredible human language ability that is our birthright as a species. You wouldn't say that some birds aren't singing right just because they're lower in the (ahem) pecking order. No more are certain ways of speaking inherently inferior. Could we not put our tremendous computing power (both human and mechanical) to better use than upholding the prejudices of a bunch of aristocrats from the eighteenth century?

Some technolinguistic tools have been attempting to do just that, albeit with mixed results. Wikipedia, whose slogan is "the free encyclopedia that anyone can edit," has been very effective at combating obvious vandalism with dedicated volunteer editors, but faces more subtle problems of bias in what it covers, because the volunteer editors it attracts are disproportionately male, well-off, and English speaking, and they tend to edit topics they're already interested in. Google Docs, where this book was written, has a spellcheck that draws on internet data, sometimes with surprising results. Once, to my great joy, it proffered a more common spelling of "Ronbledore" (an obscure Harry Potter fan theory that Ron Weasley is actually a time-traveling Dumbledore). Other times, it has persisted in suggesting the closed spelling "alot" over the open spelling "a lot" — a version that's common but more informal than I'd expect a spellcheck system to endorse. Perhaps the most promising computational tool for fighting bias rather than reinforcing it is Textio. This is a startup that assesses the text of your job posting for whether certain words and phrases are likely to put people off applying, and thereby make the position take longer to fill, by sounding sexist or corporate jargony, flagging buzzwords like "big data" and "rockstars" in favor of "caregiver leave" and "learn new things."

Just like we can use language to be elitist, we can also use language to show solidarity, like politicians who suddenly adopt a folksy way of talking on the campaign trail. In some cases, shifting language is practically universal: none of us talk to a dog the same way we talk to our coworkers ("Who's a good boss!

Do you want to go for walkies and also give me a raise?"). In other cases, our linguistic styles are bound up in a specific identity: William Labov studied residents of Martha's Vineyard and found that those who identified strongly with traditional island culture had stronger local accents than those who didn't. More recent research has shown that intonation in particular is related to social identity: young men in Washington, D.C., with one black and one white parent talk differently depending on whether they identify as black or biracial; the speech patterns of people living in Appalachia depend on how "rooted" they feel in the local community; and the speech of Jewish women in Ohio and New Jersey varies depending on their relationship with their Jewish identity.

In still other cases, the alignment is less about showing that you're part of the same group and more about borrowing coolness from another group. Research on youth language in several countries shows a parallel trend: there are distinctive linguistic forms associated with economically and racially marginalized youth in contexts ranging from the American inner city to the banlieues of Paris to the favelas of Rio de Janeiro. Elements of their language then get picked up by white middle-class youth. They don't

84

adopt enough to make them no longer seem comfortably middle class, but just enough to strike a note of autonomy from parents, teachers, and other authority figures. Of course, when a word like "lit" or "bae" gets sufficiently associated with mainstream culture — and especially when it gets picked up by brands capitalizing on trends — it then loses its appeal to hip insiders, prompting the cycle to begin again.

In English, the association of words from African American English with coolness and their subsequent appropriation by non–African Americans is much older than the internet. Terms associated with African American music, including blues, jazz, rock and roll, and rap, have all made their way into broader Western culture, while the speakers who originated them continue to be stigmatized for the way they talk. One thing that changes with the decentralization of online media is that the original speakers can become more visible. While a white person in the sixties listening to Elvis might have had no idea that he was singing a style heavily influenced by black performers like B.B. King and Sister Rosetta Tharpe, it's easier to see that mainstream America's adoption of "on fleek" came from a post on Vine (a now defunct service for sharing short videos) by the user Peaches Monroee. Still, it's tempting to mislabel the many words currently being appropriated into general American pop culture from African American English as "social media words" simply because they're used by young people, and young people are on social media, without giving due credit to the words' true origins. Fittingly, the internet has come up with a word for this: columbusing, or white people claiming to discover something that was already well established in another community, by analogy with how Columbus gets credit for discovering America despite the millions of people who already lived there.

In other languages, English itself is often a source of trendy new linguistic influence, one that signals interest in a broader, global culture rather than a smaller local one. The situation in Arabic is particularly interesting, because it involves multiple languages, multiple dialects, and multiple scripts. Most Arabic speakers know two varieties of Arabic: Modern Standard Arabic, which is the standardized, multinational version based on Classical Arabic that people learn to write in school but speak only rarely, and a local dialect, such as Egyptian or Moroccan Arabic, which is the language of everyday speech and doesn't have an official written form. Back when Arabic speakers, like most of the rest of the world, associated writing with formality and speech with informality, this worked fine. Sure, you'd have news anchors speaking the standard and advertisements written in the vernacular to add a bit of local color, but for the most part, Arabic was comfortably settled in what linguists call a diglossia: when a society has two languages or dialects that almost everyone speaks, each of which serves a distinct social function.

Then personal computers and the internet arrived, and things got really complicated, really quickly. Early computers and websites were in English and were often used by people at universities who spoke English to communicate with the rest of the world. And, importantly, these new devices generally came with English keyboards and English displays, rather than Arabic ones. So speakers figured out a way of writing Arabic sounds using the Latin alphabet, a system known by various names, such as ASCII Arabic, the Arabic chat alphabet, Franco-Arabic, Araby, Arabizi, and Arabish.

Arabizi has some distinct advantages. Most official Romanizations of Arabic use "kh" to represent the Arabic letter خ, a sound that may be familiar to English speakers as the "ch" in Scottish "loch" or the "x" in the

Spanish pronunciation of "Mexico."* But "kh" is actually a rather confusing way of representing this sound, because it looks the same as simply the /k/ sound followed by the /h/ sound, a sequence which is rare in English (found only in compounds like "cookhouse") but fairly common in Arabic. So informal writers use a different convention. Based on the similarity in shape, people instead write it as the number 5 or 7' (that's 7 with an apostrophe), which looks sort of like the خ in a mirror. They don't use plain 7, though, because that's already in use to represent ح (its dotless equivalent), another sound that's hard to transcribe — many systems use "h" for it, because it sounds kind of like a throatier /h/, but that's a problem because Arabic also has the more common /h/ sound that's in English. Using 7 instead solves the problem of one letter representing two sounds.

By similar logic, the numbers 9' and 9 can

---

*Note that North American English speakers often pronounce Scottish "loch" or German "Bach" further back in the throat than warranted, while pronouncing Spanish "Mexico" as if it's /h/. As pronounced by native speakers, all three are the same sound, which the International Phonetic Alphabet represents as /x/.

be used for the letters ض and ص, the numbers 6' and 6 for ظ and ط, and the numbers 3' and 3 for the letters غ and ع — all representing sounds that don't have ready equivalents in the Latin alphabet. What's important about Arabizi is that it assumes familiarity with Arabic already: it's a grassroots system based on the priorities of literate native speakers that each of these different sounds should be represented by a distinct symbol. Other Romanizations tend to do the opposite, rendering the same letters as variants of "d" and "s," "dh" and "t," "gh" and a backwards apostrophe (or simply omitting it altogether, as in the word "Arabic" itself, which is technically "3arabi"), based on what they sound like to non–Arabic speakers. Sure, sometimes it's useful to be able to interact on a more globalized level, like when writing about names and locations in Arabic-speaking countries for an English-language newspaper, but sometimes you also care about the local. To Arabic speakers, these distinctions are completely vital, and omitting them is like trying to convince English speakers to spell "sing" and "thing" the same way because French doesn't care about that weird English "th" sound.

Although Arabizi was initially made necessary because computers didn't support the

89

Arabic alphabet, it's now taken on a social dimension. A paper by David Palfreyman and Muhamed Al Khalil, analyzing chat conversations between students at an English-speaking university in the United Arab Emirates, gave an example of a cartoon that one student drew to represent other students in her class. One student was labeled with the name "Sheikha," using the official Romanization of the university. But the nickname version of the same name, which doesn't have an officially sanctioned spelling, was written in the cartoon as "shwee5" — using Arabizi "5" to represent the same sound as the official "kh." It's a hand-drawn cartoon: there's no technological reason for either name to be written in the Latin alphabet. But at least for some people, it's become cool: participants in the study commented that "we feel that only ppl of our age could understand such symbols" and that it makes "the word sound more like 'Arabic' pronunciation rather than English. For example, we would type the name ('7awla) instead of (Khawla). It sounds more Arabic this way."

In particular, with advancements in keyboarding meaning that it's easier to type the Arabic alphabet than it was in the 1990s, people generally use the official alphabet for the Standard variety, with its established writing system, and can now use either alphabet in a grassroots fashion for the local varieties. A study of the linguistic choices of prominent Egyptians on Twitter gives us some examples of how people decide which one to use. A politician tweeted predominantly in Modern Standard, reflecting his older age and the traditional expectation of politicians to speak the standard. A popular singer tweeted mostly in Egyptian Colloquial Arabic with some Modern Standard, both written in Arabic script, reflecting his younger age and fanbase, as well as the language his songs were in. A fancy restaurant tweeted in English and Egyptian Arabic written in Arabizi, to appeal to a wealthy, cosmopolitan clientele who would have been educated abroad. A cultural center tweeted in English and Modern Standard, to appeal to an educated regional and international audience. Egyptian Twitter users could thus potentially see four different linguistic conventions on their one feed: English and Modern Standard Arabic in their respective scripts, and Egyptian Arabic in both. And they could pick and choose between them for their own messages, depending on who they are and who they're trying to talk to.

While we may not all have multiple alphabets to choose from, we do all make linguistic choices based on our audience. Jacob Eisenstein, the linguist who was Twitter-mapping "yinz" and "hella," and his collaborator Umashanthi Pavalanathan at Georgia Tech decided to split up English tweets in a different way. Rather than look at location, language, or script, they looked at the difference between tweets about a particular topic, say the Oscars, versus tweets in conversation with another person. As it happens, Twitter has an easy way of automatically grouping these two kinds of tweets. If you put a hashtag in your tweet, like #oscars, then other people who are also interested in the Oscars know that they can click on or search that hashtag to find other tweets that also contain #oscars. If you put someone's Twitter username after an @ sign, like @Beyonce, then that user will get a notification about your message and hopefully reply to you the same way.

Since # and @ are distinct symbols, it's easy enough to automatically sort a giant pile of tweets, discarding the ones that contain both or neither. Sure, it's a bit rough — people probably aren't searching through sarcastic hashtags like #sorrynotsorry for topical information, and Beyoncé probably won't tweet you back (uh, #sorry) — but it works pretty well at a large scale. What Eisenstein and

Pavalanathan found was that people used regionalisms like "hella," slang like "nah" and "cuz," emoticons like :), and other informal language more in the tweets that @mentioned another user, while the same people used a more standardized, formal style in their tweets with hashtags. They theorized that, just as in person we'd generally talk more formally when addressing a roomful of people than when talking one-on-one, we're directing a tweet with a hashtag towards a large group of people. Our @mentions, on the other hand, are more informal, only noticed by a select few — and we adjust our language electronically the same way we do out loud.

Studies of people who tweet in other languages show a similar pattern. A study of people in the Netherlands who tweet in both the locally dominant language, Dutch, and a local minority language, Frisian or Limburgish, found that tweets with hashtags were more likely to be written in Dutch, so as to reach a broader audience, but that users would often switch to a minority language when they were replying to someone else's tweet. The inverse was less common: few people would start in a smaller language for the hashtagged tweet and switch to the larger language for the one-on-one reply.

Another study investigated how people use

informal language in Indonesian, comparing how they write in private, one-on-one text messages versus public tweets. For example, the Indonesian word *sip* means "okay, yeah, good," but to emphasize it, you can respell it *siiippp,* and "thank you" is *terima kasih,* but if you want to try to match the pronunciation of the popular Jakarta dialect, you can respell it *makasi.* If @replies on Twitter are slightly more casual than messages broadcast in hashtags, then texts are more intimate still, and sure enough, Indonesians used informal respellings like this almost four times more often in texts than in tweets. Tweets were also nearly twice as long as texts, on average, and contained more complex sentences and a larger variety of words.

From an internet linguistics perspective, language variation online is important not so much because it's new (language has always varied), but because it's only rarely been written down. Literature favors a few elite languages and dialects, even though there are around seven thousand languages in the world and at least half of the world's population speaks more than one language. So this glorious variety masks a digital divide: people who switch between languages or who speak a less written linguistic variety run into difficulties with many of the automated linguistic tools that internet residents rely on, such as search, voice recognition, automatic language detection, and machine translation. These tools are trained on large corpora, often from formal sources like books, newspapers, and radio, which are biased towards the forms of language that are already well documented. One method of bridging this gap uses public social media writing itself as training input — a promising avenue, considering that the quantity of informal writing produced on the internet exceeds the volume of formal writing many times over.

There aren't very many quadrilingual Arabic-Frisian-Indonesian-English speakers: I wouldn't expect to see a study of tweets switching between all four anytime soon. But regardless of the specific linguistic circles we hang out with online, we're all speakers of internet language because the shape of our language is influenced by the internet as a cultural context. Every language online is becoming decentralized, getting more of its informal register written down. Every speaker is learning how to write exquisite layers of social nuance that we once reserved for speech, whether we mark them by switching alphabets, switching languages, or respelling words.

All our texting and tweeting is making

us better at expressing ourselves in writing. Researcher Ivan Smirnov analyzed posts by nearly a million users in St. Petersburg on the Russian equivalent of Facebook, a social media site called VK, from 2008 to 2016. He found that average word length, a measure of complexity, increases as people get older and as they get more education, as we might expect. But Smirnov also found that messages overall have been getting more complex over time. As he put it: "15-year-old users in 2016 wrote more complex posts than users of any age in 2008."

No one who writes "u" does it because they're unaware that "you" is an option. A literacy study by Michelle Drouin and Claire Davis points out that the idea that textisms might interfere with our ability to produce the formal standard just doesn't fit with what we know about how memory works. Slang and abbreviations are for very common words: "u" for "you," "ur" for "your," "idk" or "dunno" for "I don't know," and so on. That's the point — the sender saves a bit of effort, and the receiver can interpret them because they're so frequent. We don't get internet abbreviations for longer, rarer words and phrases, like "pterodactyl" or "do you wanna start a band?" In psychological terms, shortcuts are for ideas that we've overlearned. You might forget how to find a fancy restaurant that you only go to occasionally, but you can get from your bed to your bathroom even when you're half asleep. If we were going to forget any part of language, it would be the rare, two-dollar words like "grandiloquent" or "sedulous" that we memorize with flashcards for the sake of a test, not the short words we learned as tiny children and keep encountering every day in both their abbreviated and non-abbreviated forms.

Just as conversation and public speaking have coexisted throughout human history, informal writing online can share space with more formal styles. Formal internet genres like ebooks and news sites and company websites no more resemble your quickly dashed-off text message than print books and newspapers and company brochures resembled a hastily scribbled note on the kitchen table. Several studies show that people who use a lot of internet abbreviations perform, at worst, just as well on spelling tests, formal essays, and other measures of literacy as people who never use abbreviations — and sometimes even better.

Instead, what people are doing with internet slang is a good deal more subtle. The linguists Sali Tagliamonte and Derek Denis got seventy-one teenagers to donate the written records of their instant messaging conversations so that they could disentangle what they were actually doing. They found that the teens weren't actually using internet slang all that much. Unlike examples from hyperbolic articles, where almost every word is replaced with slang (r u gna b on teh interwebz 18r?), only 2.4 percent of the actual teens' messages were slang. (I'm reminded of the surveys of perception versus reality for other kinds of youth behavior, where everyone thinks everyone else is drinking more and having more sex than them.) What the teens were doing instead was more sophisticated: they intermixed the very informal features, like smiley faces and acronyms, with very formal ones, words like "must" and "shall" that are rare in speech. Here are a few snippets from various conversations:

aaaaaaaaagh the show tonight shall rock some serious jam

Jeff says "lyk omgod omgod omgodzzzzzZZZzzzzz!!!11one"

heheh okieee! must finish it now ill ttyl

lol. . as u can tell im very bitter right now.

The most obvious thing in these sentences, from the perspective of formal written English, is the informal parts: expressive lengthening like "aaaaaaaaagh," expressive punctuation like "!!!11one," and abbreviations like "ttyl" and "lol." But Tagliamonte and Denis point out that these sentences are also odd from the perspective of informal spoken English: if you record teens sitting around talking to each other out loud, at any point in the early twenty-first century, they barely ever speak words like "shall," "says," "must," or "very" — they prefer the newer versions "going to," "is like," "have to," and "so." (Picture the difference between saying, "And then he said, 'Shall you go?' And I said, 'I must, I'm very tired,'" versus "And then he's like, 'Are you gonna go?' And I'm like, 'I have to, I'm so tired.'" The first belongs in writing, or in the speech of a previous generation, but the second is very much of our own.)

The fact that all but one of the new, informal versions is longer than the older words (two syllables instead of one) puts an immediate question mark by any assumption that the new forms could be a sign of laziness. But further, the fact that teens deploy this mix of formal and informal styles in writing suggests that what they're doing is neither an imperfect transcript of casual speech nor a failed attempt at formal writing. Internet writing is a distinct genre with its own goals, and to accomplish those goals successfully requires subtly tuned awareness of the full spectrum of the language. Media representations of chatspeak ring hollow when they borrow the exotic trappings (like "lol" and "ttyl") without acknowledging the linguistic expertise that it takes to navigate the system as a whole (the coexistence of "lol" and "heheh," or "shall" and "i'll").

Respellings and other internet styles can indicate not just informality but hospitality. Internet humorist @jonnysun tweets in a particular linguistic style, involving lowercase and creative respelling that you can see in his username, "jomny sun," and self-description, an "aliebn confuesed abot humamn lamgauge." The stylized language in jomny's tweets makes him feel approachable, unintimidating, and down-to-earth (apart from the small matter of being an aliebn). Despite his hundreds of thousands of followers, despite his day job as a grad student, you get the sense that he's the type of person who won't judge you for making a typo of your own. Some followers even tweet back in aliebn-speak: a spirit of friendly linguistic play that's more like a familect than a stuffy Oxford Common Room.

I've taken up this sense of linguistic play as a writing exercise, especially when I've just read a bunch of academic papers and I'm having trouble shaking my thoughts free of Nominalization Accumulation Enunciation Contamination. Instead, I draft in Peak Internet Style, with no capitalization or punctuation, using acronyms and creative respelling to write my way through the muddle, rather than stopping when I don't know how to articulate something or trying to sort through form and content at the same time. It's a lot harder to sound stuffy or pretentious when I've only got the tiny box of a chat window to type in and I can't go back and edit — and it's less painful to delete the necessary words when I haven't fussed with them as much. Eventually, I do figure out what I'm trying to say, and at that point it's straightforward to go back and add capitals and periods and delete things like "ugh idk what i'm doing hereeee." But it's easier to formalize the cosmetic elements while retaining an underlying clarity than it is to inject lucidity into a first draft that's classically formatted but dense and impenetrable. A paper analyzing the effects of spellcheck on writer's block suggests that I may be onto something: instantly appearing red squiggles may seem helpful, but for complex documents, they pull writers away from the overall flow and make them think about small details too early. I'm also not alone in noticing positive effects from social media on my writing style: Twitter users in particular often note that the character limits and instant, utterance-level feedback of the tweet format have forced them to learn how to structure their thoughts into concise, pithy statements.

Since long before Edmond Edmont hopped on a bicycle, people have been piecing together how various aspects of the human experience are reflected in how we communicate: our geography, our networks, our societies. There's always more to be figured out, of course, but we have a pretty solid understanding of the basics of how we use language to show our identity when we're having a conversation. And there's a tantalizing inkling that we can express our true selves through language online as well: age-old linguistic practices like language play and switching between languages and styles are becoming written down and electronic. But the youthful, the vernacular, and the digital sides of language are still too easily overlooked: let's find out what we can learn when we take them seriously.

CHAPTER 3:
INTERNET PEOPLE

Can you make friends on the internet?

This is an old question that's been a long time dying. In 1984, a researcher wondered if the internet was "ill-suited for such 'social' uses of language" as making friends, while in 2008, another mused that perhaps the internet was "basically alienating and unfulfilling. To type is not to be human, to be in cyberspace is not to be real. Rather all is pretense and alienation, a poor substitute for the real thing. Ipso facto, cyberspace cannot be a source of meaningful friendships."

And yet, as the discussion raged on, we've ended up conducting a sizeable portion of our social lives online. Close friends send funny links back and forth, grandparents and grandchildren videochat, partners text constantly about day-to-day activities, family members and old friends post photos that we like or comment on, and people join internet communities around a particular interest and end up becoming invested in each other's lives as well.

Internet friends and communities spill over into the physical world, too. I went to an early live performance of the cult hit podcast *Welcome to Night Vale* in 2014, at which Meg Bashwiner framed the preshow announcements by saying, "You know the internet, right? Many of you are even from there." The audience laughed with a note of recognition: *Welcome to Night Vale* became popular because people shared it with each other on the internet, especially on Tumblr, which rocketed it to the top of the iTunes charts and led to attention from mainstream media. The early live shows were the first physical manifestations of a community that had started online.

By one estimate, over a third of couples who got married between 2005 and 2012 met online. By another, 15 percent of American adults have used online dating, and 41 percent know someone who has. The first year that marriages from internet dating were widely reported was 1995, which means that children born of the first internet-mediated relationships are — at least hypothetically — now old enough to internet date and have kids of their own. Internet grandbabies! Pretty much the opposite of "alienating and unfulfilling."

The population of the internet is larger than any one country, and its denizens aren't just technology users; they're a kind of community. Let's call the members of this community Internet People. Sure, a few Non Internet People still conduct their entire social lives via bodily interaction and letters and landline phone calls. Some stay offline voluntarily, like older folks whose friends and family are geographically local or still willing to take landline calls, or people who've decided to live off the grid or avoid social media. Others are offline involuntarily: people in remote areas, who don't speak a language with a major internet presence, or who can't afford a device and a connection. And technically speaking, only about half of the world's population has access to the internet. But a whole lot of people — four billion in the latest count — *are* online. The cyberfriendship skeptics were right in one sense, however: our language online would need to be molded and reshaped in order to be suitable for social purposes. Luckily, Internet People have been doing just that.

FIRST WAVE

People migrate all around the world, and yet within a generation or two, their kids are generally speaking the local language the same way all the neighbor kids are speaking it. Linguists call this "the founder effect," a term borrowed from ecology by the linguist Salikoko Mufwene: the earliest members of a speech community exert a disproportionate influence on how it develops later, especially when that local norm is supported by institutions, like books and schools and signage. Most families who immigrate to the United States don't speak English — they arrive speaking the languages of Poland or China or Mexico or Senegal — and yet a kid who grows up in Texas or California will speak American English like their friends and classmates, regardless of what their parents speak. The distinctive accents in regions like Boston and Virginia can be traced to founding populations of British settlers from particular regions.

But if you get a big enough group of people moving into the same region at the same time, they can alter the local dialect. The vowels of Raleigh, North Carolina, became less Southern after a wave of tech workers from Northern states started arriving in the 1960s, and Cockney has been replaced in working-class central London by Multicultural London English, which draws on a mix of Cockney, Afro-Caribbean English, Indian English, Nigerian English, and

Bangladeshi English, especially since many Cockneys moved out to the suburbs after the Second World War.

So when we're analyzing internet dialects, it makes sense to look at it through the lens of our founding population and our waves of immigration. Social platforms often report their user numbers and demographics, but they don't know the key variable that I'm interested in: Where else have their users hung out? We saw in the previous chapter that your childhood and adolescent peers give you a linguistic base, and that joining a new social group is a prime time to adopt that group's way of speaking. So where did you spend your formative internet years, establishing your first internet-mediated relationships? The internet is a population, but it doesn't keep migration records. There's no Ellis Island of the internet — a boon to the free flow of information, but a bit of a pain for research.

To address this issue, I did a survey. I had a question of internet usage that interested me, and I had a theory, based on research and an internet lifetime of observation, about how to organize people into internet cohorts. The original question proved to not be terribly interesting, but the cohorts turned out great. I asked people to sort themselves by age range: thirteen to seventeen, eighteen to twenty-three, twenty-four to twenty-nine, and thereafter by decade: thirties, forties, fifties, sixties, and over seventy. I then asked them to select a grouping of social platforms that best represented when they first started socializing with people online. There were four options.

- Usenet, forums, IRC, BBS, listservs, or similar
- AIM, MSN Messenger, blogs, Live-Journal, MySpace, or similar
- Facebook, Twitter, Gchat, YouTube, or similar
- Instagram, Snapchat, iMessage, Whats-App, or similar

Both questions were optional and had a write-in box for other answers, but only 150 out of over 3,000 respondents either didn't answer or wrote in something else. This means that 95 percent of people felt themselves adequately described by these four clusters of social platforms. I deliberately left out generic email and texting, because an email address or mobile phone number is the prerequisite for every other platform, and they have their own cross-generational communication styles, which we'll talk about in Chapter 6. The survey doesn't represent a random cross-section of the population, but it got at least a hundred responses in each age group from teens to fifty-plus, and if it overcounts anyone, it probably overcounts people who spend a lot of time on the internet, which is essentially what I was looking for anyway.

I did the survey in 2017. Conveniently, this means we can subtract a neat two decades to get people's ages in 1997, at the very beginning of the mainstreamization of the internet in the late 1990s and early 2000s. Our teenagers weren't born yet, our twentysomethings were children, our thirtysomethings were teens, and so on. We can also subtract a decade to get their ages in 2007, the year after Facebook opened up accounts to anyone with an email address rather than just students: our twentysomethings were then teens, our teens then children, and so on.

Your experience of the internet and the language therein is shaped by who you were and who else was around at the time you joined. How much tech savvy was required to participate in conversations? Were you going online because your friends were already there, or to meet new people? Were you entering a community with established norms, or one where things were still in flux? And did you learn these norms implicitly, through immersion, or through an explicit rulebook? Your answers to these and similar questions have a big effect on what your variety of internet language looks like. In a world where, to use the expression of technologist Jenny Sundén, you're writing yourself into existence, how you write is who you are.

Broadly speaking, there are five main ways that Internet People have written themselves into existence so far.

Old Internet People

Let's start with our founding population, the first wave of people to go online. I call this group Old Internet People, because they're the people who remember the old internet, and it's the closest thing to a unified name that they have for themselves. Searching for "old internet people" brings me to a hand-coded HTML website (first created 1998, last updated 2006) defending the idea of building your own site without using graphics or templates ("some explanation from us 'old Internet people'"), a forum thread from 2011 ("us old Internet people need to get used to a social web"), and a tweet agreeing with a 2018 *New York* magazine article on the decline of typing memorized urls to get to websites directly, rather than go through a search engine or social media ("Looks like it's really hitting a note with us "old" internet people"). The self-conscious quotation marks suggest that users of this term often feel themselves to be coining it spontaneously, but the fact that several people have done so means that it's an emerging norm that I'm picking up on. Old Internet People are old in internet years: they're not actual senior citizens, but rather people who were "jacking in" to networked computers before it was cool. (Although the ones who were using computers back in the punchcard days are quite possibly real senior citizens by now.)

Because they generally went online before most of their friends and peers, they were interacting with strangers. To find strangers they wanted to socialize with, Old Internet People used topic-based tools like Usenet, Internet Relay Chat (IRC), Bulletin Board Systems (BBSes), Multi-User Dungeons (MUDs), listservs, and forums. If you don't know what some of these are, that's kind of the point. Many of these platforms remained pretty obscure even after the internet caught on. The best known was Usenet, a centralized "user's network" which let people start discussion threads and reply to each other's threads within a wide range of discussion groups of various sizes, such as rec.humor.oracle, talk.politics, and alt.tv.simpsons. Usenet was archived wholesale into Google Groups, where posts back to 1981 can still be browsed, and it's an ancestor of later internet forums like Reddit.

Old Internet People may object to being called "internet" people at all, because they remember the days when we had multiple Nets, and would like to point out that I'm actually talking about the World Wide Web, thank you very much. This is true, historically speaking, but common usage has moved on and therefore so do I. A decade or two ago, it would have made sense to subdivide this group further into people who used computers back when they occupied large rooms versus those who started with smaller personal computers, earlier LISP hackers versus later UNIX hackers, ARPAnetters from the 1960s and 1970s versus Usenetters in the 1980s and 1990s, or both of them versus those who started after the invention of the World Wide Web in 1989. But today these historic rivals have more traits in common with each other than they do with subsequent internet users: they were all ahead of their time, excited about the possibilities of technology, and highly motivated to learn how to use it.

Until the early 2000s, tech adeptness was a requirement for computer users. Before and during the technological era that would later be called web 1.0, it was still fairly difficult to get online. Actually participating required even more tech savvy: hand-coding your own HTML homepage or figuring out IRC commands wasn't for the faint of heart, but even posting on a Usenet group, installing an instant messaging client, or setting up an email server took some doing. In the 1998 email comedy movie *You've Got Mail,* one character asks another, "Are you On Line?" You can hear the space between the last two words, and it's clear from context that the question means "Do you ever use the internet?" rather than "Are you currently in front of your device?" Dialing up or jacking in was a choice of hobby rather than a rite of passage at this stage, and it was a hobby that had few restrictions on age: this cohort ranges from those who went online as precocious preteens to adults of all ages. The core members of this group were around college or working age when they first got online, since early network access often came via a university computer science department or a major tech company. Among my survey respondents, almost two-thirds of the forty-somethings selected the Usenet group as their first social platform, and so did a third of thirtysomethings and nearly half of the fifty-somethings, sixtysomethings, and older. This definitely doesn't mean that half of all senior citizens got online in the Usenet days: this means that, of the small percentage of seniors that I could reach by doing a public internet survey in the 2010s, many of them have been online longer than me.

As a group, Old Internet People have the highest level of average technological skill, generally knowing a decent inventory of keyboard shortcuts, the basics in a programming language or two, and how to look at the inner workings of a computer behind its graphical user interface. They're often skilled in some other specific area, such as computer hardware assembly, browser encryption, Wikipedia editing, or forum moderating. They've got a lot of browser extensions or other custom configuration tools on their computer and can't imagine living without them. While some people in later waves of internet adoption also have these skills, it no longer goes without saying: the average internet user no longer needs to know how to code or replace their own hard drive.

The everyday techspeak of Old Internet People overlaps a lot with programmer jargon. In the beginning, knowing how to program was the only way to get online, so it was something that everyone had in common. Much of this language was chronicled by its speakers in a document that became known as the Jargon File. At first, this was a text file of "hacker slang" maintained from 1975 onwards by a series of volunteer editors affiliated with the computer science departments at MIT, Stanford, and a few other universities connected to ARPANET. It was published on paper as *The Hacker's Dictionary* in 1983, by one of the original editors. The text file itself then stagnated for a few years until a new editor took on the project of revising and updating it, leading to two later print editions in 1991 and 1996, as *The New Hacker's Dictionary*. A website version of the Jargon File continued to be updated until late 2003.

When the Jargon File was a live index of slang, the convention was to replace older versions with the newest update. This may have made sense when storage was expensive, but it's rather a challenge for historicizing. In 2018, an archive was recovered from backup tapes dating back to 1976, and sifting through the different versions is like entering an internet time-travel machine. The oldest version of the Jargon File that's been recovered is a plain text file dated August 12, 1976, containing forty-nine words and their definitions, about half a dozen pages long. Some of its words are slang of the day, such as "win" meaning "succeed," and computer slang that later entered the mainstream, like "feature," "bug," and "glitch." Others are hacker cultural terms, like "foo" and "bar" as placeholder names. There's also a distinctly uncomplimentary definition of "user": "A programmer who will believe anything you tell him. One who asks questions." Other terms in the file are now obscure extensions of technical programming jargon: JFCL for "to cancel," from a command that quickly made a program stop whatever it was doing. But perhaps the most interesting thing about this oldest Jargon File is what's *not* in it. There's no trace of what we now think of as classic internet-speak: no acronyms like "lol" or "omg," no emoticons, not even a note about all caps indicating shouting.

The very next year, between March and April 1977, we see the beginning of the social acronyms. This version describes them as "a special set of jargon words, used to save typing" in Talk mode, an early kind of chat. These acronyms include the now unremarkable R U THERE? but also the now obscure BCNU (be seeing you), T and NIL for "yes" and "no," and CUL, "see you later." (I've kept the acronyms in all caps in this section, because that's how the Jargon File lists them, but it's unclear whether this is a reflection of how people typed them at the time or an editorial addition on the part of the Jargon File's contributors. I rather suspect the latter.) A version in December 1977 picked up the still-current BTW and FYI, but other than that, this was all we got for social slang, up to and including the first published version in 1983. Then there was a freeze on editing for the rest of the decade.

When the Jargon File resumed updating in 1990, its records started really looking like the social internet: emoticons like :-) and :-/, all caps as shouting, and a list of further acronyms, most notably LOL, BRB, b4, CU L8TR, and AFK, were all added that same year. Sure, some have gotten a bit dated (CU L8R is more an internet cliché than active slang at this point), and others haven't survived at all, such as HHOJ (haha only joking) and its mate HHOS (haha only serious). But they're clearly the underpinnings of later internet language: acronyms and all caps and emoticons are all recognizable to a mainstream internet user of the 2010s in a way that the programming jargon from only a couple years earlier is not. The 1990 edition itself reflected on this shift, saying that much of the slang was now from Usenet and that the acronyms had been reported from platforms where "on-line 'live' chat" was common but that "these are not used at universities; conversely, most of the people who know these are unfamiliar with FOO?, BCNU, HELLOP, NIL, and T." But techie communities were one of the first to adopt these new conventions: a 1991 update noted that "IMHO, ROTF, and TTFN have gained some currency there," that is, "at universities or in the UNIX world." Since Usenetters were already too spread out among different discussion topics to compile their own linguistic guide, we need to rely on this outsider perspective. But in the end, it doesn't matter so much: together, the earlier techies and the still-tech-savvy Usenetters and chatroom frequenters all make up our founding population.

The earliest internet slang could assume not just that people knew a bit about programming, but that they knew specific commands in a specific language. Technological skills and knowledge of in-group references went hand in hand: the more acronyms you could decipher, the more likely it was that you'd been online for a long time. Or at least, that you had read and reread the help documentation, whether that was a linguistic guide like the Jargon File, the readme file for an open source project, or the FAQ of a forum or newsgroup.

Some Old Internet People eventually became early adopters of blogs or Twitter, and their facility with internet-mediated social interaction often made them highly visible, influential users. Some became the first generation of internet researchers, writing up the practices of their own communities. Others just kept puttering along in their familiar internet byways, and now find themselves having to explain to young whippersnappers that just because they're older doesn't mean they don't know technology — they were programming computers and dialing in via phone lines before said whippersnappers were even born. What the Old Internet People have in common is that they still probably conduct a fair bit of their social lives online, often having a long-standing pseudonym that they use everywhere and internet-first friends that they've known for longer than some of their meatspace friends. They're the social internet users most likely to have never gotten or to have barely used Facebook, because for them the internet is a place to tap into a global community rather than reinforce a local one. (In the late 2010s, many of them started contemplating switching to Mastodon, a social networking platform with a decentralized, topic-based structure and a lack of user-friendliness which both recalled the early internet.)

As the internet's role in everyday life has matured, Old Internet People have become harder to distinguish unless you ask them. Depending on their age and who they hang out with online, some can be confused for one of their two neighboring cohorts, the people who came online in the next wave. Most of the vocabulary from Old Internet People has either been adopted by the mainstream ("btw" for "by the way," "crash" as in "my computer crashed") or fallen into disuse (the acronym UTSL for "use the source, Luke!" a Star Wars–ian way of suggesting that people read the source code before asking questions about it). Some nerdy bits of vocab remain alive in particular techy, hackerish, or other older internet communities without being common for the internet as a whole.

The biggest linguistic contribution of Old Internet People wasn't a particular word — it was a state of mind. Remember those naysayers who deemed the internet "ill-suited for such 'social' uses of language"? The speech communities of the nascent internet grappled with that exact problem: how to convey emotion in informal writing. A study of people who played chat-based online role-playing games in Germany in the late 1990s found that these factors were deeply intertwined: the participants who used the most smileys and other internet slang, and who were the least skeptical about the social potential of the internet, were also the ones who reported forming the most friendships via chat.

The story of the acronym "lol" for "laughing out loud" is a great example of emotions leaping out of the internet and into the physical world. The most commonly accepted account of the creation of "lol" comes from a man in Calgary, Alberta, Canada, named Wayne Pearson, who recalls coining it in a chatroom in the 1980s:

> A friend of mine who went by Sprout (and I believe he still does) had said something so funny in the teleconference room that I found myself truly laughing out loud, echoing off the walls of my kitchen. That's when "LOL" was first used.
>
> We of course had ways of portraying amusement in chatrooms before that (>grin< >laugh< *smile*) and the gamut of

smiley faces, but I felt that none of them really got across the fact that the other person just made you feel foolish by laughing out loud in a room all by yourself (or worse, with other family members in another room, thinking you quite odd!)

The exact time and date when "lol" was created may be forever lost to cyberspace, but Pearson's account does fit the facts we can verify. The first known citation for LOL appears in a list of already common internet acronyms in an online newsletter called *FidoNews* from May 1989, as spotted by the linguist Ben Zimmer. Regardless, Pearson's story evokes the era of Old Internet People: an internet friend, a long-standing pseudonym, laughter at the computer, the bafflement of non-techy family members. Once the next wave of internet users arrived, people would become a lot less surprised that friends and funny stuff happened online.

SECOND WAVE

The second wave of people going online was the biggest for the English-speaking world. Over a few short years in the late 1990s and early 2000s, the internet became mainstream. Internet access was no longer exclusive to tech companies, universities, and the homes of a few geeky people. Regular people started getting online at home, at high schools, and at workplaces. The first year that over half of Americans used the internet was 2000, according to Pew Research, although usage rates were already over 70 percent for those that were college-educated or between the ages of eighteen and twenty-nine. In 1995, a mere 3 percent of Americans had visited a webpage, and only a third had a personal computer. The movie *You've Got Mail,* in 1998, was at the early stages of this mainstreamization: only some of the characters were online, and they went online to meet strangers in chatrooms, but they were bookstore owners, not techies. In 1999, a journalist named Rob Spiegel wrote, "What a difference a year makes. Twelve months ago, I never would have predicted that Internet usage would become completely mainstream by November 1999. . . . I must say, it is hard to get used to everyone understanding what I mean when I say 'online' or 'Web.' "

The dominant narrative of the internet shifted from a story of hackers to a story of digital immigrants and digital natives: an older generation coming online and marveling at how a Net Generation, often the older generation's children, was "born digital," seeming to use computers as easily as they breathed. Even as this narrative was being proposed, researchers were starting to question it: one study of college students in the early 2000s found that there was no significant difference in their ability to do things like edit a spreadsheet or create a digital photo, between the twenty-year-old students and the mature students over forty. A critical review of the evidence for and against digital natives describes it as a myth, "the academic equivalent of a 'moral panic.'" That is, when a group or activity is perceived to be a threat to society, but sensationalist media is far more prominent than any actual evidence for it. Not to mention that not everyone fits neatly into a parent/child dichotomy, or that a decade or two of daily practice can make even the most floundering of digital arrivals reasonably adept.

The true difference between the groups that came online at this time was their social choices, not their technical skills. One cohort fully embraced the internet as a medium for their social lives — they became what I call Full Internet People. The other cohort used the internet as a tool but mostly kept their social lives as before, trickling into internet-mediated friendships later and more gradually — the Semi Internet People.

These groups are correlated with age but not completely defined by it: the Full Internet People tended to be younger, still in school, and susceptible to new trends and what their peers considered cool, while the Semi Internet People tended to be older, in the workplace, and with an established social life. But the important distinction lies in what they were doing on the internet, rather than their exact age: in 1999, a newbie who sought out a topic-based messageboard to meet new people would still inherit many of the cultural touchstones of the Old Internet, while a second newbie who started instant messaging daily with existing friends would become Full Internet, and a third who got into forwarding funny chain emails would become Semi Internet. These newbies could all be the same age, but the speech communities they'd be joining would be very different. As with any generalization, it's worth describing them in bright-line terms to clearly illustrate the options, but some may find themselves on the borders between one group and another.

Full Internet People

Full Internet People came of age with the beginning of the social internet in the late 1990s to early 2000s. They joined an internet that had already established many of its communicative norms, and they acquired them, not explicitly from a Jargon File or FAQ but implicitly, from their peers joining at the same time, via the same cultural alchemy that transmits which music is cool or which jeans are desirable. The internet is "full" for this cohort because they never questioned its social potential: How could they, when they began by using it to communicate more with people they already knew? It would be absurd to assert that the internet is asocial or that Internet People are somehow not real when a breakup that happened last night over IM is all anyone can talk about the next day at lunch.

IM, or instant messaging, like AOL Instant Messenger (AIM), MSN Messenger, and ICQ (I seek you), was new and at the core of the Full Internet People's first internet social experience, as were personalized homepages and profile pages where you could add neon-colored backgrounds and small, blinky gifs, such as GeoCities, Angelfire, Xanga, Neopets, LiveJournal, and MySpace. According to my 2017 survey, this group was centered around ages twenty-four to twenty-nine, over three-quarters of whom chose AIM, MSN Messenger, blogs, LiveJournal, MySpace, or similar as their first social platform. Around half of eighteen- to twenty-three-year-olds and thirtysomethings, and a quarter of forty-somethings, started with these platforms as well. That's a lot of teens, preteens, and twentysomethings in the late 1990s and early 2000s.

This group didn't keep a list of its slang the way that the Old Internet People had with the Jargon File, because by its very nature the Full Internet community was huge, decentralized, and took its discourse practices for granted. (Though, if I had a time machine, you can bet that I'd tell my fourteen-year-old self to start such a list!) As grown-ups, however, this cohort has plenty of access to media platforms and periodically gets hit by waves of nostalgia for their early internet days. A videogame called Lost Memories Dot Net by Nina Freeman draws on Freeman's own adolescent self-ies and memories of the 2004 internet: you play as a fourteen-year-old girl designing her new anime fansite-slash-blog and IMing with her best friend about the boy they both have a crush on, in a tabbed interface that resembles an Internet Explorer theme from the era. An article reminiscing about the early-2000s teen internet highlighted how it replicated offline social structures: friends would link their homepages in webrings or cliques, and decorate them with bright and pastel HTML tables and cute, tiny cartoon animal gifs. When this cohort did hang out with internet strangers, it was often on virtual-pet websites like Neopets and Petz.com, which journalist Nicole Carpenter fondly described as "a mix between Tamagotchi and Pokémon" that provided "a safe place for girls to play in an often unfriendly Internet." There were waves of nostalgia when archivists scrambled to preserve GeoCities sites after Yahoo shut them down in 2009 and when AOL shut down AIM for good in 2017. When AIM shut down, a tech culture reporter recalled how in middle school she would print out AIM conversations with boys so that she could analyze them with friends.

A few years after joining the social internet, Full Internet People also became the first Facebook and Twitter users. But here, my survey demographics are just as interesting for where this group *wasn't*. We know for a fact that they were the first users of Facebook, because it was only open to Harvard students when it launched in 2004, before expanding to universities in general, then high school students, and to the general public in 2006. The catch is that very few people in this age range (less than 10 percent) had their *first* social experiences on Facebook. The founding populations of the Usenet group and the IM group were both people who were newly online; Facebook, by contrast, was founded by people who switched from an older platform to something new.

When Facebook started, it was anomalous among social platforms for how it linked your online identity with your offline name and social networks. The assumption, carried down from the Old Internet People, had been that you went online to meet new people and experiment with identity, in which case Facebook looked like a weird rupture. But in fact, Facebook was simply making explicit something that its early users had been doing since middle school. Your friends on IM often had fanciful pseudonyms that looked superficially like the ones Old Internet People had gone by on Usenet and chatrooms, but their actual function was completely different. Whereas Wayne Pearson, the guy who invented "lol" in the 1980s, had an internet friend he only knew as "Sprout," Nina Freeman's 2004 self in Lost Memories Dot Net knew perfectly well that TarnishedDreamZ was Kayla from her class at school.

Those who joined the internet to meet new people kept the same username across platforms for years, decades even, so that their internet friends could find them. But for the internet users who joined in order to hang out with people they already knew, screennames were a way of performing identity, rather than obscuring it: your username might honor a favorite band or movie quote, and could change a few months later as your pop cultural allegiances shifted. Your friends knew it was you the whole time, but if other people lost track of your shifting names, so much the better. It wasn't so much of a stretch to start using your real name on Facebook, when your online and offline selves had been effectively linked within the minds of your primary social network for years. In fact, it could be felt to be a sign of maturity that you weren't performing your identity through your username anymore (albeit a kind of "maturity" that involved posting photos of people drinking warm beer out of red plastic cups).

A great illustration of this attitude difference between Old and Full Internet People comes from *It's Complicated: The Social Lives of Networked Teens,* technologist danah boyd's detailed and highly readable ethnography of teenagers using the internet across the United States from 2005 to 2012.

I had spent my own teen years online, and I was among the first generation of teens who did so. But that was a different era; few of my friends in the early 1990s were interested in computers at all. And my own interest in the internet was related to my dissatisfaction with my local community. The internet presented me with a bigger world, a world populated by people who shared my idiosyncratic interests and were ready to discuss them at any time, day or night. I grew up in an era where going online — or "jacking in" — was an escape mechanism, and I desperately wanted to escape.

The teens I met are attracted to popular social media like Facebook and Twitter or mobile technologies like apps and text messaging for entirely different reasons. Unlike me and the other early adopters who avoided our local community by hanging out in chatrooms and bulletin boards, most teenagers now go online to connect to the people in their community. Their online participation is not eccentric; it is entirely normal, even expected.

In our terms, this difference in attitudes is because boyd is an Old Internet Person, and the teens she surveyed are Full Internet People and younger: the sites in her book stretch from MySpace to Instagram. Boyd links the impetus for younger people to socialize online with restrictions like anti-loitering laws and car-centric neighborhoods that reduce the opportunities for physical socialization in places like malls and public parks. Similarly, a 2000 survey of students in California public schools reported that teens overwhelmingly favored private messaging with friends they already knew over going on public chatrooms and messageboards to talk with strangers.

To be sure, some Full Internet People did eventually make friends via the internet, whether for dating, professional networking, or bonding over a shared interest (just as many Old Internet People did eventually link their online and offline identities). The first generation of internet users had brought with them a certain smugness, a feeling of internet exceptionalism, the conviction that Internet People were better than regular people, and that it was just as well if the internet was a place where the previous norms of social interaction need not apply. If the language was a bit rough around the edges, prone to misinterpretations, so much the better for keeping out those who didn't get it. The first generation to join the social internet en masse had a different motivation: to maintain friendships with a local community, rather than join a global one. They weren't trying to reinvent communication; they were just trying to get on with living, to have the normal flirtations and breakups and crises using the communication tools available. But by using informal writing to convey the regular dramas of human life, they also started reshaping informal writing into something that could more deeply convey the full range of human emotions.

It is perhaps ironic that this Full Internet generation, the first to use the internet to baffle their parents collectively, is also the last to be baffled by their own children. While Fulls can draw on their own teen years to understand chat apps in the frame of instant messaging, or Tumblr in the frame of GeoCities, they didn't have a digital childhood. They're the first to reckon with unfamiliar questions like how much iPad time is too much for a toddler, what to do when a child stumbles across a disturbing parody version of a children's cartoon, and whether to post photos and anecdotes of a child on social media when faraway relatives may enjoy them but the child may grow up to find them embarrassing.

As far as internet facility goes, Full Internet People have some nostalgia for earlier technology and some insecurity about whether they've lost touch with what younger people are doing online, but they're well adapted to both social networking sites and professional electronic communication. They have at least one and possibly many social media accounts, and get a lot of their news and entertainment online, whether that's from Facebook, Twitter, Instagram, Reddit, Netflix, or podcasts. They've been serving as family tech support since adolescence and they're one of the primary vectors by which new technology percolates into the mainstream. They're comfortable with a variety of phones, computers, and other devices, as well as email, instant messaging, general internet browsing, word processing, and probably other office tools like spreadsheets and presentations. While Full Internet People may or may not remember a time before they had home internet access, they definitely don't remember an internet without basic internet slang. Abbreviations like "lol" and "wtf," emoticons like :-) and <3, and conventions like all caps for shouting were already in place. They picked up most of their internet slang from context and their peers, and associate it with tone of voice.

Their skill levels with other kinds of technology vary considerably. A study of myths and realities of tech-savviness among American college students in 2004 found that while virtually all of them had the previously mentioned skills, only a minority knew how to create graphics, edit audio or video, or make a website. Later surveys in countries like the UK, Australia, and South Africa have found the same thing — facility with technology for social purposes was nearly ubiquitous among those born after 1980, but more specialized technological skills (like coding, editing a wiki, keeping a blog, or following RSS feeds) were found among a minority, from about 2 percent to 30 percent. This percentage doesn't represent a single, savvy minority and a larger tech-clueless group, as in the early days of computers, but rather inconsistent, piecemeal knowledge: people reported learning tech skills on a need-to-know basis. And these were surveys of college students, who are already more likely to be technologically adept than the non-college-going population.

Predictions about digital natives were only partly accurate. The divide between techie and non-techie has blurred, but it didn't happen by converting the entire population into techies. The buzzword in the tech skill surveys of the early 2000s was ICT: information and communications technologies. But the information and the communication parts need to be analyzed separately. It's true that the generations born into the internet would become intimately comfortable with an online social life, just like the generations born into the telephone or the automobile didn't find themselves alienated by a disembodied voice crackling down a wire or alarmed by the prospect of traveling above sixty miles an hour. But unlike for Old Internet People, there's barely any relationship between how well a Full Internet Person can socialize via computers and how well they can talk to the computer itself. The first car drivers were all skilled mechanics, because the vehicles broke down so regularly, but as cars became mainstream, they needed to be drivable even by people who didn't know an oil pump from a carburetor. As computers, too, became usable even by people who'd never "looked under the hood," the relationship between tech skills and internet socialization loosened — a development that we'll be following for the rest of the chapter.

Semi Internet People

Like Full Internet People, Semi Internet People came online at the beginning of the social internet, in the late 1990s and early 2000s. But they don't know most of the cultural touchstones of Full Internet People, because they weren't online for the same reasons — they generally started going online for work, and shortly thereafter expanded to other functional tasks like reading the news, looking up information, shopping, and making travel plans. The social side was an area they only dipped their toes into later and more gradually. They're "semi" because they're only partially committed to an internet social life: they may have some relationships that they keep up with via the internet, especially younger family members, and some where they do so by other means, especially old friends, but they've retained a cautious attitude towards getting to know people primarily online. At any rate, they have vivid memories of what it was like to maintain relationships via letters and phone calls.

A 2007 survey of internet users and non-users in Britain found that the biggest gap in terms of internet use in general wasn't between young adults and middle-aged people, but between people who were over and under age fifty-five. We'll get to the over-fifty-fives later, but the users below this threshold still had an interesting split in terms of how they used the internet. Around two-thirds of internet users below age twenty-five used at least one social networking site, but only around half of twenty-five- to forty-four-year-olds and a third of those forty-five and over did the same. In the years after 2007, a lot of the older group started using social networking sites, or as the media put it, "My parents just got Facebook." In 2017, Pew Research estimated that over 60 percent of American adults between fifty and sixty-four had become users of Facebook, not even counting other social networks. This aligns with the survey I did of people's first social platform. We already saw that the Facebook, Twitter, YouTube, Gchat cluster is curiously hollow in the middle age ranges because its first users switched to it from somewhere else. But it does have two peaks of users who started their internet social experience there: the over-fifties and the under-twenty-threes. Of course, a forty-five-year-old and a thirteen-year-old both joining Facebook as their first social network in 2008 didn't have the same experience of it, so we're going to hold off on the younger half of the Facebook-first cohort until later in this chapter.

138

While the Full Internet People were learning internet language by immersion in the late 1990s and early 2000s, the Real Adults coming online at the same time wanted a travel guide, an explanation of the social landscape that they were only partially entering. After all, if they'd been drawn to do-it-yourself internetting and a computer-mediated social circle, they could have gotten online earlier and become Old Internet People instead. The most comprehensive of these guides was *Wired Style*.

Wired Style started as the style guide for the technology magazine *Wired,* which was founded in 1993. Normally, magazines and newspapers follow a style guide, such as *The Associated Press Stylebook* or *The Chicago Manual of Style,* in order to ensure that all the writing in a particular publication is consistent when it comes to matters like the Oxford comma, whether periods should be included in acronyms, and the spelling of words with multiple recognized options. But these existing style guides weren't keeping pace with the technological innovations *Wired* was writing about. Even when the classic style guides did have recommendations, they were often too conservative for a tech publication that considered itself on the bleeding edge. It's fine if a more staid newspaper is still writing "Web site" or "E-mail" for a few years after most of its readers have moved on to "website" and "email" (*The New Yorker*'s identity is partly defined by its deliberately conservative diaeresis on words like "coöperate"), but for *Wired* (as with this book), being stylistically behind on internet formatting would have seriously undermined its credibility.

So *Wired*'s copyeditors, Constance Hale and Jessie Scanlon, devised their own in-house style guide to provide a consistent manual on matters like whether to capitalize or hyphenate "email" (no to both) and how to capitalize and punctuate internet acronyms (caps but no dots, as in "LOL," not "L.O.L." or "lol"). Publishers saw the potential to interest a broader audience, and Hale and Scanlon's style guide was published with revisions and expansions as a book called *Wired Style* in 1996, with a second edition in 1998.

Academic papers were being written about internet language at the same time, but documents like *Wired Style* and the Jargon File are particularly important because they were written for a general audience and reflected internet practice back onto its users. While the internal *Wired* style guide had initially been created to standardize a group of writers who were already tech savvy and writing for a tech-savvy audience, *Wired Style* was aimed at the internet as it became mainstream, providing guidance on linguistic "netiquette" for new "netizens." Semi Internet People didn't necessarily read *Wired Style* itself when they first got online, but it's the most comprehensive of the many guides that were passed around via photocopy or printed in sidebars of newspapers and magazines at the time, teaching people that all caps signified shouting, that B and 4 and 2 and U and LOL were abbreviations for "be" and "for" and "to" and "you" and "laughing out loud," and that business emails weren't supposed to be as formal as a business letter. But this knowledge was sometimes more hypothetical than practical, because they were exchanging emails primarily with members of the same generation.

Just as with the hypothesized digital natives, we need to be careful not to conflate the functional side of being online with the social side: the Semi Internet group was called digital immigrants, which was supposed to represent their fundamental discomfort with technology and tendency to print out their emails. But after a decade or two of practice, Semi Internet People are broadly comfortable with the personal and

141

professional internet that they inhabit. Like Old Internet People, their level of comfort with internet slang is related to their level of comfort with other internet tools — both indicate how long they've been online and whether they feel at home there. While no other generation is going to match the average level of tech savvy of the people for whom getting online was truly difficult, the Semi Internet People tend to have depth over Full and younger Internet People's breadth. They're often highly skilled at a few technological things that they've been doing for a long time, like Photoshop, Microsoft Office, or other tools they've been using at work for a decade.

Despite their facility with familiar tools, despite the fact that they're now just as likely to be providing tech support to their own elderly parents or older friends as receiving it from younger people, they still consider themselves "not really a computer person." Their first reaction when encountering a new technological task is to ask for help from a person they know offline, such as their half-grown offspring or a younger coworker. Or sometimes merely the nearest available offline person — a middle-aged couple at a café once asked me to fix some app on their phone based on no other qualification than the fact that I was sitting next to them with my laptop. I can't say it's an ineffective strategy: I did, after all, successfully fix the phone. But it was a problem that I, too, had never encountered before, and I solved it by dint of the process described in an *xkcd* comic titled "Tech Support Cheat Sheet," which reads, in part, "Find a menu item or button which looks related to what you want to do → Click it → Did it work? → No? → (repeat) → I've tried them all → Google the name of the program plus a few words related to what you want to do." I've asked people in coffeeshops for the wifi password or if they can pass me a menu, but for tech problems I turn to digital people: googling with the hope that a helpful expert has written a comprehensive how-to article, but willing to settle for a random person on a forum five years ago who had the same issue.

Like how Old Internet People defined themselves by knowledge of technology and excitement about meeting other people through it, their age-mates who became Semi Internet People defined themselves by ambivalence towards technology and an orientation towards offline relationships over online ones. Facebook was successful among Semi Internet People because it let them replicate their offline network rather than trying to encourage them to make internet friends. I ran a follow-up survey later in 2017 using the same demographic categories to ask about a different word, but this time I posted the link on Twitter a few days before I posted the same link on Facebook. I had no shortage of forty- and fifty-somethings filling out the survey via Twitter, but they were almost all in the Usenet-or-earlier, Old Internet cohort. Within hours of posting the link on Facebook, my over-forties had balanced out again to what they looked like in the first survey, with plenty of Facebook-first joiners (despite the fact that I'd lumped Twitter into the same category as Facebook). Ten years after Facebook first became open to non–college students, the people who preferred it still had very different attitudes towards online relationships, even compared to other social platforms from the same era.

But Semi Internet People didn't start using the social internet with Facebook: they started with email, which I deliberately left off my survey because it was popular with everyone before and during the time that the internet became mainstream. In 1995, Pew found that three times as many American adults used email somewhat regularly than had ever visited a website, and email use remained saturated at around 90 percent of the internet-using population from 2002 to 2011. Semi Internet People tend to be very good at email, and often follow top-notch early email etiquette, involving a large, complicated folder system, interspersing replies to a long email after the bits that are being replied to, and sometimes even changing the subject line as the topic of the email changes. (Some Old Internet People do this, too; Full Internet People tend to be horrified by it, as it messes up the later, Gmail-style technology that automatically threads emails by subject line and hides repeated blocks of text.) Semi Internet People's early internet cultural touchstones consist more of funny chain emails than the crudely animated Flash videos of the Full Internet People.

Although they took longer to develop, by now Semi Internet People do generally have some relationships that they keep up via technology, especially using email, texting, chat apps, Facebook, Skype, FaceTime, or other video calls. They're often aware of internet slang, especially the kinds that got popularized in the late 1990s, when they were first coming online. They never quite got into as many emoticons as the more internetty cohorts, probably sticking to :-), but they leapfrogged directly into emoji. To Semi Internet People, the meaning of internet language is simply "this is a message I'm sending via the internet." All meaning is face value meaning, and if you want to convey a more subtle layer of social meaning, that's what a voice conversation is for. Their assumption is that text is fundamentally incapable of conveying the full social landscape. This is the exact opposite of what Full Internet People believe.

A closer look at "LOL" and "lol" illuminates this difference between the two second-wave cohorts. Semi Internet People learned all-caps "LOL" from lists of internet slang. It didn't stand for "Little Old Lady" or "Lots Of Love" anymore, they were told, by young people and internet manuals: it's an acronym for "laughing out loud." But words are slippery little creatures, especially online. Full Internet People learned "lol" from their peers, in the social crucible of the internet, where words — and especially time-saving acronyms — are in all lowercase unless they're emphatic. And while "lol" started out indicating laughter, it quickly became aspirational, a way of showing your appreciation of a joke or defusing a slightly awkward situation even if you didn't technically laugh at it. As early as 2001, the linguist David Crystal was doubting how many lols were truly out loud, and as one widely shared Reddit post put it, "We should change 'lol' to 'ne' (nose exhale), because that's all we really do when we see something funny online."

I did a survey of how people used "lol" in 2017, and found a word in transition. Not only was it steadily losing its capitalization, but its meaning was also evolving. Over half of Semi Internet People indicated that they used it to indicate laughing out loud, although a substantial proportion also said they could use it for general amusement that wasn't necessarily actual laughter. Other meanings, like sarcasm or wryness, were not common choices for them. The Old and Full Internet People had all three: they favored amusement when pressed to pick a primary meaning, but could also broaden it into both ironic pseudo-amusement and genuine laughter (the latter especially by expanding it into "LOLOLOL" or "actual lol"). The youngest group flat-out rejected the idea of capitalizing "lol" or using it to indicate real laughter, even when expanded to "LOLOLOL," and instead preferred the meanings of amusement, irony, and even passive aggression. This subtle new social function of "lol" raises further questions, like what exactly we mean by irony, so we'll get back to it shortly when we talk about the Post Internet People.

The third wave of Internet People trickled online after the population as a whole had already done so, when the internet had become unavoidable. Half of this wave are those who are too young to remember life before the internet and started going online as they learned how to read and type: these are Post Internet People. The second half is older, consisting of people who thought they could just ignore this whole internet thing but eventually, belatedly, decided to join: we'll call them the Pre Internet People. (Those who are still offline might be termed Non Internet People.)

The Old Internet, Semi Internet, and Pre Internet cohorts are artifacts of how the internet was introduced. Mixed-age technophiles got online much earlier, the somewhat skeptical majority waited until it was the normal thing to do, and the most technophobic delayed entry as long as they could. That's going to stop happening. Sure, an individual person can still be a luddite, just like an individual person can elect to live in a cabin in the woods with no electricity, but in wealthy societies, and increasingly around the world, the internet has become something everyone has some exposure to. Kids are all getting online at the same young age, socializing there as preteens or early teenagers, the same age when their peer groups start to take on an outsize importance in their lives offline. So for future generations, the same demographics that have always influenced language — age, gender, race, class, networks, and so on — will become more important than when you first went online.

An easy way to identify both cohorts in the third wave is by their relationship with email — or, more accurately, their lack of one. Old, Full, and Semi Internet People first went online when social media was still nascent and email was a vital part of both personal and professional communication — it still is, for many of them. For people who came online in the late 2000s and into the 2010s, social media was already ubiquitous. These users were typically either retired from work or too young to use email for professional reasons, so they often skipped directly to social media and chat apps instead.

Pre Internet People

The members of our oldest cohort are on the internet (sporadically), but they're not of it. Pre Internet People were around for the previous waves, when the internet came into existence and became mainstream, but at the time they figured they could get by just fine without it. In the 2010s, many of them gradually found their way online, as so much information and socialization had moved there. Pew Research reported that only 14 percent of Americans over age sixty-five used the internet in 2000, the first year that more than half of the general adult population was online. But that number rose to 50 percent by 2012, and that stat has continued to grow a percentage point or two per year. Pew also found that a third of seniors were using social media in 2017, a rise from just one in ten in 2010.

While not all Pre Internet People are over sixty-five, and not all those over sixty-five are pre-internet (a sixty-five-year-old in 2015 was a spry thirty in 1980, and could well have been an early adopter), the oldest demographic offers the clearest example of delayed rates of internet and social media adoption. Curiously, Pre Internet People share some commonalities with Post Internet People, who came online around the same time. They've both never really known an internet without Facebook and YouTube and wifi and touchscreens, and they're both disproportionately likely to be using their family members' cast-off electronics.

Pre Internet People generally have one

account somewhere that a more adept internet person set up for them, which may be on email, "the Facebook," a text chat app like WhatsApp, or videochat like Skype or FaceTime. They know how to do basic things like send and receive messages there, but if they ever get logged out or if the app changes its interface, they're going to have to ask for help again. They might only use the internet through a touchscreen device like a smartphone or tablet, but if they use a computer, they probably have a desktop shortcut helpfully labeled "The Internet" or "E-Mail," and woe betide them if anything ever happens to it. They definitely can't code, and they may not even know how to copy-paste, but some do know how to touch-type: they learned on an actual typewriter.

Late internet arrivals aren't studied or worried about as much as tech-happy youth and early adopters, but one source of information comes from Jessamyn West, a librarian (and Old Internet Person) who has been running weekly drop-in tech help sessions in rural Vermont since 2007. West periodically documents these sessions online so that the internet at large can better understand this population. Most of the people West works with are between fifty-five and eighty-five, and while the percentage of the population that doesn't use the internet had been dropping, between 2015 and 2018 it remained steady at around 11 percent of Americans. This rate is higher among people in rural areas with slow connection speeds, people who prefer to use the internet in a language that isn't English, and people with failing eyesight or who are hard of hearing. All of these characteristics are more common among older people. West emphasizes that you don't get to being a non–internet user in the 2010s simply by accident: the people she works with have had some exposure to computers and decided it wasn't for them, but now they're faced with something that can only be accessed online, like a government service or photos of a grandchild. Her role becomes as much about coaching them through their anxiety about technology and confusing user interfaces as it is about the specific tasks at hand.

While Semi Internet People associate internet slang with any kind of informal communication via technology, and the younger cohorts of Internet People use internet slang to convey tone of voice, Pre Internet People simply don't use "LOL" and other internet acronyms (much less their hipper, lowercase versions) and may not even recognize them. Adopting the language of a particular community, as we saw in the previous chapter, is as much about believing that it is a desirable thing to be a member of that community as it is simply being exposed to it: despite their internet use, Pre Internet People do not accept the internet as a legitimate source of social influence — they're the primary cohort that leaves the internet again, once they've joined, because it's not necessarily a high priority to get their devices fixed. If they use any written slang, it might be rebus forms that predate the internet, such as B, U, and 2 for "be," "you," and "too," or emoji that get brought up automatically by an auto-predict keyboard and seem readily interpretable as little pictures.* Internet slang like acronyms and emoticons is not just unfamiliar to them, it signals membership in a group that they have no desire to be a part of. To put it in the words of an older person who talked to me after using Facebook for a year or so, "I keep seeing people writing a colon and then a parenthesis. . . . What do they mean by that?" But even after I explained ("Oh, that's rather

*Though the seeming obviousness of emoji can be deceptive, as we'll see in Chapter 5.

clever!"), I have never once seen this person use a smiley.

This cohort may not have the same linguistic norms online as Internet People proper, but that doesn't mean that they're typing in newspaper-ready formal English any more than anyone else is online. By nature, these are the kind of internet residents that you can't reach with a large internet survey, but the most common piece of linguistic anecdata that I kept seeing myself and hearing about from other Internet People concerns their use of separation characters. Many people in this group use hyphens or strings of periods or commas to separate one thought from the next ("i just had to beat 2 danish guys at ping poong.....& ..they were good.... glad i havent lost my chops" or "thank you all for the birthday wishes - great to hear from so many old friends - hope you all are doing well -- had a lovely dinner" or "Happy Anniversary,,,Wishing you many more years of happiness together,,,,").

We don't have statistics about the exact prevalence, but the dash or ellipsis as generic separation character seems to be found throughout, at least, the English-speaking world. When I asked for more anecdotes on Twitter, someone commented, "So you've texted with my in-laws?" Why do all these people, who primarily went online to reach younger family members, still type more like each other than like their interlocutors? Our first clue comes from a senior that Jessamyn West videoed at one of her library drop-in tech sessions, sending his very first email. The man, Don, says to West behind the camera, "First time I ever typed a thing in my life." Then he pauses and asks, "Something I use a lot of times, when I'm writing by longhand, is rather than normal punctuation, when I get to the end of a thought, I go 'dot dot dot.'" He gestures to the computer: "Is that just period, period, period?" When West says it is, Don turns back to the keyboard and triumphantly types dot, dot, dot.

Don's expression of triumph contrasted sharply with the bafflement that I heard from younger Internet People about separation characters, so I took the hint and went searching for more longhand. Where I ended up was postcards. One particularly fruitful source was a book of scanned postcards sent to Ringo Starr by the other three members of the Beatles. John Lennon and Paul McCartney tended to write longer messages with relatively standard punctuation, but George Harrison's shorter messages read, in transcription, almost exactly like a

155

text from a Pre Internet Person. A postcard sent to Starr from Harrison in 1978 has a whole five dots:

Lots of Love from Hawaii. . . . .

George+Olivia

Other postcards in the book have emoji-like sketches — a bear with a speech bubble, a smiley face below the signature. I found more postcards from Harrison on auction sites: one to his father has all the dashes you could ask for, as well as "xx" for kisses at the end, which is still common in British text messages:

Hi Dad - Eileen -

Hope you are O.K. and had a good drive back. We came to North Sweden for a week - Pretty Cold. But very nice - makes a change - Be back next week - speak to you then

Love George + Olivia xx

It's not just a Beatles thing, or even just an English thing. A corpus study of over five hundred Swiss postcards from the 1950s to the 2010s notes two common features of the genre: repeated punctuation marks, like . . . . . ., ???, and !!!, as well as smiley faces, hearts, and other emoticon-like doodles. Indeed, this influence goes in both directions: a study comparing the postcards and text messages of Finnish teenagers in 2003 noted that they had begun writing sideways emoticon faces like :) in their postcards.

Other genres of informal writing also show dashes or ellipses as a generic separation character, especially when space is constrained. For example, this scanned, type-written recipe card for "BONNIE DOON OATIES" cookies, attributed to one Joyce Viele, uses repeated dots, this time with spaces between them, while other handwritten recipes use dashes to separate each step.

```
Combine shortening, sugars, eggs,
salt, and vanilla and beat thor-
oughly . . . Sift flour and soda
together; add to first mixture
with coconut and oats and mix
well. . . . Drop level table-
spoons of dough on greased bak-
ing sheets . . . Bake in moderate
oven (350°F). 10-15 minutes. Makes
3 dozen cookies.
```

Postcards and recipe cards have a couple key features in common with social media posts. They're both written by a single person, without editing — not like a published cookbook or a novel told in letters. Both provide a constrained space to write in, which encourages a certain breeziness, and both are often semipublic: directed at a specific person or two but implicitly viewable by a much larger group. It's not an invasion of privacy to pick up and read a postcard or recipe card lying on a table the way it would be to unfold and read a letter addressed to someone else. These similarities explain both the generic separation characters as well as the surprisingly rapid adoption of emoji by older groups in comparison to internet acronyms like "lol." Pre Internet People (along with some Semi and Old Internet People who also use the dot dot dot, though not quite as extensively) are faithfully reproducing the conventions of a genre that they're fluent in but that their baffled younger audience has lost in our digital age. This genre already contained a mental "slot" for little doodles, and emoji fit right in. This group provides an intriguing bridge between digital and analogue informal writing: even people who are almost completely at sea with the technical side of things have correctly identified the social framework and mapped it onto familiar linguistic practices.

In many ways, this oldest internet cohort is more interesting than the younger ones. We have some idea of what it means to be a young person with internet-mediated friendships. There's not that much difference between a late-1990s teenager constantly sending mundane but vital updates via AOL Instant Messenger and creating social drama about who was in their top eight friends on MySpace and a mid-2010s teen who's constantly sending mundane but vital updates via Snapchat and creating social drama about who liked whose selfie on Instagram. But we haven't seen an older generation mass-adopt a large-scale communications technology in quite a while — perhaps not since the invention of the telephone. So far, we're only getting the first glimmerings of what it's like for a whole cohort of seniors to be longtime Internet People, but small-scale efforts to teach older folks how to use the internet do suggest it can lead them to feeling more socially connected. I'd love to see a proper corpus study comparing postcards and texts from younger and older people, to see what else we can learn by drawing together informal writing across different generations and mediums.

Post Internet People

When I was growing up, my family didn't have a television. This made me a trifle eccentric among my peers, but I nonetheless picked up, by cultural osmosis and glimpses at other people's houses, the essentials of TV culture: how to operate a remote control, the *Jeopardy!* theme song, and the social progression of *Sesame Street* from "the best" to "a thing for babies" to the nostalgia-fueled best again. I grew up in a post-television generation, irrespective of my own (lack of) participation in it. The Pre Internet People don't feel socially connected to the internet even when they do use it, and the Post Internet People are the inverse: socially influenced by the internet regardless of their own level of use. They don't remember the first time they used a computer or did something online, the way that earlier generations don't remember when they first watched a television or used a telephone, and they can talk about the social implications of following and liking even if they don't personally have an account on a given platform or even use social media at all. It's just part of the social landscape.

Practically speaking, the bright line question that divides Full and Post Internet People is often, did you get Facebook before or after your parents? Or in more general terms, did you arrive on the social internet after it was already ubiquitous, or were you on it when it was still a niche or young-person thing? In the survey that I did in 2017, the first social platform of the thirteen- to seventeen-year-olds was a pretty even split between either the Facebook, Twitter, YouTube, Gchat cluster or the Instagram, Snapchat, iMessage, WhatsApp cluster. About a third of eighteen- to twenty-three-year-olds joined them in selecting the Facebook cluster. (Another half of the eighteen- to twenty-three-year-olds selected the IM cluster and are thus grouped with the Full Internet People above.)

Digital residency tends to start around age nine to fourteen. Small children use touchscreens as media devices, for playing games and watching videos. But their use of the internet for communication is still mediated by their caregivers, just like their offline relationships: parents coordinate a videochat with grandparents or arrange with another parent for their kids to be able to videochat just as they're in charge of playdates or going to the park. This is partly for practical reasons: internet communication still often takes knowing how to read and type, there are real concerns about age-appropriate material, and the age requirement for most social networking sites is thirteen.* But even for open platforms like texting, and even assuming some users lie about their ages, the switch to regularly carrying a device and using it for your own, autonomous communication happens in the tween or early teen years. This is the period when parents want to be able to coordinate logistics directly with their kids rather than through other adults, and kids start asking for phones because the social life of your peers becomes more enticing than hanging out with your parents.

Since this is the youngest cohort, it's tempting to treat them as our crystal ball, and try to divine from their social media practices what we're all going to be doing in another decade or two. But it's important to be cautious about any attempt at Divination By Teenager. We need to separate out the linguistic and social features that are characteristic of this stage in life from those that will follow them as they age.

*The Children's Online Privacy Protection Act has various regulations for websites catering to those aged twelve or younger, and for ease of enforcement many sites simply require users to be thirteen or older.

A certain genre of trendy article pops up every couple months in which the writer explains how teens are using social media right now — sometimes by interviewing a teenage relative, sometimes by profiling a handful of supposedly representative teenagers, sometimes by being an older teen and reflecting on the usage of their friends. What these profiles inevitably find is that popular teenagers are texting or snapping or other-kind-of-messaging each other, for seemingly no reason, at rates completely unfathomable to the adult writer. Thousands of texts a month! Running up data bills! If they dig a step deeper, they may also find that shyer, nerdier, or more introverted teens are doing less of all this.

But none of this is unique to the internet. As the linguist and internet researcher Susan Herring points out, her generation of baby boomer teens hung out "aimlessly" in malls, at drive-in movies, at sock hops and school sports games and public parks. They created codes and wrote backwards to pass notes, the same way kids in internet generations create inventive language for texting, and they decorated their lockers or bedrooms like a younger generation takes great care with their social media profiles. Whether they're spending hours on the landline telephone, racking up a massive texting bill, or being "addicted" to Facebook or MySpace or Instagram, something that teens want to do in every generation is spend a lot of unstructured time hanging out, flirting, and jockeying for status with their peers.

Herring also points to a French sociology study from 1981, which found that sociability is highest among teenagers and young adults, and declines as people get older. "All else being equal," writes Herring, "this suggests that one should interpret observed differences in digital sociability between younger and older users as life-stage related, rather than as indicating an ongoing change in the direction of increased sociability for all digital media users." Even the fact that teens use all kinds of social networks at higher rates than twentysomethings doesn't necessarily mean that they prefer to hang out online. Studies consistently show that most teens would rather hang out with their friends in person. The reasons are telling: teens prefer offline interaction because it's "more fun" and you "can understand what people mean better." But suburban isolation, the hostility of malls and other public places to groups of loitering teenagers, and schedules packed with extracurriculars make these in-person hangouts difficult, so instead teens turn to whatever social site or app contains their friends (and not their parents). As danah boyd puts it, "Most teens aren't addicted to social media; if anything, they're addicted to each other."

Just like the teens who whiled away hours in mall food courts or on landline telephones became adults who spent entirely reasonable amounts of time in malls and on phone calls, the amount of time that current teens spend on social media or their phones is not necessarily a harbinger of what they or we are all going to be doing in a decade. After all, adults have much better social options. They can go out, sans curfew, to bars, pubs, concerts, restaurants, clubs, and parties, or choose to stay in with friends, roommates, or romantic partners. Why, adults can even invite people over without parental permission *and* keep the bedroom door closed!

The true influence of Post Internet People on general internet socialization was both more subtle and more important than simply a shiny new social networking site. By joining the social internet after their parents were already there, they faced an especially dire version of "context collapse." This is danah boyd's term for when people from all your overlapping friend groups see all your shared posts from different aspects of your life. For adults who occasionally see a coworker's personal photos or political updates, context collapse is a fairly minor issue, a problem of specific individuals being indiscreet. For young people, context collapse is a collective problem: they need space to figure out who they are, where they aren't being constantly supervised by authority figures.

The Full Internet People solved this problem by using social tools that their parents weren't on, jumping ship for a new one every couple years to remake their networks afresh, and leaving their cringiest moments buried on defunct platforms. Friendster gave way to MySpace gave way to Facebook. Social networking sites tried to solve this and prevent themselves from being abandoned by letting people set privacy settings and pick a specific list of people to share each post with. But switching platforms every couple years and keeping all your friends sorted into lists gets tiring. Post Internet People instead came up with a more durable strategy, organized along three principles.

First, things should disappear more, the way conversations throughout history have naturally not left records. Private messages that vanish after they're seen, live video streaming, manual deletion of old posts, and story-style posts that only stay visible for twenty-four hours all reduce the likelihood that messages will be encountered outside their intended context. Second, not all social networks need to be all things to all people. Rather than using a single dominant social platform, or maintaining an account on every single one, you pick and choose your platforms to help control your contexts, perhaps interacting with school friends on Instagram and fandom friends on Twitter, or doing more résumé-safe activities with a public account under your real name but putting more private activities into a locked or pseudonymous account. Finally, social groups also need to be organized at levels more fluid and granular than an entire platform, including both large, open options like hashtags and public groups, and small, closed options like groupchats or secret groups.

The Post Internet People have also continued the semantic shift of "lol." We know that lowercase "lol" hasn't necessarily indicated full-on laughter since the early 2000s, but what does it mean when the Facebook- and Instagram-associated young people indicated that it has shades of meaning around softening, irony, and passive aggression? The linguist Michelle McSweeney decided to find out. She created a corpus of 45,597 text messages donated by fifteen Spanish–English bilinguals in New York City between the ages of eighteen and twenty-one, and analyzed how "lol" was used in it in collaboration with the youths themselves.

The first thing McSweeney and her collaborators noticed is that "lol" only appears once per phrase: people say "feeling a bit sick lol" but they don't bracket it on both sides of a simple utterance ("lol sounds good lol") or stick it in the middle ("sounds lol good"). If there was more than one "lol" in a single message, the message would have multiple parts that could have each stood alone, each one with its own lol: "Yeah lol / my mom was annoyed when I said it lol." The other thing she noticed is that "lol" occurs with certain types of emotions, like flirting, requesting or offering empathy, alluding to undisclosed information, repairing a previous message, or softening a confrontation, but not with others, like expressing love, exchanging information, and small talk — people say "got a lot of homework lol" or "you look good in red lol" but they don't say "i love you lol" or "good morning lol." The youth explained that you could technically say "good morning lol" as a way of ribbing someone if it was actually the afternoon (where it's alluding to undisclosed information rather than simple small talk), but you really shouldn't say "i love you lol" — you'd be making fun of someone in quite a mean way.

McSweeney reasoned that "lol" must be conveying a message about the phrase as a whole, a meaning that's compatible with flirting, softening, and empathy but not with love, directness, and checking in. The difference between flirting and saying "I love you" is plausible deniability. Likewise, using "lol" can soften what might otherwise be interpreted as a confrontation ("what are you doing out so late lol"), but would undermine a serious direct statement ("you hurt me so much in our relationship"). "Lol" can subtly request empathy ("Lol I'm writing an essay :'(") but isn't necessary when asking a direct question ("Can you tell me your schedule so I know when to text you").

Some statements are direct; others wrap their meaning in layers. Including "lol" indicates there's a second layer of meaning to be found, telling the recipient to look beyond the literal words you're saying. The exact nature of that second layer depends on the meaning of the first: it's reassuring when your statement might otherwise be perceived as rude, sarcastic, or confrontational, but "I love you" is already maximally warm and fuzzy, so if you add a second layer of meaning to it, things can only get worse.

In some ways, "lol" hasn't changed its meaning so very far from its roots in laughter. Sure, sometimes we laugh at a direct joke, something we can point at and say, "That's funny." But there's also nervous laughter, social laughter, and polite smiles. We laugh more at a comedy performance if we have other people to laugh with: even a studio audience or a laugh track helps. One study of natural conversations found that only 10 to 20 percent of laughter was actually in response to humor. Flirting often involves laughing at nothing in particular, but when someone says "I love you" for the first time, you probably want it to be delivered with a straight face. On the internet, real laughter calls for a representation that hasn't become trite through overuse. In my survey of 2017, people favored the ever-increasing repetition in "hahahaha" or expanded, ad hoc phrases such as "I actually just spat water on my keyboard from laughing." But, by necessity, the way we express genuine laughter keeps changing.

Just as the older half of the third wave of people to go online have managed to participate in online social activity without

170

becoming tech people, young internet people's social savvy is also no guarantee of technological skill. Post Internet People may know the latest cool apps and be able to derive tone of voice from an errant comma or period, but their levels of technological knowledge vary dramatically. Some enter the working world without technical skills that seem basic to digitally adept older folks, like organizing documents in folders or adding up a column of numbers in a spreadsheet, while others have coded their own apps or websites. Some have a sophisticated knowledge of internet culture and social media strategy, and have made memes or accounts seen by millions of people; some don't know how to write an informative email subject line. Some are highly skilled in one area and don't even know what they don't know in another. As with many societal divides, those kids with parents who can afford the latest devices, send them to coding camps, or advise them on professional etiquette often do better than those stuck with secondhand phones or filtered computers at schools and libraries.

This high degree of variance, both within and between Post Internet People, tends to be the hardest thing for their parents and teachers to grasp. Social and technological savvy online were virtually the same for Old Internet People and still loosely linked for Full and Semi Internet People, but they've become completely decoupled for the Post cohort. This defies predictions that digital natives would pick up technological skills as easily as speaking. Rather, "computer skills" have become as meaningless a category as "electricity skills." Like children of the off-line kind of immigrants, second-generation internet kids do grow up fluent in the communication styles of their peers, but no generation anywhere has ever mastered the skills of adulthood without mentorship. The Post Internet challenge is to parse out which tech skills are acquired incidentally while socializing and which skills were incidental a decade or two ago but now aren't, and so need to be taught.

On the other side of the age divide, Posts often assume that because older people in their lives seem to be familiar with Facebook and texting, they also share certain baseline assumptions about the meanings of associated communicative signals like "lol" and punctuation marks. The dot dot dot is especially perilous. For people with experience of informal writing offline, it's a generic separation character, as we just saw. But for internet-oriented writers, the generic separator is the linebreak or new message, which has left the dot dot dot open to taking on a further meaning of something left unsaid. When dealing with the generations above them, the Posts often overinterpret: they infer emotional meaning from minor cues that are more subtle than the older folks ever dreamed of sending. This level of nuance conveyed through choices in punctuation and capitalization is so varied and interesting that it deserves its own chapter, and we'll get to that next.

But in a discussion of generations and cohorts, here's the sharpest line dividing internet writers: Who is the imaginary authority in your head when you choose how to punctuate a text message? Is it the prescriptive norm of an offline authority, like your former English teacher or a dictionary? Or is it the collective wisdom of your online peers, the anticipation of their emotional reaction to your typographical tone of voice? The difference between how people communicate in the internet era boils down to a fundamental question of attitude: Is your informal writing oriented towards the set of norms belonging to the online world or the offline one?

CHAPTER 4:
TYPOGRAPHICAL TONE
OF VOICE

"Does. Not. Compute." "Your call has been forwarded to an automated voice messaging system." "I'm sorry, I didn't catch that." The words themselves are often pronounced right, but a robotic voice is flat: there's no rising or falling in pitch, speeding up or slowing down, getting louder or softer, emphasizing some words more than others, or undercurrents of growling or giggling, to indicate what the robot's thinking or feeling.

We don't want to sound like robots to our internet friends. (Even robots themselves are sounding less stereotypically robotic.) Traditionally, bridging that gap between writing and emotions has been the task of novelists and poets — writing that line that makes a character sympathetic rather than annoying, or providing that flash of insight which perfectly expresses a feeling that's gone unnamed for too long. Artistic writing about feelings isn't easy, but in a way it has lower stakes. If you write bad poetry or stiff characters, you can work to improve your craft or shove it in the bottom of a drawer and decide to become a linguist instead (oh hi). But if you can't socialize well via text, in this era, you might start feeling like an abandoned drawer-manuscript yourself, suffering a dire lack of human companionship.

How is J. Q. Notapoet, our average internet person, supposed to express these all-important nuances using informal internet writing? Formal writing gets help along the way: you can take time to revise it and enlist other people to edit. But informal writing happens in near-real time: not only does this make it hard to go through multiple drafts, but you also need to express your emotions in writing while you're still in the grip of them. Even the most professional of writers can't use all their handy tools and tricks when the other person can see that you've started typing into the chat box. (In other words, J.Q.'s literary cousin, Poety McWritersBlock, needs the same casual expressive options as everyone else when it comes to everyday use.)

To start, we need to establish a baseline, a normal kind of communication from which any deviation has an emotional impact. In speech, our baseline is the utterance — a burst of language bounded by pauses or interruptions. Sometimes an utterance corresponds to a full sentence; sometimes it doesn't. Most of the time an utterance is a string of words, but sometimes we even cut ourselves off in the middle of one (for examp —). Talking exclusively in complete sentences sounds stilted in all but the most formal of prepared speeches. (Sentence fragments! How useful!) We use utterances in casual writing as well. For people whose linguistic norms are oriented to the internet, the most neutral way of indicating an utterance is with a new line or message break. Each text or chat message in a conversation automatically indicates a separate utterance. Here's an example:

hey

how's it going

just wondered if you wanted to chat sometime this week

maybe tuesday?

This is efficient in a digital medium, where scrolling down is easy and unbounded: not a waste of pixels the way it might be a waste of paper. Linebreaks come for free: they don't take up any more bytes than a period and a space, and they add a lot in readability. Both "new line" and "send message" take a single keystroke, often the same enter key, so the muscle memory is easy. Plus, it helps the conversation flow better if you hit "send" after every utterance rather than waiting and sending a whole essay: the reader can start thinking of a reply sooner. Even in more formal genres online, such as news articles, paragraphs have gotten shorter and are separated by a blank line rather than a space-saving indent as they are on paper.

For people whose linguistic norms are oriented towards the offline world, the most neutral way of separating one utterance from the next is with a dash or a string of dots. After all, you definitely wouldn't want to send each of these phrases as a separate email, let alone as a separate text in the days when we were billed per message. You'd take up four times the space on a postcard if you started a new line every time! Here's the same example in the punctuation style of the offline-oriented:

hey...how's it going.....just wondered if you wanted to chat sometime this week......
maybe tuesday....?

This, too, has a logic to it: while some kinds of punctuation are traditionally reserved for joining full clauses (periods) and others for dependent clauses (commas), ellipses and dashes are deemed acceptable for joining both sorts, even in the most conservative styles. So if you're writing informally and you don't want to bother deciding whether your string of words is a full sentence or merely a clausal fragment, one way to split the difference is to punctuate ambiguously — to use an ellipsis or dash. Sure, classically speaking, the ellipsis indicates omitted text or a trailing off, but that's fine: in speech we sometimes trail our sentences off for casual effect. And sure, classically speaking, the ellipsis gets three dots in the middle of a sentence and four dots at the end and gets a slightly different spacing from simply three periods, but that's the kind of rule that copyeditors care about, not composers of casual emails who have no dedicated ellipsis character on their keyboards. Informal writers who are oriented towards offline norms, like the 1970s Beatles postcards we saw in the previous chapter, sprinkle in dots and dashes to show they're not standing on ceremony by committing to formal, clause-typing punctuation. It's exactly the same motivation younger folks have for separating utterances by linebreaks or message breaks. The same reason, in fact, that Jane Austen sprinkled her original manuscripts with what seems to the modern reader to be an absurdly high number of commas, or that Emily Dickinson's poetry contains a metric ton of dashes, if you can get ahold of an edition where they haven't been edited out. Pause marking is really intuitive, and it always has been.

The problems start when you combine multiple sets of norms. A message like this, say, from an older relative to a teenager, or a boomer boss to a millennial employee, reads quite differently depending on what you think of as neutral.

hey.

how's it going....

just wondered if you wanted to chat sometime this week......maybe tuesday....?

For some, it reads as a compromise between the new text messaging linebreak style and the older dot dot dot. But if you're solidly in the linebreak camp, you see those extra dots or even just a single period where a linebreak or message break would have sufficed, and assume that anything that takes more effort than necessary is a potential message. The dots must be indicating something left unsaid: "how's it going [there's something I'm not telling you]." From a peer, something left unsaid might indicate flirtation. But from an older relative, that would be weird. What other kinds of hidden messages are left? The most common assumptions are either passive aggression or sheer confusion.

The passive-aggressive potential of the single period started being reported in thinkpieces in 2013, in a list at *New York* magazine and then later the same year as a full article in the *New Republic,* before popping up in a handful of other publications in subsequent years. The string of dots got a thinkpiece in 2018, though it has been popping up in comment threads since at least 2006, while its cousins, the hyphen and string of commas, have been less extensively reported but have occasioned long comment threads on blogs and internet forums. Despite the fears mongered by headlines, it's not the case that the passive-aggressive meaning has completely killed all other uses of the period. The linguist Tyler Schnoebelen, who's definitely younger than the peak dot-dot-dot generation, did a study of periods in his own 157,305 sent and received text messages. He found that, true, periods were rare in short, informal messages — ones less than seventeen characters or containing lol, u, haha, yup, ok, or gonna. But they were still often found in messages longer than seventy-two characters or containing words like told, feels, feel, felt, feelings, date, sad, seems, and talk. The added weight of the period is a natural way to talk about weighty matters.

So how is a person to tell whether a given period is supposed to be passive-aggressive, sad, or merely formal? The jumble of meanings associated with the period became clear to me when I started interpreting it as a marker of typographical tone of voice. Just as a question mark can indicate a rising intonation even without a question (Like so?), the period can indicate a falling intonation even when it's not serving to end a statement (Like. So.). When I put on a newscaster voice, I deliver every sentence with falling intonation. Solemnly. Portentously. But in an ordinary conversation, we don't speak in full sentences, and we especially don't round them all off with a distinct fall. ("And now over to: The Weather.") Instead, we speak in utterances, and our intonation is neither rising nor falling: by default, it's flat or trailing off, like a dot dot dot or an unpunctuated linebreak.

Both the dot-dot-dotters and the

linebreakers have instinctively brought us back to an idea from the very beginning of punctuation. The first kind of punctuation marks indicated breaks between utterances, and medieval scribes were the ones who first used them. One important medieval punctuation mark was the *punctus,* a dot which was placed in the location of the modern comma for a short breath, midway through the line for a medium breath, and up around the position of the apostrophe for a long breath. Before that, ancient Greek and Roman writing had all the formatting of a wordsearch puzzle grid, with no punctuation, paragraphs, or even spaces between words, in all caps (carvings) or all lowercase (ink). Like a wordsearch, the reader had to figure out where one word stopped and another began — and also like a wordsearch, they often did this by muttering under their breath. (Mercifully, unlike a wordsearch, the words didn't appear diagonally and there weren't additional distractor letters.)

With the rise of the printing press and dictionaries in the sixteenth and seventeenth centuries, spelling and punctuation became more complicated and standardized. Scribes had spelled and punctuated idiosyncratically, but printers could — and did — change things while typesetting to match everything else they were printing. People may never have wholly followed these elaborate guidelines in their personal correspondence — Austen, Dickinson, and the Beatles certainly didn't, and the handwritten notes of famous writers are among the most analyzed. But when a printing press was the easiest means of reaching a large audience, edited and formal punctuation became the main kind that people saw. The internet made our personal punctuation preferences public, and brought with it a different set of priorities: writing needs to be intuitive, easy to create, and practically as fast as thinking or speaking. We drew these requirements together to create a system of typographical tone of voice.

STRONG FEELING

WHEN YOU WRITE IN ALL CAPS IT SOUNDS LIKE YOU'RE SHOUTING.

All caps to indicate strong feeling may be the most famous example of typographical tone of voice. But there are several kinds of strong feelings. Linguist Maria Heath asked a cross-section of internet users to rate the difference in emotion between a message in all caps and the same message in standard capitalization. She found that all caps made people judge happy messages as even happier (IT'S MY BIRTHDAY!!! feels happier than "It's my birthday!!!") but didn't make sad messages any sadder ("i miss u" is just as sad as I MISS U). When it came to anger, the results were mixed: sometimes caps increased the anger rating and sometimes it didn't, a result which Heath attributed to the difference between "hot" anger (FIGHT ME) and "cold" anger ("fight me"). A single capped word, on the other hand, is simply EMPHATIC. Looking at examples of all-capped words on Twitter, Heath found that the most common single ones included NOT, ALL, YOU, and SO, as well as advertising words like WIN and FREE: the same kinds of words that are often emphasized in spoken conversations (or commercials). When we want to emphasize something in speech, we often pronounce it louder, faster, or higher in pitch — or all three at once. All caps is a typographic way of conveying the same set of cues.

Emphatic caps feel like the quintessential example of internet tone of voice, and sure enough, they've been around since the very early days online: linguist Ben Zimmer found people in old Usenet groups explaining that all caps meant yelling as far back as 1984. What's more intriguing is that capitals were available for emphasis long before the internet as well. The linguist John Mc-Whorter dates shouty caps back to pianist and writer Philippa Schuyler in the 1940s, while author L. M. Montgomery has a character use both capitals and italics for emphasis in her fictional diary entries of the 1920s, which another character criticizes as "Early Victorian" — meaning old-fashionedly melodramatic, even back then. Going yet further back, a newspaper in 1856 described a line of dialogue with the phrase "This time he shouted it out in capital letters."

Back in the heyday of personal letter-writing, all caps were just one part of a broader emotional ecosystem for expressing strong feeling, along with italics, underlining, larger letters, red ink, and other decorative formatting options. The emotional use wasn't even the most prominent option: all capitals were widely used to avoid the idiosyncrasy of joined handwriting, such as in comic strips, on forms ("Please fill out your name in block capitals"), or in official documents by lawyers, architects, and engineers. Similarly, several of the postcards that I looked at for the previous chapter were written in block capitals, especially in the address field. Typewriters and early computer terminals made illegible handwriting less of a problem, but they also introduced a new one: they wouldn't let you type italics and underlines and font sizes (for that matter, many social media sites still don't). This created a vacuum into which the preexisting but relatively uncommon shouty caps expanded.

This brings us to a puzzle. Early internet guides like the Jargon File, *Wired Style,* and website FAQs mentioned all caps, but not to facilitate shouting, the way that *bolding asterisks* or _italicizing underscores_ were recommended to compensate for the lack of other formatting that can indicate emphasis, or a smiley face was recommended to facilitate sarcasm and joking around. No, they were generally trying to *discourage* it, meaning that a fair percentage of eighties and nineties computer users were writing their routine correspondence in all caps.* Where did the idea that it was ever okay to type a full message in block capitals come from? After all, people have been handwriting in lowercase for over a thousand years, and even the melodramatic early Victorians didn't capitalize *everything*. Why would anyone suddenly switch to all caps on a computer?

*The nineties version of "oh my god, my boss doesn't realize that periods are passive-aggressive" was "oh my god, my boss doesn't realize that all caps is shouting."

186

Part of the blame may go to Morse code, that dashingly dotty system used for sending telegrams. Morse code represents every letter as a combination of dots and dashes, suitable for transmitting as long or short taps along an electrical line: A is dot dash, B is dash dot dot dot, and the rest of the twenty-six letters can all be represented as combinations of up to four dots and/or dashes. But if we wanted to include lowercase letters, we'd need a fifth and a sixth dot or dash, because we'd be representing fifty-two symbols, and telegraph operators would have to memorize twice as many codes. Unsurprisingly, people decided it wasn't worth it — if all caps was good enough for the Romans, it would be good enough for telegrams.

Early computers were very similar. Some used teletype machines — the mechanical descendants of telegraph operators — as a way to transmit or print out information. The classic first command that you learn when you start to code is something like PRINT("HELLO WORLD"), which causes the computer to display HELLO WORLD onscreen. It doesn't make the computer print out on paper HELLO WORLD, but at one point it did — back before screens, when we commanded computers by keying words into a teletype machine and received their replies printed out onto rolls of paper. Even once computers had screens, storage space was still expensive, as precious as the brain cells of a telegraph operator, so many of them, such as the Apple II, displayed everything in just one case — all caps. Relicts of this setup are still in place on some commercial computer systems: teletypes are uncommon, but your grocery store receipt, bank statement, or airplane ticket might very well appear from a roll of shiny paper, printed in all caps.

By the time computers did start supporting lowercase characters, we were faced with two competing standards: one group of people assumed that all caps is just how you write on a computer, while another group insisted that it stood for yelling. Ultimately, the emotional meaning won out. The shift in function happened in parallel with a shift in name: according to the millions of books scanned in Google Books, the terms "all caps" and "all uppercase" started rising sharply in the early 1990s. By contrast, in the earlier part of the century, the preferred terms were "block letters" or "block capitals." People tended to use "all caps" to talk about the loud kind, while block capitals more often referred to the official kind, on signs and on forms. But the addition of all caps for tone of voice didn't eliminate the official kind of capitals, which remain common on EXIT signs and CAUTION tape and CHAPTER ONE headings: they may be emphatic, but they aren't interpreted as especially loud. Rather, our interpretation seems to flip depending on whether we read the text as formal or informal: HOME in a website's menu bar is a mere graphic design choice, while HOME in a message like "ugh I want to go HOME" is typographical tone of voice.

Another way to do emphasis online is by repeatingggggg letterrrrssss, especially for emotive words like "yayyyy" or "nooo." Just like shouty capitals, the origins of this practice predate the internet by maanyyy years. I searched the Corpus of Historical American English for sequences of at least three of the same letter (to eliminate common English words like "book" and "keep"). The corpus contains texts from 1810 to 2009, but to my surprise, there were hardly any results in the first half of the corpus. The few earlier examples were mostly just typos, like "commmittee," or numerals, like "XXXIII." Here's the oldest real example I could find, a character pretending to be a candy-seller in a novel published in 1848:

"Confectionary, confectionary," he cried, bursting into a louder tone of voice, which rang forth clear and deep-toned, as a bell. "Confectionary!" and then he added with grotesque modulations of his voice, "Confecctunarrry!"

"By Jove, how this reminds me of the little fellow in London. I'll go the complete candy-seller. I might as well."

"Ladies and gentlemen! Here's your fine candy, lozenges, apples, oranges, cakes and tarts! Heeeere's your chance!"

The "grotesque modulations" of this 1840s faux confectioner were an anomaly, ahead of their time. The author respells the elongated "confectionary" with a "u," rather than preserve the component letters like a modern writer would do. Even now-commonplace elongations of sounds like "ahhh," "oooh," "hmmm," "ssshh," and "brrr" don't start showing up in this historical corpus until the decade before and after 1900, whereupon they increase steadily for the next hundred years, displacing word-like versions such as "ahem" and "hush." Rare, one-off elongations of full words like "confecctunarrry," "evvveryone," and "damnnn" follow in substantial numbers a few decades behind, starting to rise in the 1950s and 60s and really getting popular in the 1990s and 2000s. The period when lengthening became popular lines up with the rise of recorded speech, such as phonographs, records, cassettes, and CDs. It might be coincidence, but it might also be that when we started being able to play and replay recorded speech, we started paying more attention to representing it precisely. At any rate, it's clear that the goal of repeated letters is to represent speech in writing because the early examples show up in fictional dialogue, especially in play scripts and novels.

Repeating letters is an expressive tool that's been growing for over a century in informal writing, not just on the internet. And it isn't haphazard. One study looked at the most commonly lengthened words on Twitter and found that they still tend to be sentiment words. The top twenty most lengthened words are a cornucopia of emotions: nice, ugh, lmao, lmfao, ah, love, crazy, yeah, sheesh, damn, shit, really, oh, yay, wow, good, ow, mad, hey, and please. Several studies have found that this expressive lengthening, as linguist Tyler Schnoebelen named it, is sensitive to social context: people lengthen more in private texts or chat messages than in public posts.

People are also sensitive to linguistic cues.

In a study I did with the linguist Jeffrey Lamontagne, we found that while people generally lengthen the rightmost letter in a word, they'll also lengthen the rightmost letter in a smaller unit of sound. For example, in the word "dream" the "ea" together indicates the vowel sound, so people will lengthen this word as either "dreaaam" or "dreammm." But in the word "both," the two middle letters "ot" are not a unit (the "t" belongs with the "h" instead), so people lengthen it as "bothhhh" or maybe "boooth," but never "bottth." But people aren't completely tied to phonological feasibility. They often write things like "stahppp" or "omgggg," but it's not physically possible to hold ppppp or ggggg for more than an instant. Even more improbably, people sometimes "lengthen" silent letters, writing "dumbbb" or "sameee." What's cool about expressive lengthening is that, although it started as a very literal representation of longer sounds, it's ended up creating a form of emotional expression that now has no possible spoken equivalent, making it more akin to its typographical cousins, all caps and italics.

On the whole, indicators of strong feeling have remained remarkably stable since the early days of the internet, and for much of the past hundred years. Catullus or Chaucer would have been at a loss, but L. M. Montgomery from the 1920s would have had no particular difficulty telling when a modern text message wanted to express excitement or emphasis. Perhaps this stability is because we don't feel as creative when we're in the grips of strong emotion, or perhaps it's because strong feelings are SO CLEARLY IMPORTANT that we had to figure out SOMETHING.

A Kinder, Gentler Internet

Internet researchers who looked at the flamewars, shouty caps, and misunderstood sarcasm of early electronic communication might have been justified in wondering if the internet was doomed to remain a place of shouting or alienation, with nothing softer in between. But the coldness of the early internet was a temporary learning curve rather than a permanent state. A study from 1999 by Susan Brennan and Justina Ohaeri analyzed how groups of people collaboratively retold a story, either speaking in person or chatting via instant messenger. In the spoken version, everyone talked approximately the same amount, and they all used polite hedges like "kind of" and "thingy" rather than baldly stating their own opinion as if it was the only possible option. In the written version, there were fewer polite hedges overall, which looks at first as if people are simply blunter when typing: bring on the flamewars! But when the researchers drilled down and looked at the individuals, they found something quite different. Both the number of words typed and the politeness level of the typists varied widely, but the people who typed the most words also produced a significantly higher ratio of polite ones.

In other words, people who were more fluent at typing used their increased facility to be more polite, just as polite as they would have been while talking. Of course, bringing people into the lab and paying them a couple bucks to tell a story is hardly the kind of scenario designed to foster rude behavior, but this study gives me hope. Even without being consciously aware of it, people were aiming to be polite just as soon as they had the typing skills to do so. The way we convey our tone of voice changes when we're typing versus speaking, but the internet doesn't have to be a rude or shouty place.

At a larger scale, we've all had a lot of practice at typing since 1999. Twenty years of experience tends to transform even the slowest "hunt and peck" into two-finger idiosyncratic typing that can be quite rapid, especially when your motivation is having a conversation rather than typing up a boring report. My experience here is common for Full Internet People: I did a formal touch-typing program so that I could type up my own essays for school, but I only really got super fast at typing when I was trying to keep up with friends on instant messaging.

As we've become better typists, we've also increased our ability to produce and appreciate the nuances of informal written language that allow us to be kind, humorous, or polite online. The politeness literature offers a couple main strategies for being nice. One is to make an extra effort, using hedges, honorifics, or simply more words: "Doctor, could I possibly trouble you to open the window?" versus "Open the window!" Another is to indicate solidarity, using endearments or in-group vocabulary to indicate that you're on the same side and don't have to stand on ceremony: "Honey/mate/dude/luv/bro, d'you wanna open that window?" Both of these show up online. Many internet acronyms make polite hedges accessible even to slower typists, such as "btw" (by the way), "iirc" (if I recall correctly), "imo" (in my opinion), and "afaik" (as far as I know), but writing them as acronyms rather than in full is also in-group vocabulary, saying, in effect, "We're all internet people here. I trust you to get this."

Research on politeness in internet communities finds that many elements of it mirror politeness offline. It's well established that politeness decreases with power — you're more polite to your boss than to your underling. One group of researchers looked at polite words like "thanks" or "nice job" and indirect politeness strategies like "sorry" or "by the way..." in messages exchanged between volunteer editors on Wikipedia and in questions asked on the Q&A website Stack Exchange. Just like offline power relationships, the more powerful Wikipedia administrators and those with a high "karma" rating on Stack Exchange tended to be less polite than regular users. Furthermore, both offline and online politeness is situational: controlling for karma level, the text of questions asked on Stack Exchange was more polite than the text of the answers. Online politeness also has real effects: Wikipedia administrators were more polite before they'd been elected as admins, back when they were simply normal editors — more polite, in fact, than their fellow editors who'd run for adminship and lost.

The exclamation mark is frequently repurposed to indicate warmth or sincerity, rather than just excitement. After all, to be excited to meet someone or help someone is also to be sincere about it. This change is well under way: a 2006 study by Carol Waseleski found that in emails, exclamation marks were infrequently used to indicate excitement, occurring only 9.5 percent of the time with either strong language, like "These damn programs are out of touch with reality!" or effusive thanks, like "Thank you so much for your comments — they are very, very helpful and the list of resources is wonderful!" In comparison, exclamation marks indicated friendliness 32 percent of the time ("See you there!" "I hope this helps!") and emphasized statements of fact another 29.5 percent of the time ("There's still time to register!").

An article in the satire newspaper *The Onion* comically exaggerates the quasi-obligatory nature of the sincerity exclamation point:

> In a diabolical omission of the utmost cruelty, stone-hearted ice witch Leslie Schiller sent her friend a callous thank-you email devoid of even a single exclamation point, sources confirmed Monday. "Hey, I had a great time last night," wrote the cold-blooded crone, invoking the chill of a thousand winters with her sparely punctuated missive.

To solve this problem, Stone-Hearted Ice Witches might consider installing Emotional Labor, a Gmail add-on that promises to "brighten up the tone of any email" — largely by adding exclamation marks at the end of every sentence. I confess, I have recently been getting a kick out of deliberately replying to emails from people who don't use exclamation marks without using any in return, rather than using one every other sentence, as is my usual practice for professional correspondence. At first, it felt stiff — was I now a cold-blooded crone? — but after a while, I started enjoying how it seemed to increase my gravitas. After all, why should I tolerate an inequitable distribution of the typographical emotional labor?

The situation with multiple exclamation marks is less stable. Hyperbolic adjectives lose their force through overuse ("awesome" is no longer the same as "awe-inspiring"), and hyperbolic punctuation seems to do the same. Multiple exclamation marks were considered part of an early internet slang known as leetspeak, which featured numbers and other special characters substituting for similar-looking letters, such as 1337 for "leet," or "1 4m 133t h4x0r!" for "I am an elite hacker!" and incorporated common typos such as "teh" for "the" and "pwn" for "own." The common typo for the exclamation mark was the number 1, since English keyboards typically place these two symbols on the same key. The typo !!!!1!11! was then parodied by writing out "one" and "eleven" as full words: !!!one!!eleventy!! Leetspeak and multiple exclamation marks were genuine indicators of computer proficiency and excitement, respectively, in the netspeak of the 1980s and 90s, but both gradually became ironic through continued use. A 2005 paper about leetspeak and online gamer slang characterized statements like "OMG, D@T is teh Rox0rz!!!111oneeleven" (oh my god, that rocks!!!!) as used by "newbs and wannabes." Ouch. But then, after a period of dormancy, multiple exclamation marks reemerged as a marker of genuine enthusiasm, according to a trend piece from 2018 ("Sounds good!!!"). History suggests that they won't stay sincere forever.

Another way to be polite is to directly evoke the gesture of delivering words with a cheery smile, lest your recipient think you're forcing them out between clenched teeth. One example we've seen of this in the previous chapter is the way "lol" takes on the polite function of laughter as a social lubricant, rather than its purely humorous function. Smileys can have a similar effect, as we can see in a study by the linguist Erika Darics on emoticons in work communication. An example that Darics compiled from her corpus of workplace messages includes this hypothetical deadline reminder from your boss:

Everyone else has already submitted their report. You are the LAST!:)

But, Darics says, "even if you are on very good terms with your boss, the emoticon here clearly doesn't function as a representation of a smile or signal a joke, and capitals are not meant to be read as shouting." Instead, it "could be read as a friendly nudge or teasing. . . . The emoticon isn't relaying a full-on smile but it is tempering the tone of the message." (We'll dive into emotions in more detail next chapter.)

Politeness in writing is hardly unique to electronic communication, but before the internet, cheery, informal, mundane requests were primarily oral or notes scribbled on scraps of paper. ("Here's the book you asked for! -GM" "Have fed the dog.") You're likely to already share a certain rapport (not to mention the same physical space) with anyone you're leaving a sticky note for, and even so, a look through scans of dozens of notes that people have left for their family members or roommates shows that people often sign them with a heart or smiley face or "xo." It's hardly a coincidence that our repertoire of upbeat, sociable typography expanded precisely when we needed it to build near-real-time relationships with unseen others.

Another method of building solidarity online is to joke around and create shared references that only an in-group truly understands. In-jokes are hardly exclusive to the internet, but they have a particularly internettish manifestation: we can bend the functional and technical tools of hypermediated text to a more social purpose, indicating that we're the type of people who understand a particular tool so well that we can play around with it.

One way of creating in-jokes is to play with the language of the computer itself, writing humorous pseudo-code in the style of a programming language. Let's say you wanted to mark a particular string of text as italic in HTML: you could put <i>*where you want the italics to start and*</i> where you want the italics to end. This naturally lends itself to creative uses, like <sarcasm>I fail to see the problem with this</sarcasm>, or in abridged form, THIS IS TERRIBLE /rant.

The computer, humorless beastie that it is, does not recognize a /sarcasm or /rant command. But your fellow humans who are used to talking to computers may think you're rather clever, especially if you can find a novel way to use it. A deeply nerdy example comes from the programming language LISP. The way to ask yes/no questions in LISP is to add -P to the end of a statement, such as TRUE-P (Is this true?). One time, the story goes, a few LISP programmers were out at a restaurant, and one of them wanted to know if anyone else was interested in sharing a two-person dish, so he asked, "Split-p soup?"

As we saw in the previous chapter, the average internet person no longer knows how to code, and so code-based internet slang remains limited to Old Internet People and techy subcultures of later generations. A more common typographical tool is *asterisks* and _underscores_ as a way of emphasizing in environments that don't support proper bold or italic. But asterisks also look like tiny stars, and early internet denizens seized on their decorative potential as well, especially when combined with the fanciful swoop of the ~tilde~. In the plain text of late 1990s and early 2000s instant messenger status messages, sparkle punctuation would range from ~*just one*~ of each all the way up to ~~~~~~~******~~~~~~so many sparkles~~~~~~~******~~~~~~; ~*~*~*~alternating~*~*~*~ or ~**~~*~~in combination~~*~~**~~; mixed with wOrDs iN mIxEd cAPiTaLiZaTiOn, e x t r a s p a c e s, and ◇·: ⋆ *◇·:* ⋆ extra star symbols ◇·: ⋆ *◇·:* ⋆. With advances in technology, people also made the text multicolored, uʍop ǝpᴉsdn, or used emoji, ʙᴜɪʟᴛ-ɪɴ ꜰᴏɴᴛꜱ, ⓔⓝⓒⓘⓞⓢⓔⓓ ⓛⓔⓣⓣⓔⓡⓢ, or øʙꜱᴄᴜʀ℮ ꜱYᴍbol𝐒 for aesthetic effect.* It's unsurprising, then, that aesthetic typography became especially popular with successive generations of teens on instant messengers and MySpace and Tumblr, digital versions of the elaborate doodles and intricate folded paper notes once passed in class. While the heyday of sparkles may have been in the 1990s and early 2000s, they still resurface occasionally in certain contexts. In this example from 2017, a Twitter user expressed sparkle excitement upon encountering a registration dropdown menu that included, after Mr/Ms, a vast array of titles like Group

*And ẕ̐a̋l̶g̈o̊ or g̓l̶i̱t̸c̈h text, a uniquely internet style which exploits the fact that Unicode lets you stack marks above and below letters infinitely.

Captain, His Excellency, and Professor Dame.

registering for a conference in the UK is

,-~*˜·'*·~-MAGICAL-~*˜·'*~-,

A shared set of references can also center on social networking rather than programming or formatting. The most prominent example here is hashtags. Hashtags started out as a practical way of finding and grouping social media conversations about a similar topic. I could post "Just arrived at #EmojiCon" and then anyone who clicked on or searched for #EmojiCon would find all the posts that had been tagged as relevant to a real conference that I attended, which was entirely about emoji (plus a bunch of typos from people who intended to type "#emoticon"). Or I could post "Watching #superbowl!" if I wanted to join the conversation about a certain football event or call attention to my superlative collection of owl photographs. And, just like <sarcasm> or </rant>, I could hashtag my sentences with #sarcasm or #awkward or #NovelWittyHashtag or other metacommentary — labels that add a note of irony instead of categorization.

The hash mark itself, also known as the

number sign, pound sign, or octothorpe, dates back hundreds of years, originally a hastily written version of the abbreviation *lb* from Latin *libra pondo,* "a pound by weight," as in 3# potatoes @ 10$^{¢}$/#. In the early days of the internet, the hash mark, as a relatively underutilized symbol available on a standard QWERTY keyboard, was repurposed for a variety of technical functions. One of these was organizational. In chatrooms, you could type in "join #canada" or "join #hamradio" to talk with Canadians or ham radio enthusiasts. On the early social bookmarking site del.icio.us and the early photosharing site Flickr, you could "tag" your links or pictures with relevant categories like #funny or #sunset, borrowing a metaphor from how a tag on a shirt labels it with metadata about its price or creator. So when Twitter users started casting about for a way of grouping together related tweets, it's not surprising that technologist Chris Messina reached for the #, in a tweet dated August 23, 2007. Twitter didn't officially support hashtags until 2009, but #sarcasm and other joke hashtags showed up almost immediately after Messina's proposal.

There's not much point in vocalizing the organizational kind of hashtag: there isn't (yet) a technology letting us search all our spoken conversations by keyword, which is probably a good thing for privacy. But the metacommentary hashtag was never for searching in the first place, so it's sometimes spoken. What's good for privacy is less good for history: it's hard to track down the first instance of "hashtag" spoken out loud. We do know that some people were using it as early as 2009, the year blogger Mariana Wagner reflected, "When hanging out with other Twitter users IRL, I will actually SAY 'Hashtag [insert witty phrase here]' to emphasize/categorize something I just said. Dorky? Yes. Absolutely. But all my Twitter friends 'get' it and that makes it fun."

By the mid-2010s, spoken "hashtag" to indicate metacommentary had spread to people who weren't even online yet, with parents reporting that they were hearing it from their seven- or eight-year-old kids. One linguist parent was delighted by her kid saying "hashtag mom joke," but another parent was jokingly unimpressed by her own kid's use of "hashtag":

My daughter just finished a sentence with 'hashtag awkward!'

8 years. It's been a good run. But the orphanage will suit her much better.

At first glance, this kind of repurposing might seem like a purely internet invention, and it is, insofar as people weren't peppering their speech with code snippets or hashtags before we had any such thing. But English has a long history of verbalizing punctuation: think of "that's the facts, period" or "these quote-unquote experts." Or to take two examples from the 1890s, that dangerously modern decade: "He would not flinch one comma of the law" and "There was a very big question mark in [her] voice." Spoken "hashtag" is just the latest in a long list of creative strategies to say without saying, add context, control the flow of information, or indicate that something is of more or less importance. In speech we also have options like the stage whisper, silly voices, putting on an accent, and speaking from behind your hand or with a different posture. Who hasn't reproduced a line from a song or movie while imitating its original intonation? Inconceivable!

Not all creative typography crosses over into the mouths of babes. Some simply serves to reinforce the social ties of a particular community. In spoken Japanese, for example, people associate lengthening at the end of a word or phrase with sounding cute or playful. But in written Japanese, each symbol stands for a syllable rather than an individual sound the way a letter does. And people generally aren't trying to indicate that the whole syllable is being repeated. So while English writers lengthen by repeating a letter, writers of Japanese add a different symbol entirely: the wave dash ～ (or the slightly narrower tilde ~, depending on what the keyboard supports). The Japanese word for "yes" is written はい and pronounced "hai." If you want to write the equivalent of "yesss" or "haiii" using tilde lengthening, you'd write "yes~~," "hai~~," or "はい〜〜." The word-final tilde to indicate lengthening became popular throughout Southeast Asia, in Japanese, Chinese, Korean, and even nearby languages written with Latin script, like Tagalog and Singlish. But since English already had a way of indicating length, the lengthening tilde became associated in English with bilingualism in one of these languages, being a fan of Japanese cultural exports like anime or manga, or even just the secondary association with cute sparkles and ignoring length altogether.

Another repurposed technical tool for adding playful commentary is the exclamation!compound used to refer to different versions of a particular person, such as past!me or CAPSLOCK!Harry.* Exclamation!compounds take us into a fascinating corner of technological history. Back before we were all on one thoroughly interwoven internet, in order to send someone an email you had to specify exactly which path of connected computers it should take. Alex in the math department at Princeton might be princeton!math!alex — so your computer sends it to the big Princeton server, which passes it to the "math" computer, which contains an "Alex" account. This system was easily extended to personal descriptions. Just as you could keep track of your various friends named Alex depending on their interests (Alex the mathematician versus Alex the artist), you could also distinguish them based on their computer paths (art!alex versus math!alex).†

Technically speaking, this system was rather clumsy. Who wants to memorize paths of networked computers just to send a message? By the time most people started going online, internet architecture had gotten

*Referring to Harry Potter in the fifth book, where he spends a lot of time yelling in capslock.
†This system isn't so dissimilar from that which gave us many common surnames, such as Alex (the) Smith or Alex (who lives by the) Wood.

more densely webbed and invisible to its users, so all you needed to do was specify a username at a domain, and hidden technology would route it through an appropriate path. But fans of the 1990s hit TV show *The X-Files* had started chatting with each other on Usenet discussion boards during the heyday of bang!path email addresses, so they also began referring to different versions of the main characters as Action!Mulder and Action!Scully, to differentiate them from the scenes where the characters were just standing around talking. *The X-Files* eventually went off the air, fan communities moved from Usenet to LiveJournal to Tumblr, and email addresses gained their user@domain. com format, but fans persisted in the social convention of referring to versions of people and characters as angst!Draco or future!me, even though many fans of Harry Potter and more recent stories had never even seen a bang!path email address.

Some expressive typography emerged into the mainstream, like spoken hashtag and sparkly punctuation. Other kinds remained a marker of a particular community, like joke code, lengthening tildes, exclamation!compounds, and others not catalogued here or even invented yet. But regardless, the repurposing of technical tools as social in-jokes goes a long way towards making the internet feel not chilly and impersonal, not shouty, not even just politely cheerful, but like a place where we can belong.

MEANING IN ABSENCE

Sarcasm, online as well as off, involves saying the opposite of what you mean in a way that still conveys your true opinion: "Well, isn't that just terrific!" in response to bad news, or "Thanks, Sherlock!" in response to a very obvious deduction. In writing, it's harder to make your true intention shine through without the full range of eloquent pause, verbal inflection, arched eyebrow, and wry lip we can employ in person. Irony is subtle and contextual, the ultimate in-joke.

People noticed this problem long before the internet, and many had attempted to remedy it, a history chronicled in the book *Shady Characters* by Keith Houston. There was Henry Denham, a British printer who used a mirrored question mark (⸮) to distinguish rhetorical questions in 1575, and John Wilkins, a British natural philosopher, who proposed an inverted exclamation mark (¡) to indicate irony in 1668. After them, there were three centuries of French writers proposing variously shaped *"points d'ironie"*

— Jean-Jacques Rousseau noted the need for one in 1781, Alcanter de Brahm in 1899 proposed another version of ⸮, and Hervé Bazin in 1966 proposed the Greek letter Ψ with a dot below. In more recent years, a backwards-slanting italics known as "ironics" or "sartalics" was attributed to several American newspaper columnists in the latter half of the twentieth century, the upside-down exclamation mark (¡) was again proposed in 2004, this time by a former writer for *The Onion,* and in 2010, a swirl with a dot in the middle was patented under the name SarcMark and sold for noncommercial use at the bargain (⸮)price of $1.99.

All to no avail.

The problem with adopting new irony punctuation is that if the people reading you don't understand it, you're no better off than without it. Pointing out after the fact that you're using a new sarcasm punctuation mark is about as much fun as explaining the joke. It's even worse if the people receiving your sarcastic messages have to pay two bucks and install a new font just so they can have your joke explained.

Mock </sarcasm> code or #sarcasm hashtags require no explanation, fee, or font installation, and have indeed caught on to some extent, but both can be a trifle obvious.

After all, the point of sarcasm is the double meaning, the innuendo, the sous-entendu. If we wanted to make all our messages completely lucid, we already have a very effective tool for that, and it's called Not Being Sarcastic. Rather than a single bright flag to festoon all our ironic sentences, we needed a range of ways to gently hint that there was more meaning than one might assume at first glance.

Fortunately, the range of expressive punctuation had expanded enough to do just that. Some ironic indicators that play around with typographical signals of authority predated the internet, like "scare quotes" and Satirical Brand Names and Legalese™. Ironic Capitals may be Very Old Indeed, such as this 1926 quote from *Winnie-the-Pooh*.

"Thank you, Pooh," answered Eeyore. "You're a real friend," said he. "Not like Some," he said.

The ironic punctuation mark that the social internet can truly claim as its own is the ~sarcasm tilde. It derives, in broad terms, from the enthusiastic ~*sparkles*~ that had decorated status updates on AOL and MSN Messenger or profile pages on MySpace or Xanga. Excavating how it became ironic is a walk through the history of this social corner. We begin on Urban Dictionary, that user-contributed slang website which is probably where you end up when you finally admit defeat and google some new acronym you can't quite figure out.

But to use Urban Dictionary for data, we must first acknowledge its limitations. Entries on Urban Dictionary do pass through the barest of volunteer editor checks, keeping out spam and complete nonsense, but there's no "citation needed" on Urban Dictionary the way there is on Wikipedia, despite both being user-edited projects. This openness is both Urban Dictionary's greatest strength and its greatest weakness. A word can be added years before it hits the kind of mainstream sources required by a conventional dictionary, when it might be popular only with a single friend group. But other words are added that never gain popularity or were jokes from the beginning. This means we can't use Urban Dictionary to prove that a term is genuinely being used: just look up practically any first name and you'll get the same sorts of entries, either highly flattering or highly insulting, all presumably targeted at specific, unknown people whose friends apparently wanted to tell them, "Look, it's in the dictionary that you're like that!"

Looking up a word that we've already seen, as many of us do from time to time, avoids this problem because we can weigh the definitions against the context we already have. But here, too, there's an important caveat to make: many definitions are overtly racist, sexist, or otherwise offensive. It's not just people pranking their friends: the entries for names of celebrities that are black, female, or both show levels of vitriol that would put a YouTube comments section to shame. The same goes for slang that is associated with young women or African Americans: for example, in the entries for "bae," although several definitions accurately note its connections to "babe" and "before anyone else," many also seem to take a perverse delight in mentioning that *bæ* is the Danish word for "poop." There seems to be a correlation between how genuinely popular a word is and how much Urban Dictionary's definition writers despise it and the people who use it.

For the sarcasm tilde, I'm interested in an Urban Dictionary strategy that goes a level deeper still. In this case, we already know both the item and its meaning, and all we're looking for is the automatically generated, unfakable datestamp for when the two first became associated. As long as we also bear in mind that the site was founded in 1999 and took a few years to accumulate a base level of entries, Urban Dictionary can offer a unique perspective on tracking the history of slang that entered English after the early 2000s, several years before social media sites became popular. What's key here is that Urban Dictionary includes entries for a wide range of special characters, making it especially useful for tracking down rising meanings of symbols that had long been in use for other purposes.

As a proof of concept, let's compare the Urban Dictionary timelines for two relatively known quantities: passive-aggressive uses of "lol" and the period symbol. In 2003, a user defined the symbol . as "Ends a fucking sentence." But in 2009, another user defined it as: "the new cool way to emphasize (usually moody-ass) sarcasm." We can see how disdain maps onto popularity: in 2003, the disdain is for the reader, for looking up a punctuation mark with no slang meaning, while in 2009, the disdain has shifted to the user of the slang. Once present, the sarcasm meaning showed up again in definitions from other users, suggesting that the trend was gaining hold. It took a solid couple years before *New York* magazine ran a thinkpiece about the rising passive-aggressive potential of the period in 2013. In contrast, "lol," which we know from the previous chapter arose in the 1980s and was dubiously sincere by 2001, contains no such shift: from its earliest entries, users note that it officially stands for "laughing out loud" but "nobody laughs out loud when they say it."

For the tilde ~ symbol, there were several Urban Dictionary entries for it before 2008, such as "used at the end of words to make them longer" in 2007, but none of them mention sarcasm. The first time an Urban Dictionary entry mentioned sarcasm was in 2008 (giving the example "OMG that's soo cool~"), followed by two more entries mentioning sarcasm in 2009. There's our timeline. But for meaning, what's interesting about the evolution of the ~sarcasm tilde~ was that you could figure it out without Urban Dictionary at all.

In fact, we have evidence that several people did. Two LiveJournal threads from 2010 and 2012 discussed this new use of the tilde, in contexts like "Well, isn't that ~special" or "Every character on that show has a ~tragic past~." Both threads were started by people asking about the meaning of this new use of the tilde that they'd been seeing, and yet both askers correctly deciphered its meaning in their original questions. One said, "It seems to designate some sort of irony or disagreement with what is said," and the other, "what I am guessing is the equivalent of scare quotes." In the discussion threads that followed, a few people still primarily recognized the tilde as "approximately" (as in ~20) or as the cheerful decorative ~*~sparkles~*~ or Japanese cute lengthening~~~ of previous years, but many also recognized them as sarcastic. How is it that sparkle sarcasm achieved such an edge over six centuries of philosophical proposals? And why did it succeed so quickly where ؟ and ¡ and fellow symbols had all failed?

The trick lies not just in ease of typing, but in layers of meaning. Sparkle sarcasm derives from sparkle enthusiasm, and it does so by the following semiconscious calculation: "You might have used this word seriously here, but I know you wouldn't use it excitedly. And yet you've added sparkles anyway, and they're definitely not a serious thing. So if you're not sincere, and you're not truly excited, then it must be ironic excitement." Like "lol," sparkles are an anti-seriousness marker, leaving space for the precise nature of the anti-seriousness to be determined by context. The previous meaning and the calculation step are what made sparkle sarcasm, along with "scare quotes" and Ironic Capitals, survive where official proposals failed — they're ambiguous and context-dependent, like irony itself.

Why the tilde in particular? After all, asterisks are also a crucial part of the ~*~sparkle ecosystem~*~. But the solitary asterisk had long been committed to other meanings, like *bold* and *narrates own actions in the third person* — neither of which are relevant on the irony-to-enthusiasm scale. More intriguingly, the tilde might have been helped by its visual resemblance to a particular type of sarcastic inflection. The posters on the 2010 LiveJournal thread consistently describe it as "a sarcastic sing-songy voice." I share this intuition, but "sing-song" is not exactly the terminology of proper linguistics. So I tried to pin it down more specifically, and nearly fell off my chair in excitement when it dawned on me: when you say a word like "sooooo" with a sing-song sarcastic inflection, the pitch of your voice literally rises, then falls, then rises slightly again. In other words, your intonation makes the shape of a tilde.

The full-fledged state of sparkle sarcasm was described by a *BuzzFeed* reporter in 2015 as "somewhere between sarcasm and a sort of mild and self-deprecatory embarrassment over the usage of a word or phrase." In theory, sparkle sarcasm has as many possible

219

typographical variations as sparkle enthusi-asm. But in practice, it tends to veer more towards the subdued side: a pair of ~tildes~, perhaps up to a ✦ sparkle emoji ✦ or ~*as-terisk plus tilde*~, but often simply an ini-tial ~tilde. There may not be quite as much space for ~*~*true sparkle exuberance*~*~ in deadpan snark.

A still more deadpan kind of irony is cre-ated in the lack of punctuation and capi-talization altogether, what I call minimalist typography. How do you search for this sort of thing, the inverse of all caps and multiple exclamation marks? All caps or block capi-tals is lucky to have a few established names, and has had decades to attract interest from internet advice manuals. For minimalist ty-pography, this is not yet the case. There's no entry for it in Urban Dictionary or the Jar-gon File, and it's the only one I've needed to propose a name for. So instead, I turned to two sources: people complaining and people analyzing. Let's start with the complaints, to establish a timeline.

As we saw above, computers based on teletype machines in the 1960s and 70s sup-ported only uppercase letters. But a little later, in the 70s, 80s, and 90s, the popular computer operating system Unix was case-sensitive — very sensitive. If your username was "foobar," and you tried to log in as "FooBar," then you might as well be a different person. If the way to open up the internet browser was to type "netscape" and you told the computer "Netscape," then you might as well have typed in "firefox" or "chrome" (neither of which existed yet). All of these case-sensitive Unix usernames and commands were in lowercase, so Unix users got in the habit of keeping such technical vocabulary in lowercase, even at the beginning of a sentence. After all, if you type "foobar should've used netscape" even in social messages, then the newbie reading your post is far less likely to get confused and type the wrong capitalization into the terminal.

At the same time as computer users influenced by teletype machines and Apple IIs continued typing in all caps for a while after other users had decided that caps meant shouting, Unix hackers became known for the inverse — the type of people who would type in all lowercase all the time. (As well as the type who would explain with great earnestness that a hacker is just a person who likes figuring things out about computers, and the Hollywood cybervillains are actually *crackers*.) For the general, non-Unix-coding population, minimalist typography also gradually became something associated with technology: email addresses and urls were generally all lowercase, and usernames often followed this trend as well.

But in the opinions of a whole decade of people posting on internet forums, the greatest cybervillains may well have been the people committing crimes against standard capitalization. From "Netiquette" guides in the 1990s to forum posts into the mid-2000s, a hot topic for griping was other internet users who typed in all lowercase. Both those who liked it and those who didn't spoke about it in terms of ease of use: "lazy" or "constantly hitting shift puts a lot of strain on the ol' hands." The complaints themselves don't matter: disdain for a bit of language is no more relevant to linguistics than a personal distaste for broccoli is relevant to food science. Rather, like how a food historian might use a historical figure's diatribe against broccoli to establish that broccoli was indeed being eaten in a particular place at a particular time, the linguistic forms that people complain about can tell us which linguistic forms were becoming popular when. No one bothers with tirades against vegetables they've never heard of or words they've never encountered.

What's curious here is that after 2006, there was a marked decrease in people complaining about when people don't capitalize. Okay, we might think, maybe they just got used to lowercasing, the way that people have chilled out about emoticons or internet acronyms since they first became popular. But then, a few years later, a new under-capitalizing supervillain began ravaging cyberspace. This time, the people complaining weren't forum posters. They were publications that cater to young people, like *Teen Vogue, BuzzFeed,* and the *Crimson,* Harvard's student newspaper. And the crime associated with lowercasing wasn't laziness but passive aggression. Trend pieces about passive-aggressive texting started around 2013 and really got going in 2015 and 2016. These pieces pointed out that this same minimalist typography was liable to make your friends wonder why you're mad at them. Typing in lowercase was no longer an issue of laziness or efficiency: it became a way of indicating attitude.

So what happened between 2006 and 2013? The rise of smartphones — phones with large touchscreens, internet access, and on-screen keyboards that were much better at predictive text than the previous generation of non-touchscreen, many-buttoned cellphones — neatly correlates with the exact time span we're interested in. The first iPhone came out in 2007, and American smartphone sales first surpassed sales of non-smart cellphones in 2011, with the same shift happening globally in 2013.

A predictive keyboard automatically adds capitals at the beginning of messages and after a period, and it only predicts words in its dictionary. Suddenly, instead of lowercasing taking less effort, it often took more. I did an informal poll on Twitter in 2016, asking, "When you write on your phone, do you ever undo the autocapitalization for the sake of aesthetic?" and the results were very clear: of the five hundred–plus people who replied, over half said that they do so all the time, with another third saying "sometimes" and only 14 percent saying "never." Several people, unprompted, even commented that they'd gone into their phone settings and turned off autocapitalization permanently — a far cry from the "lazy" stereotype of the pre-2006 lowercaser. In the words of Dolly Parton, "It costs a lot of money to look this cheap." Of course, the people who reply to a random Twitter poll one day are probably not a balanced sample of internet residents, so we should take those percentages with a grain of salt. But it's clear a substantial number of people choose minimalist typography deliberately, to create a specific effect. If people are going to all this effort, what is it that they're signaling?

The social significance of minimalist typography is too broad a question for a corpus or a dictionary. It operates on a sentence level or a whole utterance level, so you can't just search for words that aren't capitalized: you'll filter through scores of entirely unremarkable uncapitalized and unpunctuated words from the middles of formal sentences. Moreover, we know that there was an earlier stage where people didn't bother with capitals and punctuation for reasons of economy, not to convey a particular tone of voice. Some internet users may still be lowercasing for this earlier reason. To answer this question, what we need is a view into the minds of the people who were typing this way.

Based on the locations of these early trend pieces, it seems that minimalist typography is a younger-people thing. But there's a catch-22 when it comes to analyzing youth language: your intuitions about it are inversely proportional to your ability to write about it. I can assert things with confidence about the slang of the 1990s and 2000s, but as the 2010s continue, I'm already feeling myself slipping out of touch, even as my platform to write about it grows larger. The point at which you're a native speaker with the sharpest intuitions, the most deeply embedded into your particular youth sub-culture, with friends your age who think it would be a lark to let you analyze their posts or texts, is also the point when you're likely to be writing your very first research paper or conference presentation, if you're lucky. You know what's cool, but no one knows who you are or why they should be reading you.

Some linguists work on youth language by involving their undergraduate students; others by partnering with local schools. I do it via the internet. I started a blog called *All Things Linguistic* when I was still in grad school, and I made it on Tumblr because I was familiar with the platform from previous meme blogs. Initially, the blog was a way of not getting too high up the ivory tower. I started posting tips for students I was teaching, links to articles I was reading, and fun linguistic things that I came across in my everyday life. As I realized that I enjoyed this public-facing writing more than the academic kind, and began writing about linguistics for a general audience full-time, the blog and social media became a line back into academia rather than just my window out of it. It became the way that I found out about conferences to attend and papers to read.

The blog is also a crucial way that I bridge some of the gaps in internet linguistics citations. I started to keep a file of posts under a tag I named "language on the interwebz" in the very first week of the blog, long before I realized that I'd be writing this book or how important it would become to my research. As of this writing, it contains nearly three hundred posts, my third-largest tag after general linguistics and "linguist humour" (tagged with Canadian -*our*, thank you!). Some of the posts are my own open questions, some of them are links to academic or popular articles, some of them are reblogs of other internet users reflecting on their language use. Sometimes, browsing Tumblr leads me to come across junior scholars sharing their research; periodically, I post a call for people to send me their class papers and honors theses and conference handouts about internet linguistics; increasingly, people know me by reputation and come right up to tell me about relevant projects at conferences or in my inbox. Some of these papers have also informed other sections of this book; others I didn't end up citing at all, but I've never met one that didn't give me fresh perspective into which communities the authors as speakers find interesting enough to investigate, which examples they pick as representative of the whole, or how to approach data collection in new communities. In this way, I'm building on a tradition in internet linguistics. David Crystal, in his 2011 book *Internet Linguistics: A Student Guide,* includes a call to action, saying, "The one thing Internet language needs, more than anything else, is good descriptions." When I see this quote cited as motivation in many student papers, it seems to me that the next step is surely to fold those papers back into the literature. In the internet era, an observation need not appear even in an academic journal to be citable.

For minimalist typography, there are two linguistics master's theses that are particularly relevant, a 2015 thesis by Harley Grant and a 2016 thesis by Molly Ruhl, both about Tumblr. Tumblr is understudied compared to Twitter (or rather, Twitter is overstudied compared to every other social network) because Twitter makes it very easy for researchers to collect a large, random assortment of tweets and search through them by date posted. Tumblr is easier to study than Facebook or Snapchat, because at least the posts are generally public, but it doesn't have any means of pulling out a random sample. You either need to be an active participant-observer and study whatever happens to be posted or shared by the people you follow, or you need to pick a particular subcommunity to analyze. Both of these methods mean that you need to already have a sense of which communities might be linguistically interesting.

Tumblr is of particular interest for the period when minimalist punctuation was developing, in the years between 2006 and 2013, because its user base was young (nearly half were between ages sixteen and twenty-four in 2013), oriented towards the internet as a source of community (in comparison to Instagram and Snapchat, popular for connecting with existing friendship networks), and self-reflexive about their own language use. In her thesis, Grant cites several meta-commentary posts about the linguistic style of Tumblr from 2012, which are also self-referential examples of typographical minimalism. The most popular such post, with over half a million likes and reblogs, begins as follows:

when did tumblr collectively decide not to use punctuation like when did this happen why is this a thing

it just looks so smooth I mean look at this sentence flow like a jungle river

The popularity of this and similar posts both confirms that the posters were describing a phenomenon widely recognized by fellow users and helped acculturate new users into the norms of the platform, such as signaling that a question is rhetorical or ironic by asking it without a question mark. Ruhl cites another self-referential, widely shared, multiauthored post, this time from 2016. At first glance, it seems like it's primarily an example of different kinds of emphasis, but those examples are interspersed in a neutral, minimalist carrier sentence:

i think it's really Cool how there are so many ways to express emphasis™ on tumblr and they're all c o m p l e t e l y different it's #wild

#E m p h a s i s™

WHAT HAVE YOU DONE

The hashtagged, initial-capped, space-stretched, trademarked #E m p h a s i s™ is a break in the system: it's got too many things going on at once to be interpretable as more than a joke. But the reply, all-capped WHAT HAVE YOU DONE, is simultaneously emphatic and minimalist: it signals strong feeling from the all caps and a rhetorical question from the question syntax without a question mark.

Tumblr users were particularly self-reflexive about minimalist typography, but it wasn't just a Tumblr thing: it also started flourishing on Twitter around the same period. The minimalism brings in a poetic effect in this surreal tweet by absurdist co-median Jonny Sun in 2014 (who we saw in Chapter 2 being hospitable with typos).

"i just want to go home" said the astronaut.

"so come home" said ground control.

"s o c o m e h o m e" said the voice from the stars.

If sparkle punctuation is overt artistic ornamentation, then minimalist punctuation is an open canvas, inviting you to fill in the gaps. In less than 140 characters, this tweet tells a story about the conflict between longing for the familiar and the unknown, about our dual identities as earthlings and as stardust. Sun's tweet also showcases an example of using the expanded Unicode character set to convey tone of voice, in this case using fullwidth characters to make the letters appear wider and with more space around them, as if they're echoing from between the stars. This eerie, melodic, compelling narrative has inspired other Twitter users to create more than fifty original paintings and drawings.

I asked Jonny Sun when he started using this distinctive style, and he said 2012 — the same year that many people were noticing it on Tumblr — but no, he'd never been a Tumblr user. Sun cited instead a soft/weird aesthetic that people were using on Twitter at the time, as well as a callback to the 1990s tendency to lowercase everything on instant messaging. Like how sparkle sarcasm can be derived from sparkle enthusiasm by a calculation, the aesthetic and ironic effects of minimalist typography are derived from knowledge of its earlier connotations (laziness, antiauthoritarianism) and the explicit choice to embrace them in an age of auto-capitalization. Glitchy, pixelated, and badly photoshopped internet art came back into popularity in an age of high-definition cameras and smooth Instagram filters, and so did the written equivalent: stylized verbal incoherence mirroring emotional incoherence.

In my quest to seek out internet linguistic papers on minimalist typography, I inadvertently produced a useful example myself.

One of the places where I asked about student papers was in a Facebook linguistics meme group in 2018, since I'd noticed that the linguistics meme energy had been shifting from Tumblr to Facebook groups (more about memes in Chapter 7). Someone commented that they'd been about to send me something that I'd actually written myself before they put two and two together and realized we were the same person. I replied, without thinking too much about it, "my Brand is Strong" — a few people acknowledged the humor, and that was that.

Later, I got to thinking about it. I realized that I'd replied from my phone, but I'd had to go to extra effort in order to do so. If I hadn't been able to override my phone's default formatting — if I'd had to type "My brand is strong." rather than "my Brand is Strong" — my irony could have been read as sincere arrogance. I can't see that phrase with default capitalization and not want to wipe that smarmy grin off someone's face: there's no way I'm going to let it issue from my own. Of course, I could have typed something else that was sincere and non-smarmy using formal typography. But the irony gains me something here: with ironic capitals on the "brand" part, I align myself with internet people, all facing the same weird pressures of social media on our self-presentation. With minimalist lowercase at the beginning, I make myself approachable: like a self-deprecating joke at the beginning of a public speech, I remove myself from the position of being able to lecture others about their writing style by preemptively adopting features that someone else might lecture me for. At one level, I acknowledge that it's true, the other person has heard of me, but at the same time, I defuse the awkwardness of that moment by signaling that I don't take myself too seriously: it's okay, I've got an ordinary internet user's ironic ambivalence towards the idea of a personal brand.

Irony, paradoxically, creates space for sincerity. If you and I can have the same web of complex attitudes towards one thing, then maybe we can also share more straightforward attitudes towards others. In this thread, irony did just that: the original poster replied again sincerely, thanking me for taking young people's slang seriously. At first glance, it might seem like I hadn't done that at all: Wasn't the whole point of my reply that it was ironic? But at a deeper level, what I was taking seriously was aligning myself with the internet fluent, demonstrating such fluency myself, and signaling that I understood how vital it is to be able to convey a typographical tone of voice.

In that moment, this thread was the fulfillment of a dream belonging to centuries of writers, from Rousseau to *The Onion:* a successful communication of irony in writing between two complete strangers. That commenter and I are not alone: people now communicate in this ironic dance every minute of every day. We succeeded, in fact, precisely because we're not alone, because we're not solitary intellectuals writing up abstract proposals for ironic punctuation, but social people trying our damnedest, paying attention to how our messages will be read, extending the grace of assuming that the other is also choosing their typography with intent. We succeeded because our linguistic norms were both oriented towards the social internet rather than the prescriptive red pen.

Irony is a linguistic trust fall. When I write or speak with a double meaning, I fall backwards, hoping that you'll be there to catch me. The risks are high: misaimed irony can gravely injure the conversation. But the rewards are high, too: the sublime joy of feeling purely understood, the comfort of knowing someone's on your side. No wonder people through the ages kept trying so hard to write it.

If polite typography, as we saw earlier, is about making extra effort, using initial capitals and friendly exclamation marks to signal cheerful distance or genuine enthusiasm, then ironic typography is the opposite on both counts: it introduces a note of dissonance that makes the reader look harder to find the double meaning. Any variation from an expected baseline will do, whether that's lowercasing, sparkle sarcasm, asking a rhetorical question by omitting the question mark, or ironically using outdated slang (one much-reblogged post on Tumblr noted that saying something is "great" indicates that it's genuinely good, whereas something that's described as "gr8" is a guilty pleasure or appreciated sarcastically). But crucially, irony requires this baseline in the first place. It required us to develop a set of typographical resources for indicating straightforward types of voices, like shouting and enthusiasm, before we could creatively subvert them.

It's easy to analyze different types of computer-mediated communication in terms of platform, splitting up the short texts from the long blog posts. Less often do we consider the importance of time, the fact that CU L8R and #E m p h a s i s™ belong to very different eras of internetspeak.

Minimalist typography is a key example of a time-based internet style: its beginnings are recorded across Tumblr and Twitter and texting within the same span of around 2012–2013. In comparison, a study conducted around a decade earlier by psychologist Jeffrey Hancock asked undergraduate students to talk about scenarios designed to induce irony, like fashion fails, in either written, computer-mediated communication or spoken, face-to-face communication. Hancock found, to his surprise, that people were just as likely to use irony in both circumstances, even though, he noted, there weren't very many typographical tools to use in conveying it — the only one he found to report was the dot dot dot. I'd love to see this study replicated for the era of ironic typography, but it's useful as a reminder that internet language, like every other linguistic style, changes across time. Future eras may create ways of expressing meanings that are still more exquisite, making our current system of irony one day seem as blunt as a simple dot dot dot.

Looking back at the proposals for backwards question marks and upside-down exclamation marks as irony punctuation, we can see that many of them were halfway there in trying to trade on double meanings.

Perhaps their problem wasn't just in trying to impose a novel symbol that would need to be explained, it was also in dreaming too small: a single punctuation mark is not enough to convey the full range of possible irony. Ironic typography is complicated because irony itself is complicated: its linguistic signals aren't as straightforward as a LOUD voice or a rising? pitch. Sometimes, the irony literature tells us, a double meaning is purely derived from context, like saying, "What a nice sunny day!" when it's pouring rain outside. Other times, irony is signaled by overstatement: "thank you very much" is more likely to be ironic than simple "thanks." But in many circumstances, irony is signaled by a constellation of features from the voice and face: smiling, laughing, raising an eyebrow, talking more slowly and intensely — the kind that ironic typography can help us with. Even in face-to-face conversations, for all their generations of practice, irony isn't always successfully transmitted: an ironist still relies on feedback like a smile, a laugh, or the continuation of the irony in order to make sure that the double meaning has truly been conveyed.

Ironic typography merely gives written irony a fighting chance: in any medium, irony requires trust. Not signaling all one's emotions with overt punctuation can be a sign of faith that someone won't take things the wrong way, because we're already friends or we're part of the same speech community — or conversely, a way of repelling outsiders, of saying, "I don't care if you take this the wrong way." It's like how a pet name is both a sign of intimacy and a way of being rude when the presumed intimacy isn't there. It may be a sign of Stone-Hearted Ice Witchery to not punctuate a polite social email with exclamation marks, but with a truly close friend, I don't need to send a polite social follow-up email in the first place.

But even as this system of typographical tone of voice is developing so beautifully, it's also under threat. When asking about the future of technolinguistic tools, like speech to text or predictive smart replies, we need to ask not just how they can be used, but how they can be subverted; not just how designers can help users communicate their intentions, but how users can help them communicate more than the designers intended. It's all very well to be sincere when asking a voice assistant for the day's weather, but for technology that aims to help us write messages to other people, the next great challenge is not just the words we say but how we say them. It was the subversion of autocapitalization, after all, that paved the way for ironic mini-malism, and the subversion of traditional handwritten means of calling attention that paved the way for #E m p h a s i s™. For typographical tone of voice, training on formal datasets from books and newspapers is not going to be enough. This kind of subtlety must be part of the future of any system that aims to facilitate writing, and it's not yet clear how to do so effectively: IBM experimented with adding Urban Dictionary data to its artificial intelligence system Watson, only to scrub it all out again when the computer started swearing at them.

It's important, in the meantime, not to overstate what's changed. Many features of internet tone of voice have been around for over three decades, if we take those 1984 Usenet posts as a starting point, and yet if E. E. Cummings or L. M. Montgomery were to pick up a modern book or read a modern newspaper, they'd see edited prose that looks quite familiar to their 1920s eyes. In formal writing, periods are still emotionally neutral,* questions and question marks

*Or at least, I sure hope they are, because otherwise you're halfway through a book where I've been passive-aggressive to you the whole time. SORRY.

still march hand in hand, uppercase still demarcates sentence beginnings and proper names, and one must still rely on clever phrasing to communicate sarcasm. (Alas ⸮)

It's not that writing has completely changed, it's that writing has forked, into formal and informal versions. But this forking didn't coincide with the invention of the internet, or even of the computer. All caps, expressive lengtheninggg, ~irony punctuation~, minimalist punctuation, and capitalization paired with linebreaks all have direct ancestors in the early twentieth century, not the twenty-first. Think of the minimalist punctuation and capitalization of E. E. Cummings or the stream of consciousness used by James Joyce in the last chapter of *Ulysses,* which is 4,391 words long and punctuated only by two periods. The principle of the stream-of-consciousness writing style was that it represented the flow of thoughts in one's head better than rigidly conventionalized formal writing, so if we're looking to make our writing closer to our thoughts, perhaps it's not surprising that we'd end up sounding modernist or postmodern.

We could even trace this fork back to the beginning of grammatical typography. When grammarians decided that the scribal, pause-based punctuation needed to be reformed under the model of Latin grammar, they may have been able to change the practices of schoolteachers and editors, but they never wholly held dominion over private letters, handwritten signs, or notes left on the kitchen table. In the future, the era of writing between the invention of the printing press and the internet may come to be seen as an anomaly — an era when there arose a significant gap between how easy it was to be a writer versus a reader. An era when we collectively stopped paying attention to the informal, unedited side of writing and let typography become static and disembodied.

The internet didn't create informal writing, but it did make it more common, changing some of our previously spoken interactions into near-real-time text exchanges. At the same time, keyboards took away some of our previous repertoire for expressive writing, like multiple underlines, colored ink, fancy borders, silly doodles, and even subtle changes in someone's handwriting that might allow you to infer their mood. But the expanded system of conveying emotional nuance through text we've come up with instead is so nuanced and idiosyncratic that if I'm typing a personal sort of communication for someone — say, when I'm in the passenger's seat and a text on the driver's phone needs to be replied to right away — I find I need to inquire in great detail how exactly they want me to type. Period, exclamation mark, or simple linebreak at the end of the utterance? How much capitalization? Do any letters need to be repeated? Likewise, if I receive a message authored by someone other than the owner of the phone, I can often tell the difference. Expressive typography makes electronic communication anything but impersonal.

I, for one, think this change is fantastic. Even if this increased attention to typographical tone of voice did mean the decline of standard punctuation, I'd gladly accept the decline of standards that were arbitrary and elitist in the first place in favor of being able to better connect with my fellow humans. After all, a red pen will never love me back. Perfectly following a list of punctuation rules may grant me some kinds of power, but it won't grant me love. Love doesn't come from a list of rules — it emerges from the spaces between us, when we pay attention to each other and care about the effect that we have on each other. When we learn to write in ways that communicate our tone of voice, not just our mastery of rules, we learn to see writing not as a way of asserting our intellectual superiority, but as a way of listening to each other better. We learn to write not for power, but for love. But for all the subtle vocal modulations that typography can express, we're not just voices. We still need a way to convey the messages that we send with the rest of our bodies.

CHAPTER 5:
EMOJI AND OTHER INTERNET GESTURES

Our bodies are a big part of the way we communicate.

If someone stamps into a room with a furrowed brow, slams the door, and proclaims, "I'M NOT ANGRY," you believe their body, not their words.

If someone is sobbing and wiping away tears as they say, "No, no, there's nothing wrong," you don't reply, "Great, glad to hear it, that's a relief, let's go dancing!" You say something like "I mean, it sure looks like something's wrong, but if you don't want to talk about it I understand."

If a good friend looks you in the eye, grins, and says, "You're the most terrible person I've ever met!" you don't think, "Oops, I guess this person isn't my friend after all." You think, "Awesome, we're such close friends that we can mock-insult each other and we both know we don't mean it!"

Likewise, a lot of our language about

emotion is embodied — our hearts race, our eyebrows arch, our cheeks flush, our stomachs butterfly, our throats, um, frog. Writing is a technology that removes the body from the language. That's its greatest advantage — it's easier to transport and store words written on paper or in bytes than embodied in an entire living human or a hologram of one. Sometimes, you wouldn't even want the body component: just because I ambitiously decide to keep a copy of Plato's *Republic* beside the toilet does not mean that I want Zombie Socrates taking up residence in my bathroom.

But the lack of a body is also writing's greatest disadvantage, especially when it comes to representing emotions and other mental states. In the early days of going online, it seemed like we had a very clear eventual answer to the question of virtual embodiment. In the future envisioned by Neal Stephenson's 1992 novel *Snow Crash,* or the 3D virtual world Second Life, launched in 2003, it seemed like we'd all be making full-bodied avatars for ourselves, with hands and feet and hairstyles, to bodily interact with each other in virtual space. The idea was that these avatars would project in cyberspace whatever we'd do in the physical world, whether logistical or emotive: thus we'd enter rooms and shake hands and roll on the floor laughing.

On a technical level, we've gotten quite good at projecting and manipulating a virtual body. It's a central feature for entire genres of videogames, from first-person shooters to The Sims. But for general socializing, it never quite took off. Second Life made a lot of headlines, but it remained popular only in a smallish subcommunity of internet users, and similar efforts are even more obscure. The closest thing most of us have to a social avatar is the profile picture we use on social media apps — hardly the ambitious three-dimensional graphics that Second Life or *Snow Crash* imagined. True, profile pictures do provide some sense of who you're talking to and what they (or their dog) look like. But they're static. My profile pic has the same fixed, photographic smile, regardless of the message I type beside it. What we really need is a dynamic system. Punctuation is good at representing tone of voice, but we're still missing something, something embodied. This was the void that emoticons and emoji stepped into, those smiley faces made from repurposed punctuation marks and those small pictures of faces and hearts and animals and all manner of other objects.

I first got involved with the linguistics

of emoji in 2014. I'd written some articles about meme linguistics and internet linguistics, and as emoji started hitting the news in a big way (over six thousand articles were written about the emoji released in 2014 alone), I became one of the people who journalists and tech companies called up to analyze emoji. I did a talk at South by Southwest, a tech culture conference, in partnership with smartphone keyboard app SwiftKey, looking at the overall picture of how people used emoji based on SwiftKey's billions of anonymized data points. When we put the proposal together in 2015, I was slightly worried that emoji would have blown over by the time of the conference, a whole eight months away. But instead, they were more popular than ever, and the jam-packed room of people who came to our talk agreed, as did the newspapers in six countries that reported on the talk later.

The question on everyone's mind was: Why? Why were emoji so popular, so quickly? By the time you've called up a linguist to answer this question, you've pretty much decided that the answer is "because they're a new language." But as the linguist being called up, I wasn't so sure. I was just as fascinated as anyone by emoji as a phenomenon, but linguists have a definition of what language is, and it's very clear that emoji don't fit in it.

Here's a demonstration: when we were coming up with the South by Southwest talk, we spent about half a minute batting around the idea of whether we could give the talk entirely in emoji, before realizing that it would be impossible to convey anything useful or interesting that way. Even just putting the slides entirely in emoji was too much: we needed to be able to label our graphs and ask focusing questions. In comparison, I also speak French, and I could definitely have given the talk in French, even though I would've had to look up a few words. I could've also attempted to give the talk in Spanish or German, and the fact that I couldn't give a talk in the rest of the world's seven thousand languages is not due to any failing on their parts, simply my lack of fluency. (Alas, being a linguist has not conferred upon me the ability to speak all the languages.) Yet no matter how "emoji-fluent" we and our audience were, there was no way to give the presentation entirely in emoji: a whole hour of reciting emoji might be an interesting piece of performance art, but there was no way for it to be the funny, informative talk we'd promised. There isn't even a clear way to say "emoji" in emoji, let alone a way to render, say, this paragraph. Real languages can handle meta-level vocabulary and adapt to new words with ease: every language has a name for itself, and many have recently acquired a word for "emoji," just to take one salient example. Emoji aren't capable of either.

WHAT ARE EMOJI FOR?

Emoji aren't the same as words, but they're clearly doing *something* important for communication: I just needed to articulate what that was. Inspired by the fact that the face and hand emoji were consistently the most popular, I began talking about emoji as gesture. I made lists of common gestures and emoji to find correspondences. The lists got long: shrug, thumbs up, pointing finger, rolling eyes, middle finger, winking face, clapping hands, and so on. All of these exist in gestural and emoji form, but there were also many that didn't: the eggplant emoji and the fire emoji didn't have equivalent gestures, and nodding "yes" or shaking one's head "no" didn't have emoji. I was at a standstill.

That's when I sent a draft of my emoji analysis to Lauren Gawne, an Australian linguist who's also a good friend and my cohost on the podcast *Lingthusiasm*. She highlighted my list and commented, "You know there's a name for this kind of gesture in the literature, right? They're called emblems."

I did not.

Oh, I knew Gawne did gesture research, but we'd never really talked about it much. After all, it's not like we could gesture on the podcast. I assumed she didn't care to talk about the gesture side of her research. She assumed I wasn't interested. Suddenly, I was very interested.

You know how when you learn the word "schadenfreude," and something clicks into place? You're not uniquely terrible in occasionally taking pleasure in someone else's misfortune: other people have been there before you. I'd been spending months and years with emoji, categorizing and analyzing them, and here was this one word that blew them all open. Someone has been here before me, a whole body of scholars, in fact, and they'd figured stuff out. I dived head-first into the gesture literature. By the time Gawne was awake again in Melbourne, I'd exhausted Wikipedia and sent her a dozen questions. Delighted, she forwarded me the reading list for her whole gesture course.

I spent the next week in a daze. It was like I was thirteen again, encountering linguistics for the very first time: eavesdropping on people in public places with fresh ears and eyes, thoughtfully examining the positions of my hands and fingers in cafés the way that I'd once experimented with sounds and sentences under my breath in libraries. (I became utterly incapable of having a normal conversation, because I kept getting derailed by analyzing the gestures — it was hard enough when I only got derailed by the words!) When I discovered linguistics, I learned that language isn't just a squidgy mess of opinions and impressions: there are real patterns here that I've been subconsciously following all along! Even if we don't know them all yet, they're fundamentally knowable, and there's a whole community of people whose mission it is to figure them out. What I hadn't realized until now was that the same thing is true for gesture. Like I can listen to a person's vowels and plot out which parts of the mouth it takes to make them and where that means they might have lived, thanks to my linguistic training, I could also learn to spot the different kinds of gestures and what each was for.

You might ask, as I asked myself, how did I manage to get two degrees in linguistics and go to dozens of linguistics conferences but never learn anything about gesture? I'm not alone: gesture studies has been gaining ground, but it's still a smallish subfield.

There are some universities that have gesture linguists and offer a course or a unit on gesture, but many still don't: Gawne happened to go to universities that had gesture studies, and I happened to go to ones that didn't. If there were gesture talks at any conferences I went to, I didn't have enough context to know why I should make a point of attending. Neither, Gawne and I suspected, did many other linguists, because we hadn't seen anyone else drawing these parallels between emoji and gesture either. So she started in on an academic paper using the examples I'd collected, and I rewrote this chapter with her guidance on the literature.

I've always been a sucker for a good taxonomy of everyday life, and gesture gave me a great one. But what was even better was that the same taxonomy worked just as well to describe how people use emoji. This was the missing link. Looking for a grand unified theory of emoji had been dooming me to failure because emoji don't just have one function, they have a range of them. But crucially, it's the same range that gestures have, and that's why emoji caught on so quickly and so completely: because they gave us an easy way of representing the functions behind the gestures that are so important for our informal communication. Without realizing that either gestures or emoji were potentially systematic, a couple billion internet users had subconsciously, collectively, and spontaneously mapped the functions of the one onto the capacity of the other.

Let's get back to emblems, the word that cracked everything open. I'd been making a list of gestures, like thumbs up, waving, winking, shrugging, jazz hands, rolling one's eyes, giving someone the finger, tugging out an imaginary collar to indicate awkwardness, playing a metaphorical tiny violin in false sympathy, brushing imaginary dirt off one's shoulders, dropping a metaphorical mic, making a heart with one's fingers, and so on. Many of these gestures have direct emoji equivalents: peace sign ✌ and thumbs up 👍 and crossed fingers 🤞 and rolling eyes 🙄 and winking 😉.

But what I'd also been doing, without realizing it, was making a list of gestures that have common names in English. I don't have to describe to you that a wink involves the deliberate closing of one eye or that a thumbs up involves the four fingers curled in on the hand, the thumb protruding and oriented to the sky, with the palm of the hand facing towards the speaker — as a speaker of English, these are things you already know. I was doing this for purely practical reasons (describing gestures in detail takes effort), but it turns out that these nameable gestures have some important things in common. Many theorists call them emblems, the way that a Jolly Roger is an emblem of a pirate. Emblem gestures can all fit easily into a linguistic frame (try any of them in a sentence like "If we're late, then ___"), but they're also perfectly meaningful without speech at all. The same thing goes for many emoji (you can say "If we're late, then 👍" or "If we're late, then 🙁"), but it's also sufficient sometimes to reply with just a thumbs up or eye-rolling emoji.

Emblem gestures have precise forms and stable meanings. They may seem universal because they often cover different territories than languages do: the middle finger, or *digitus impudicus,* was also considered rude in ancient Greece and Rome, while the palm-inwards V sign means "up yours" in some English-speaking nations but not others. But ultimately, emblems are arbitrary and culturally specific: obscene emblems from around the world include thumbs up ("sit on this" in many Arabic-speaking countries), the ok sign ("asshole" in many Latin American countries), an open hand thrust forward (the Greek *mountza*), a fist with the thumb between the index and middle finger (the Russian and Turkish "fig" gesture), and a gesture known as the *bras d'honneur* or Iberian slap (common to many Romance-speaking countries), which consists of extending one arm palm-up in a fist while the other hand is placed on the upper arm at the crook of the elbow. Perform one of these inside its region and you'll get anything from a rude gesture in return to legal prosecution for obscenity; perform it outside its region and no one will care. (An American recently told me about how, when visiting Japan, she was surprised to see people casually using their middle finger to press buttons on elevators and microwaves.) Perform one of them in a subtly wrong way (try flipping someone off with your palm facing towards them, instead of towards yourself), and you'll get laughed out of town.

The kinds of emoji that end up in emoji trend piece articles ("10 Emoji You Should Be Using Right Now!") sometimes also have taboo meanings. The eggplant emoji 🍆 is a prime example: widely used as a phallic symbol, it's a natural heir to the obscene gesture list above. The smiling pile of poo emoji 💩 is another: in deciding whether to include it in Gmail, the Japanese engineers had to explain its importance to the head office. They described it as: "It says 'I don't like that,' but softly," and " 'That's unfortunate, and I would like to punctuate my comment with a reiteration that I am displeased at what has just been expressed.' It's the anti-like." (For me, what made the poo emoji "click" was parsing it as "a bit shitty.") But what's crucial about emblem emoji is that they also have precise forms: some designers initially implemented the poo emoji without the smiling face, but this leaves out an essential aspect of its meaning. When emoji were first catching on internationally, a surprisingly big problem was emoji fragmentation: different app or device manufacturers were displaying the same underlying emoji with different designs. Platforms had not anticipated how much people would hate it when sending a lady in a red dress could result in their friends seeing a disco man or a blobby figure with a rose in its mouth: designers thought they were free to put their own company's spin on the general idea of "dancer." People felt as foolish sending the wrong dancer emoji as you would giving the middle finger backwards or crossing the wrong two fingers, and companies eventually backed down: the *Emojipedia* blog hailed 2018 as "The Year of Emoji Convergence." If we think of these emoji as emblems, we know that the range for variation is tiny indeed.

257

Thinking of certain types of emoji as emblems can also make it clearer what they're doing with respect to language. The key feature of emblems is that they're nameable gestures, and dictionaries naturally have entries for gestures like "wink" and "thumbs up" in their status as English words. Similarly, the names of certain emoji (already English words or phrases) are taking on additional connotations which originate with emoji but don't require the emoji itself. I've noticed a few people using nonculinary "eggplant" with no mention of the emoji at all: in one headline, a singer "Mistakenly Shared Photo Of His Eggplant On Instagram." If this usage continues, it will clearly be necessary to add a new subdefinition under "eggplant" (joining the existing euphemistic senses of words like "banana" and "sausage"). But this doesn't mean that dictionaries necessarily need to keep an inventory of all emoji, even the non-emblem ones, any more than they already do for the non-emblem gestures.

Emoji aren't the only way to express emblems in internet communication. An early fan of Snapchat described the appeal of sending messages overlaid on top of a photo you've just taken as "like texting, but you get to use your face as the emoticon instead of an actual emoticon." In other words, texting but with emblematic gestures. Animated gifs, while technically looping, silent animated image files that can display any image, are often used in practice to display emblems. The most engaging gifs have been found to be those with faces in them, a feature that's come to be reflected in user interfaces. When you go to insert a gif on Twitter, the built-in categories of gif that you're offered are nameable, stylized gestures by humans, cartoon characters, or occasionally animals, such as applause, eww, eye roll, facepalm, fistbump, goodbye, happy dance, hearts, high five, hug, kiss, mic drop, no, omg, ok, popcorn, scared, shocked, shrug, sigh, wink, and yawn. Certain gifs are so emblematic that they can be invoked by name, without an image file at all, just like a thumbs up or an eggplant emoji: when you want to convey your excitement in observing other people's drama, you can send a gif of Michael Jackson eating popcorn in a darkened movie theater, eyes avidly glued to the screen, but you can also simply say #popcorngif or *popcorn.gif*.

It's not an accident that the most iconic popcorn.gif is one of Michael Jackson. Both gestural and digital emblems participate in cycles of appropriation from African American culture: the high five came from a Jazz

Age gesture known as the low five or "giving skin" and spread via sports teams, and the fistbump came from the "dap" among black soldiers during the Vietnam War. Similarly, the painting fingernails emoji entered the mainstream by its association with the black drag queen expression "throwing shade," for giving a subtle, cutting insult. In an article called "We Need to Talk About Digital Blackface in Reaction GIFs," Lauren Michele Jackson pointed out that black people are overrepresented in gifs used by nonblack people, especially those that show extreme emotion. She linked this stereotype to the exaggerated acting of minstrel shows and scholar Sianne Ngai's term "animatedness" to describe the long-standing tendency to see black people's actions as hyperbolic.

There are other gestures that don't have conventional names, which I'd been ignoring entirely because they're hard to describe in words. But we use them even more than we do emblems, because they come with us in practically everything we say. You'd probably gesture when saying, "Keep going that way and turn at the lights" and "The fish was THIS big" and "The person sitting next to me just kept going on, and on, and on . . ." but your gestures don't have specific names, only descriptions. For directions, you'd point to indicate which way is "that way" and which direction to turn at the lights; for indicating size, you might put your hands flat, facing each other some distance apart; and for "going on and on," you might make some sort of open hand shape, moving repeatedly in a rough circle.

If you try talking with your hands tied down (recruit a friend to make sure you get untied!), you'll probably have a hard time with it. Researchers have done this: they showed people cartoons of Wile E. Coyote chasing Road Runner and asked them to describe them to someone else. Half the time, the describers had their hands fastened to the chair, ostensibly to take physiological measurements, but really to see what happened when they weren't able to gesture. The researchers found that when you can't gesture, you have a harder time telling the visual and spatial parts of a story: people talked slower, paused more, and were more likely to say "um" and "uh."

Every culture that's been studied has gesture, and we gesture along with our speech even when it's communicatively useless, such as when we're talking on the phone. Even people who have been blind since birth do it, even when they're talking with people who they know are also blind. But it's not so much about an irresistible temptation to wink or flip someone the bird: the gestures we can't help doing are the ones without specific names. So linguists think that this other kind of gesture, called co-speech or illustrative gesture, is more about the thinking of the speaker than the understanding of the listener. Sure enough, people who are encouraged to gesture do better at solving math problems and mental rotation.

The next time you're in a restaurant, have a look around you at the groups of people at other tables. You probably won't see a lot of emblems, but you're guaranteed to see some co-speech gestures. Look at some people at a table far enough away that you can't hear them: you can tell who's speaking when by who's gesturing. You can probably get a sense of how well they're getting along, whether they're laughing merrily or you're about to witness an awkward fight, but the content of their conversation remains private because the meaning of co-speech gestures is more dependent on their surrounding speech. For example, the thumbs up sign could also be used as a co-speech gesture to indicate "up there." But "up there" could just as easily be illustrated by the index finger or whole hand pointing up, using one or both hands, the eyes or eyebrows pointing up, or any of these things combined — none of which work as a substitute for the thumbs up emblem.

We can see this same flexibility at play when it comes to illustrating birthday greetings with emoji. People wish others a happy birthday using the cake with candles 🎂, the slice of cake 🍰, the balloon 🎈, the wrapped gift 🎁, the bouquet of flowers 💐, or general positive emoji such as hearts, sparkles, happy faces, confetti, and positive hand shapes like the thumbs up or fistbump. These emoji showed up in the SwiftKey dataset in a wide variety of combinations and orders. When you're illustrating your speech, you're more willing to accept a range of options as suitable for "birthday" or "beach" or "fun" or "danger." The birthday cakes display variously as chocolate, vanilla, or strawberry, with an inconsistent number of candles, across different platforms, and yet "The Year of Emoji Convergence" did nothing to make them more similar.

People were bothered by variation in the form of the dancer emoji because it was serving as an emblem, and emblems add their own separate meaning to the words they go with. But people were unruffled by variation in the form of the birthday cake emoji because it's an illustration, and illustrative emoji instead highlight and reinforce a topic that's already present. It's okay if illustrators aren't quite exactly on target: the surrounding words will provide enough context to interpret them correctly. For the emblem emoji, we tend to know exactly what we're looking for because we've seen other people using it first. For illustrative emoji, we often go browsing through our keyboards instead.

But sometimes, when we go fishing for an illustration, we realize in surprise that there's nothing at all suitable: "What?? How is there no _____ emoji??" The problem here is that emoji were added through a hodgepodge of historic compatibility and individual request, not designed as a systematic attempt to cover all areas of semantic space. (More on this later, when we get to the history of emoji.) Birthdays are a well-filled-in area of emoji illustration, but other domains are less so, especially those beyond emoji's original roots in Japan or first transplant in the United States.

The illustrative, co-speech emoji are interpretable at face value: it takes cultural knowledge of birthday traditions to interpret a cake and a balloon, sure, but it doesn't take any particular internet literacy to know that sending these items as emoji is intended to evoke birthday wishes. Illustrator emoji are readily used even by people who are less familiar with internet cultural norms: it's easy to add a cat emoji to "Have you fed the cat yet?" But many an inadvertent grocery-store innuendo has been texted by someone who was treating the eggplant as an innocent illustrator rather than a suggestive emblem.

The final emoji puzzle is how we use them in combination with other emoji. One type of sequence, which gets a lot of attention, is the retelling of familiar stories in emoji: *Emoji Dick* is a retelling of *Moby-Dick* in emoji, the #EmojiReads hashtag featured people's renditions of stories like *Lord of the Flies* and *Les Misérables,* and Emoji Karaoke is a game where you see who can come up with the best emoji version of a song before it stops playing. It's easy to see how these fit in with the idea of emoji as gesture: they're like playing digital charades or pantomiming to a friend across a loud bar. Emoji pantomime and other "stunt" uses of emoji are fun, but what I wanted to know was, is this truly a reflection of the generic, day-to-day use of emoji? How do emoji interface with our normal, casual writing?

To answer this, I got SwiftKey's engineers to run two queries. The first thing I wanted to know was, what percent of things that people write are describable as emoji stories: emoji-only utterances that are at least five or ten emoji long? If emoji storytelling were truly common, if (as the headlines would have it) emoji were taking over from English, we should find lots of emoji-only messages. We did not. The vast majority of messages were text only. Of the ones that contained emoji at all, the vast majority put them alongside words. And of the messages that were only emoji, the majority were just one or two emoji long — presumably replies to something else. Less than one in a thousand messages were long enough that they might qualify as a potential emoji story. In fact, the only people I've been able to find who regularly communicate with extended emoji sequences are preliterate children. Many parents have told me about how their two- to five-year-old kids enjoy texting them messages full of dinosaur or animal emoji — but then these same kids start sending words instead of emoji once they learn how to read.

So, long emoji sequences weren't common, but our dataset was still really large. What did these rare sequences of potential emoji storytelling look like?

This was my second question. I got Swift-Key's engineers to extract the most common sequences of two, three, and four emoji.

This is a common way of analyzing a large body of writing. The difference between a mere list of words and a story is that a story's words are arranged in sentences and paragraphs: a collection of narratives has subpatterns among its common words that reflect the basic structure of the language itself. If you look at the most common sequences of two, three, and four words for the half-billion words of the Corpus of Contemporary American English, you get sequences like "I am," "in the," "I don't," "a lot of," "I don't think," "the end of the," "at the same time," "as well as," "for the first time," "one of the most," and "some of the." They're not riveting prose by themselves, but you can feel how well they'd work as glue to hold a more interesting story together. If people are commonly writing stories in emoji, looking for patterned emoji sequences is how we'd find them. We might expect, for example, a lot of the red circle with a line through it 🚫 to indicate negation, or that emoji representing people, like 👩 or 👨, would often be followed by the arrow emoji ➡️, indicating a person going somewhere.

Instead, what we found was repetition. Looking at the top two hundred sequences of each length, about half were pure repetition, such as two tears of joy emoji 😂 😂, three loudly sobbing emoji 😭 😭 😭, or four red heart emoji ❤ ❤ ❤ ❤. Those that weren't simple repetition were often complex repetition, such as snow around a snowman ❄ ⛄ ❄, the see-no-evil, hear-no-evil, speak-no-evil monkeys 🙈 🙉 🙊, and kiss faces with kiss marks 😗 💋 😗 💋. Even the most heterogeneous strings of emoji were always thematically similar, such as heart eyes and kiss face 😍 😗 or single tear and loudly crying 😢 😥 😭 😭, strings of related objects like birthday 🎂 🍾 🎉 or fast food 🍕 🍗 🍗, and strings of hearts in different colors or sizes such as ❤ 💕 💚 💞.

Emoji aren't behaving like words in this respect: there are no repetitions at all in the top two hundred sequences of two, three, and four words in the Corpus of Contemporary American English. We don't even get strings of all nouns or all adjectives the way we got strings of thematic emoji. Sure, words are sometimes used repetitively (very very very, higgledy-piggledy) and emoji nonrepetitively (🚫 ❄ to mean "no snow" or ❤ 🍕 to mean "I like pizza"). But nothing like this shows up in the top lists. You might use several similar adjectives to reinforce each other (such as "big bad wolf"), but you wouldn't intertwine them in complex repetition (there's no "big bad big wolf"). Furthermore, emoji ordering wasn't very important (different kinds of hearts or birthday-related emoji appeared in all sorts of orders), whereas word ordering is often important ("bad big wolf" and "red small car" just feel wrong). It's essential to look at what's common if we want to understand how emoji fit into our communicative systems; after all, what distinguishes emoji from any other set of little pictures is that billions of people use them on a daily basis. The true emoji question is what billions of people are currently doing with emoji, not what an advertiser or a philosopher thinks they could hypothetically do with them. The part of communication where we repeat stuff all the time isn't in our words, it's in our gestures.

Look over to your imaginary co-patrons at the imaginary restaurant again. Here's someone with a hand loosely curled, palm upwards, moving it up and down to make a point. Someone else nods vigorously. Another person's finger loops the air emphatically several times. Someone taps the table in quiet boredom. A politician on TV brings an open hand down on the podium over and over again to drive home a point. These repetitive gestures are known as beats. You can do any shape of gesture in the style of a beat, whether it's repeatedly flipping someone off, pointing emphatically several times, or simply an open-handed beat that comes along for the ride in our regular conversations. What's important about the beat is the rhythm: when you stutter out loud, your beat gestures stutter with you. When you hold a vowel for a loooong time, your beat gestures hold a silent scream for just as long.

Emoji have the same rhythmic tendency as beat gestures. That's what the repetition is telling us. We type 😗 😗 😗 because we might also blow multiple kisses, we type 👍 👍 👍 because when we give the thumbs-up gesture, we sometimes do it rhythmically or hold it up for several seconds to emphasize it. Like how we can extend the letters of a word for emphasis, even when the result is unpronounceable ("sameeeee"), we can repeat even those emoji that don't have direct gestural correlates, like the skull 💀 or the smiling pile of poo 💩 or the sparkle heart 💖, because we've generalized this behavior to the category as a whole.

One use of emoji that's explicitly beat-related comes when each word is followed by a clapping hands emoji, as in WHAT 👏 ARE 👏 YOU 👏 DOING 👏. This started as an emoji representation of a beat gesture common among African American women.

270

Comedian Robin Thede described the "double clap on syllables" in a *Nightly Show* segment on "Black Lady Sign Language." But as writer Kara Brown put it when the gesture started making mainstream news headlines, "This — this clapping on every word for emphasis — is something that I have done since I was a cantankerous youth." In 2016, it started spreading to mainstream Twitter users unaware of its offline, African American origins. But whether online or offline, it's a beat.

The emoji combinations story also explains a puzzle that I encountered when analyzing the SwiftKey data: the case of the missing eggplant emoji. We knew that people were fond of the eggplant emoji as a phallic symbol: heck, you can buy eggplant emoji plush toys and keychains. And yet, when we looked at the top two hundred most common sequences of two, three, and four different emoji, the eggplant was nowhere to be found. We did find other, less famous, sexual combinations, such as the tongue emoji with water droplets 👅 💦, or the pointing finger and the ok sign 👈 👌. But the eggplant emoji only showed up as pure repetition 🍆 🍆 🍆 in our Top 200 lists. Same for the smiling pile of poo, another classic emoji that you can buy as endless novelty items: people were happy to repeat it 💩 💩 💩, but reluctant to combine it. What gives?

This mysterious absence of these classic emoji makes sense if we think about the difference between how emblems and co-speech gestures deal with sequences. Co-speech illustrative gestures are fluid, going smoothly from one into the other, with lots of possible shapes and variations for essentially the same meaning. If you describe the path of where you've gone today, you'll use many gestures in a row and you could easily gesture it slightly differently when you tell me about it now and when you told someone else about it a few minutes ago. Same with illustrative emoji: you can depict "Happy Birthday" or the weather with different sequences on different days, and that works fine. Emblems, on the other hand, are discrete, individual gestures: they can repeat, but they don't combine. You can applaud for a long time or flip someone off repeatedly, but you can't un-applaud someone or un-flip someone the bird, even if you combine them with the widely understood head shake that means no. In the same way, both the eggplant and the smiling poo emoji are emblem emoji: they have conventional meanings not immediately obvious from their literal origins, and they don't combine readily either. That's why we tend not to see them in interesting emoji sequences like we saw the birthday party emoji. Sending someone all of the possible birthday party emoji is extra festive: great! But sending someone all of the possible phallic emoji (say, the eggplant and the cucumber and the corncob and the banana 🍆 🥒 🌽 🍌) is NOT extra sexxaayy: that's a weird salad. There are multiple kinds of gestures and multiple kinds of emoji. Paying attention to how emoji fit with each other can give us a renewed appreciation for the gestures we make every day.

How We Got Emoji

When we think of emoji as gesture, it's clear why they caught on so quickly. But it leaves us with the inverse question: What took us so long to figure out a way to write our gestures?

Well, we tried.

Writing used to have illustration all the time. Medieval scribes illustrated their manuscripts with everything from the classic illuminated capital letters to a bizarrely popular motif of knights fighting giant snails at swordpoint. It was really the printing press that made us think that books should be composed primarily of walls of text: letters became significantly easier to produce than drawings. After all, once you've cast a set of metal letters, you can type any arrangement of words you could possibly want, but each new picture has to be engraved from scratch for printing. In theory, early printers could have created small, versatile metal drawings, too. In practice, they tended to be conservative about making new pieces of type: the first English printers imported their presses from Continental Europe, where no one used the English letter þ (thorn), so English printers substituted either the "th" letter sequence (which won out in most places) or the similar-looking letter "y" (which survives in a few limited contexts like Ye Olde Tea Shoppe). If printers weren't willing to cast a genuinely important letter, well, you can see why pictures were banished to book jackets and frontispieces and children's books. But the other factor preventing us from obtaining a delightful inventory of Renaissance emoji was psychological. What we thought we wanted out of writing was still very different: printing was a formal context, and handwriting was still around for informal doodles. We didn't yet have the sense that we could demand emotional expression in the same place as our standardized typesetting.

The chief variety of written gesture for a long time was the manicule, or printer's fist ☞, a pointing finger drawn or typeset in the margins of manuscripts to call attention to a particular passage. It was in widespread use from the twelfth to eighteenth centuries, used by medieval monks adding notes, printers calling attention to corrections or additions, and Victorian readers highlighting passages they wanted to remember. It only fell out of use around the same time that the stylized arrow shape was developed in the early nineteenth century.

Informal writing, however, retained a considerable array of ways to ornament our text: doodles were popular with authors from Lewis Carroll, who himself drew a series of sketches for the original handwritten version of *Alice's Adventures in Wonderland,* to Sylvia Plath, who drew in both her own diaries as well as the margins of books she owned. (She was especially fond of cows.) Even if you lacked their doodling skills, you could express your aesthetic sensibility by ornamenting your personal correspondence with different-colored ink and monogrammed, bordered, textured, or even scented paper. You could also borrow images from other people, by cutting out printed photographs and quotes and gluing them onto your pages, as people did with commonplace books in the eighteenth and nineteenth centuries, and with printed stickers and scrapbooks in the modern era. Some of the 1970s postcards that we saw in previous chapters had handwritten smiley faces and doodled animals.

Early computers weren't much better than printing presses, as we saw in the previous chapter, with even fewer character and font options. But people did make borders, words, and artwork using punctuation symbols, a style known as ASCII art after the ninety-five printable characters defined by the ASCII encoding system of early computers, and later extended once more characters were available to mean any sort of art created with text-based symbols. (Text-based art itself is older, dating back to the limited graphics capabilities of typewriters.) The ASCII art below, for example, uses slashes, backslashes, underscores, and the occasional parenthesis and apostrophe to make hollow letters reading "ASCII art" and a slightly wider array of symbols including double quotes and equals signs to make a simple bunny rabbit. More ambitious examples could contain thousands of symbols and portray elaborate shading or an entire scene.

```
  (\_/)
 (='.'=)
 (")_(")
```

One major advance in internet gesture happened as the result of a serious miscommunication on the Carnegie Mellon University computer message system. Most of the time, the message system was pretty serious: announcements of talks in the computer science department, lost and found items, and heated discussions about politics and which keyboard layout was the best. But one day in September 1982, messageboard users started goofing off by posting absurd hypothetical questions about the physics of elevators in free fall. What would happen, wondered one person, if you put a helium balloon in an elevator and cut the cable? Or what if, wondered a second person, you put a bunch of pigeons in a free-falling elevator? Okay but what if, wondered a third, the birds were breathing the helium? Would their cheeping get higher-pitched? A fourth person had an idea for a similar experiment: What if you put a tiny drop of mercury with a lit candle in the free-falling elevator?

Alas, I am a linguist and can provide the answer to none of these questions. What I care about is what happened next. First, the setup: someone continued the joke: "WARNING! Because of a recent physics experiment, the leftmost elevator has been contaminated with mercury. There is also some slight fire damage. Decontamination should be complete by 08:00 Friday." Then, the problem: other people logged into the message system and saw only the fake warning, minus its necessary context. A few hours later, someone had to get back on and clarify that the warning was fake: "My apology for spoiling the joke but people were upset and yelling fire in a crowded theatre is bad news. . . ."

Finally, the solution: the CMU users switched to brainstorming ways to indicate that a particular message was intended as a joke (this wasn't the first time a user's attempt at humor had been taken seriously). Various options were proposed — putting an asterisk * or a percent sign % or an ampersand & in the subject line, posting all messages with a numerical 0–10 "Humor Value," creating a separate messageboard just for jokes, or using the sequence {#} "because it looks like two lips with teeth showing between them" or the sequence

__/, which looks like a smiling mouth. But the idea that caught on was a suggestion by a professor named Scott Fahlman. Here's the original message that he posted, dug up from dusty 1980s archives, from back when computer records were preserved on reel-to-reel tapes:

```
19-Sep-82  11:44  Scott  E  Fahlman
:-)

From: Scott E Fahlman <Fahlman at
Cmu-20c>

I propose that the following char-
acter sequence for joke markers:

:-)

Read it sideways. Actually, it is
probably more economical to mark
things that are NOT jokes, given
current trends. For this, use

:-(
```

The idea of a simplified smiling face already had a considerable history, so Fahlman's sideways proposal was straightforward to interpret. It was also easy to type, and was thus quickly picked up by other participants in the message thread, and within a couple months people were using sideways text faces beyond Carnegie Mellon and had come up with a wide variety of creative expansions on the sideways idea, including non-face examples like the heart <3 and the rose @>-->--. Many of the more elaborate examples, like sideways portraits of famous people, circulated more in lists of clever faces than in actual usage. (It's unclear when a person would ever need to invoke Abraham Lincoln by smiley, but here he is ==(:-)= complete with tall hat and beard.) A few classics like :-) :-(;-) :'-(:-P, and later their noseless variants :) :(;) :'(:P, remained the most popular.

Symbols like :-) were named emoticons, a combination of the words "emotion" and "icon." One useful side effect of emoticons is that they let you incorporate the facial part into your running text, right alongside your words, rather than using a large, unwieldy image that has to go on a new line — even if it's made out of the same ASCII characters as the rest of your message. Just like gestures and facial expressions fit seamlessly with spoken words, punctuation-based emoticons can directly accompany typed words.

Filling an important niche, the text-based emoticons grew and changed. The meaning of the basic smile shifted after Scott Fahlman's original proposal, from indicating a joke to indicating a more general positive sentiment, a marker of sincerity: "that's great :)" is sincere, not sarcastic. The nose fell out of favor among younger people: in 2011, a study of emoticons on Twitter by linguist Tyler Schnoebelen found that noseful emoticons were used by people who also tended to tweet to celebrities like Pepe Aguilar, Ashton Kutcher, and Jennifer Lopez, whereas those who tweeted noseless emoticons tended to prefer to tweet to Justin Bieber, Miley Cyrus, the Jonas Brothers, and Selena Gomez. (For the benefit of readers from the future who don't have a degree in Early Twenty-First Century American Pop Culture, I'll point out that Justin Bieber and the like were very popular among teenagers in 2011, while Kutcher, Lopez, et al. were an older set of celebrities. This strongly suggests that younger people were dropping the noses in their emoticons.)

Around the same time as emoticons were developing in the United States and on English-speaking networks, another form of digital face was developing on an early Japanese computer network known as ASCII Net. They were called kaomoji, from the Japanese *kao* (顔, "face") and *moji* (文字,

"character"). Kaomoji are like emoticons, but you don't have to turn your head sideways to read them, allowing for virtually any pair of symbols to be used to represent the shape of the eyes, not just symbols like :) and =) that are already found in a pair. Classic kaomoji such as ^_^ (happy), T_T (crying), and o.O (wide-eyed) are nearly as old as emoticons — there are claims of them appearing on ASCII Net as early as 1985 or 1986.

The emphasis on the eyes was important for kaomoji because of a broader cultural difference in how emotions are represented. When researchers show East Asian and Western Caucasian people photos of faces displaying different emotions, the Asian participants tend to make conclusions about the emotions based on what people are doing with their eyes, whereas the Western participants look to the mouth to read emotions. This tendency is reflected in the different conventions for portraying emotions in manga and anime versus Western cartoons, and it shows up again in the stylized faces of emoticons and kaomoji. Happy :) and sad :(emoticons can have the same eyes but must have different mouths, whereas happy ^_^ and sad T_T kaomoji can have the same mouths but must have different eyes. Some kaomoji have caught on more broadly among English speakers, especially those that narrate actions of the whole body rather than relying solely on the eyes, such as shruggie ¯_(ツ)_/¯ since 2014, flower-in-hair (⚘‿⚘❀) since 2013, and table flip (╯°□°)╯︵ ┻━┻ since 2011. But the kaomoji that purely convey emotion through the eyes seem to require a certain minimum level of fluency with a set of cultural conventions that most English speakers simply don't have (unless they're manga or anime fans).

By the late 1990s, you could include images on your website just by digging out the connection cable for your newfangled digital camera or combing through other people's GeoCities pages for exactly the right "under construction" gif to borrow. In Japan, something new had caught on beyond kaomoji: sending picture messages back and forth on cellphones. Unfortunately, it was impractically popular, because it took a lot of data to send and receive them. So in 1997, the Japanese cellphone carrier SoftBank found a solution: What if they encoded some common pictures the way they encoded text characters? After all, when you text a friend the letter A, your phone doesn't send pixel-by-pixel each tiny dot in the grid that would make up a *picture* of the letter A, your phone just sends one short number code like 0041 and your friend's phone knows that 0041 makes an A and displays it. If you could send a simple number like 2764 to display a heart ♥, things would go much faster than sending a whole image file. So designers at SoftBank created short number codes for ninety small pictures, including icons for weather, transit, time, and sports apps, as well as hearts, hands, and a few faces that looked a lot like the existing kaomoji. This was the origin of the emoji that we started talking about earlier.

Although the word "emoji" resembles the English "emoticon" ("emotion" + "icon"), the word actually comes from the Japanese *e* (絵, "picture") and *moji* (文字, "character"), the same *moji* as in kaomoji. This coincidence did probably help the word catch on among English speakers, but typing the symbols wasn't quite as straightforward. These small, easy-to-send pictures quickly became popular in Japan, and other Japanese cellphone carriers got busy adding their own sets of emoji. But here they ran into a problem. The whole point of emoji was to save space by assigning number codes to small pictures, but different phone manufacturers were using different sets of images and different number codes for them. So if you had a phone with DoCoMo and you texted a heart emoji to your friend whose phone was from SoftBank, your friend might see an indecipherable box, nothing at all, or worse yet, an entirely different symbol like an umbrella or a music note. (One common point of confusion was that people who thought they were sending a Taurus zodiac sign from DoCoMo phones would end up appearing to have sent a picture of a normal cow when received on a KDDI phone. Which could be . . . awkward.)

The organization that's in charge of standardizing the number codes for normal letters and numbers and punctuation characters is called the Unicode Consortium. The Unicode Consortium is a small committee of people who live at the intersection of tech geek and font nerd, and are mostly employees of major tech companies trying to make sure that, say, when you copy and paste an apostrophe from one program to another, or type an apostrophe on one device and view it on a different one, it doesn't mysteriously change into â€™ instead. This problem is fairly rare and confined to punctuation symbols for English, which was privileged to have its letters ubiquitously encoded very early. But the names for this problem in other languages speak to the frustration: Japanese *mojibake,* "character transformation" (that's the same *moji* as in *emoji*); Russian *krakozyabry,* "garbage characters"; German *Zeichensalat,* "character salad"; and Bulgarian *majmunica,* "monkey's (alphabet)." Multiply that by all the symbols in all the scripts of all the languages around the world, add in special symbols for mathematical notation and music notes and over six hundred styles of arrows (seriously), and you have the unglamorous but very important monkey-salad-garbage-transformation job that Unicodeâ€™s been doing since 1987.

The members of the Unicode Consortium had definitely not signed up to become the smiley faces people. In 2000, as emoji first started taking off in Japan, they politely declined to get involved, leaving DoCoMo and SoftBank and KDDI to hash out between each other the compatibility of picture messages (or, in some cases, the lack thereof). If sending small images encoded like text was just going to be a momentary fad in one country, that was below the pay grade of an international standards organization. But emoji hung on in Japan, and multinational companies started getting involved. Gmail needed its Japanese users to be able to send and receive emails with emoji in them. Apple wanted people in Japan to buy iPhones, but they wouldn't buy a phone that didn't support emoji. Ten years later, perhaps emoji weren't just a fad anymore, so in 2010, into Unicode they went.

But which emoji? By this point, SoftBank's initial set of ninety emoji had expanded as other Japanese carriers had come up with their own additions, so the initial set of emoji that were added to Unicode contained 608 symbols that were common in Japan. Now encoded, emoji arrived on Apple devices in 2011 and Android in 2013. The international support and cross-device compatibility solved a problem for Japanese texters, but it also helped emoji become popular outside of Japan. And become popular they did. Just five years after emoji entered the international stage, in early 2015, the most popular emoji, tears of joy 😂, surpassed the usage level of the most popular emoticon, :).

As more and more people from around the world began using emoji, however, it became more and more apparent that even 608 symbols weren't enough. People started questioning — If there's a unicorn and a dragon, why no dinosaur? If there's a man in a turban, why not a woman in a hijab? If there's sushi and hamburgers, why no taco or dumpling? All of these emoji have been added, many in response to proposals from ordinary people who figured out the process from the Unicode website or with the help of grassroots emoji proposals organization Emojination. But the set of emoji remains a work in progress: the Unicode Consortium is still taking requests, still rolling out a hundred or so new emoji each year.

Even with these expansions, the official Unicode process is slow and deliberative by design. At its core, Unicode is still a unique, uniform, universal encoding system. The goal is to create symbols that work on every device in the world long into the future. No more blank boxes. This means that once Unicode adds a symbol, they never remove it — doing so would defeat the purpose of a unified standard. That's also why Unicode doesn't accept emoji proposals for celebrities and pop culture references. They'd be fun for a while, but our great-grandchildren won't really need their keyboards cluttered with the faces of one-hit wonders from the early twenty-first century. To get around this, there are individual apps that use an emoji aesthetic with larger, more of-the-moment pictures, which are sent as normal image files rather than encoded like letters, known as customizable emoji keyboards and sticker apps. Plus of course, there are still gifs, and even the regular kinds of images that you find or make for yourself.

As the hype settles down, as we move into a stage where emoji use is becoming ordinary and unremarkable rather than the subject of daily news articles, we need to reckon with the enduring legacy that the first emoticons, and then even more strongly emoji, have left us with. In a few short years, in the span of an internet generation, we've radically changed our expectations for what we should be able to do with informal writing. We're no longer content to leave full communication only to channels that allow faces and voices. We demand that our writing also be capable of fully expressing what we want to say and, most crucially, how we're saying it. Any solution to this problem would have had to solve some similar problems to what emoji have, but why did emoji in particular catch on so quickly? What qualities do they have that any future would-be rival must meet or surpass?

WHY EMOJI WON

At a purely technical level, emoji come with some significant advantages, which we can see by comparing emoji to punctuation-based emoticons on the one hand, and animated gifs on the other. Emoticons are supremely easy to type, since they're made of punctuation already on your keyboard, but there's only so many recognizable figures you can make out of punctuation characters. Emoticons are good for your basic couple of smiley faces, but they become less practical as they get more elaborate — users of kaomoji inevitably find themselves either installing a kaomoji text expansion app or repeatedly googling "shruggie" and copy-pasting from the top search result. Gifs, on the other hand, are infinitely complex, with real faces and animations and full lines of dialogue written on as captions. But they have the inverse problem: there's so many of them that it's hard to get the one you want, and they're so large and distracting that they don't integrate seamlessly with a line of text (they take up their own line even when you're in an app that has a built-in gif search). Gifs are fun to use occasionally, but they're impractical to incorporate in every other sentence. Emoji strike a happy medium between the two: your most-used emoji show up in their own, easy-to-access section of your emoji picker, but there's also more there if you want to go exploring. They intermingle easily with everything else you're typing, rather than demanding their own new line, and they're easy to copy-paste and send from one app or device to another, at least as long as Unicode has the ones you want.

But it's certainly true that emoji, emoticons, and gifs all exist in the same ecosystem, and even certain words seem to have a related function. Instagram engineers looked at the most popular emoji used on their app and created a list of words people also use in a similar context. They found that people use the face with tears of joy emoji 😂 in the kinds of sentences where they might otherwise have used lolol, lmao, lololol, lolz, lmfao, lol, ahahah, ahaha, lmaooo, or lolll; they use the heart emoji ❤ in the same contexts as words like xoxoxox, xoxo, xoxoxoxoxo, xxoo, oxox, babycakes, muahhhh, mwahh, babe, and loveyou; and they use the loudly crying emoji 😭 like they use ugh, ughhhhh, wahhhh, agh, omgg, omfg, and whyyy. When one format isn't available, the others can work as substitutes: a study by linguists Jacob Eisenstein and Umashanthi Pavalanathan showed that people who use more emoji rely less on other expressive resources, like plain text emoticons :), repeated letters (yayyy), acronyms (lol), and other creative respellings (wanna).

There's a deeper question about the appeal of digital embodiment, though, regardless of whether it surfaces as emoji, emoticons, gifs, or another form. The facial expressions are by far the most popular, and yet there's an important way in which they're not like our ordinary kinds of facial expressions. When we're interacting with other people, we find the most trustworthy kind of facial expression to be the kind that's given off involuntarily: the burst of laughter or sob in the throat that's difficult to fake. And yet you can't involuntarily give off an emoji. They're all given out deliberately — you choose exactly which one to send, and you know that everyone else does, too. Emoji and all of their relatives are fake by definition. If we try to say that they map directly onto our emotional facial expressions, then we have a weird mismatch. How is it that we're so keen on such disingenuous symbols? What's to enjoy about a world where everyone is wearing a mask?

A paper by linguists Eli Dresner and Susan Herring has a compelling answer. Rather than think about emoticons as emotional, they argue, we should think about them as deliberate cues to the intention of what we're saying. Sometimes that intention does align with an emotion: if you say "I got the job :)" you're indicating that you're happy about it. But sometimes you put on a facial expression aspirationally, the way you might put on a polite social smile during a customer service interaction, even if you're having a terrible day, just to make things proceed smoother. A smiley face might be used in a context like "I'm looking for some suggestions :)" — you might be anxious rather than happy about requesting feedback, but you're using the smiley to make the request more polite. Moreover, people sometimes use smiley faces in contexts that aren't happy at all. Dresner and Herring quote a person saying "I feel sick and tired all the time :)" — the speaker isn't happy or even smiling about feeling sick and tired, but might include the smiley to indicate that they don't want their words to be read as a complaint. The same statement with :(, on the other hand, could be intended as a request for sympathy.

The basic smile emoticon :) or emoji 😀 is a versatile tool for this kind of contextualization. It can soften other kinds of harsh statements: making a demand into a softer request, or a seeming insult into softer teasing. As psychologist Monica Ann Riordan points out, saying an insult plus a smiley doesn't mean smiling while insulting someone, or being happy about how terrible someone is: the smiley changes the intention behind the whole insult into a joke. A smiley can even indicate outright rejection, in a polite sort of way. Journalist Mary H.K. Choi did a series of interviews with a diverse cross-section of American teenagers about how they use technology and emoji for a 2016 article in *Wired*. One teen explained that he would exchange various heart emoji while flirting, but the worst emoji for a girl to send back was the smiley face — "Yeah, that's the 'Thank you, but I'm not interested.'"

Dresner and Herring point out that spoken language already has a well-established distinction, dating back to a British philosopher of language named J. L. Austin in the 1950s, between the actual words you're saying and the effect that you mean to have on the world in saying them. (Whether you actually succeed, says Austin, is a slightly different philosophical category.) If I say, "There's a car coming," I may be intending a warning (Step back!), an insult (road rage), a promise (I have booked it for ten o'clock tomorrow morning), or a complaint (I thought we were alone on this desert island!). Or if I say, "That's a nice shirt," I could be complimenting it, hinting that I want to borrow it, or even criticizing it by calling attention to it at all (But why are you wearing it in this sauna?).

We have a lot of tools at our disposal for conveying our intended effect: we can add explicit, clarifying words like "Watch out!" or "I promise . . . ," we can add strategic pauses and vocal inflections, we can rely on our shared knowledge of context, and we can gesture. It turns out that gesture linguist Adam Kendon has also invoked Austin's idea of clarifying the intentions behind an utterance as a way of explaining what emblems do in communication. Think about saying "Good job!" along with a nameable, emblematic gesture: with a thumbs up, it's a congratulations; with a wink, it's a sly prod; with a facepalm, it's a sarcastic acknowledgment of failure; with the middle finger, it's an insult.

We've circled back to another reason why it makes sense to think of emoticons and emoji as gestural rather than emotional: thinking this way resolves the apparent contradiction between emotional facial expressions and the emoticons that supposedly represent them. Sure, it's constructed, but a thumbs up is constructed, too, and both can still be genuine. If we say instead that people are consciously using them to guide their readers to the correct interpretation of their words, then emoticons become a positive, helpful, social behavior, a way of saying, "I want to clarify my true intentions for you." It's not the more negative behavior of putting on a mask. It's true that a smiley face doesn't always mean that the speaker is happy (an uncontrollable, genuine smile), but it does align with a deliberate, social smile, or the exclamation mark that proves you're not a Stone-Hearted Ice Witch. All three can indicate that I'm asking politely, I don't want to impose, I'm actually joking, I'm letting you down gently, or a passive-aggressive, "Oh no, of *course* I'm not mad." It's not so much that every emoji has a direct analogue in gesture; it's that we can use them both to accomplish similar communicative goals.

Bodies don't just communicate gesture: they also exist in space and time, and emoji can help us get across similar meanings in virtual space. Sometimes, you don't actually have anything informative to say to the other person, and all you're looking to communicate is subtext: "I see this," "I'm listening," or "I am still here and I still want to be talking with you." In physical space, we often convey this through the body: you know when other people are near you and you can tell whether they're paying attention to you or whether you're looking at the same thing. Even if neither of you is saying anything, you can make eye contact, touch, or even just look over and see that the other person is still there. (Unless someone is being very,

very sneaky.) In virtual space, sneaky happens by default. You're only felt to be present when you're saying something (save for a few limited exceptions, like videochat and avatars in Second Life or social games).

A simple way to let someone know you've seen their post is by liking it. This can be used for acknowledging big life events, like a wedding or a baby. Liking can be the precursor to something more: if you like a few of someone's posts and they like yours back, you might take that as a sign they're open to further conversation. It can also be a way of trailing off: by liking the final post in a thread, you indicate that you've seen the other person's message and decided there was nothing left to say. Liking can also backfire: the "deep like" refers to a possibly accidental like on someone's post from a long time ago, which implies that you were creepily looking back through their profile.

Emoji and gifs offer a way to indicate more active listening responses: not just "I've seen this," but "I hear you and understand you." In speech, we often indicate understanding by repeating the important part or mirroring each other's gestures. If I say, "Sorry I'm late, I had a flat tire," and you reply, "A flat tire!" you're not being superfluous, you're indicating understanding. Similarly, therapists and active listening coaches often recommend making people feel heard by restating their emotions to them. Thus, I could say, "Ugh, I got a flat tire on the way here," and you might say, "Ooh, that's frustrating." Emoji can accomplish both kinds of reaction: if you say, "I want to go to the beach this weekend," I can acknowledge the topic you've introduced by replying with fish and shell and crab emoji 🐟 🐚 🦀. Or if you say, "I miss you 😭," I can share your sadness by echoing the same emoji 😭 😭 😭 or go one step further by finding a sad gif. Human-computer interaction researchers Ryan Kelly and Leon Watts interviewed a cross-section of young adults, primarily from the UK, about how they used emoji. One of their participants clearly illustrated the use of emoji to acknowledge a topic and close a conversation: "Yesterday we were talking about pancake day, so I just sent some pancakes [an emoji] and that kind of just, finished the conversation. It kind of just, yeah I think it says you have nothing else to say."

Beyond single responses, sending messages back and forth can be a way of digitally hanging out: even when your messages have barely any textual meaning, they convey an important subtext: "I want to be talking with you." The sending itself is the message, whether it's emoji or stickers or selfies or gifs. This practice is especially common among teenagers, who often want to hang out with friends for hours on end in ways that seem trivial to adults around them. As a participant in the Kelly and Watts study put it: "You just start playing around with the emojis . . . like send a picture of a moon with a face on it, and then they would send me back like a cow, and I would send them back a turtle, and it doesn't mean anything, but it's just sort of funny. . . . Or like a little game, where you have to like guess what they're trying to say with all the pictures." One way that social tools catch on is when they facilitate conversation for the sake of conversation, allowing social interaction with less pressure, such as by encouraging us to send selfies or photos of our surroundings. We can't be witty conversationalists all of the time, and embodied communication tools like emoji mean that we don't have to be.

Sometimes even the fun of sending emoji or selfies back and forth pales. Our bodies — and the worlds they inhabit — are themselves colorful, animated, and interesting to look at. Words on a page, less so. After all, in the physical world, we don't often sit around in undecorated, windowless rooms and simply talk at each other. We do things together — we prepare and eat food together, we watch a show and talk about it later, we go for a walk or a car ride, we trade compliments, we point out the cute antics the dog or cat is getting up to, and so on. In digital conversations, we also bring in external objects as excuses to start up a conversation and ways to keep it flowing: a gif of a tiny turtle eating a strawberry, a sticker that makes a pop culture reference, a video that reminds us of someone's interests, a link that supports an argument we're trying to make, a camera filter that appears to give us cute animal ears. Studies find that looking at cute cat videos improves mood and that people have similar reactions to cute puppy photos as they do to cute baby photos, so gifs become a kind of emotional currency, a way of sending someone a tiny zap of positive feeling. A more involved way of digitally hanging out is by playing online games with your friends, whether that's immersive-style games like Fortnite, League of Legends, and World of Warcraft, or casual games like Pokémon Go and Words with Friends.

Embodiment and projecting a virtual body may sound dangerously space-age — holograms! — but in many ways, embodiment is very old. Older than writing, as old as stories, perhaps as old as language itself. What does a storyteller do other than use their voice and body to project characters and feelings into the minds of their listeners? What is language other than a tool for transmitting new mental representations of the world into the minds of other people? Many theories about why language was evolutionarily useful involve things like collaboration and gossip — being able to plan together to hunt a mammoth, remember where the good berries are, or who can be trusted.

Like the failed proposals for sarcasm punctuation that we looked at in the previous chapter, generations of people have tried to reform English spelling, but eeven wen speling reeform iz perfektlee lejibl, sumhow it nevr katshiz on. The most we get is fragmentation, for example when some parts of the English-speaking world switched to *-or* or *-ize* while others stuck with *-our* and *-ise,* but multiple competing systems is not really an improvement. Same with other attempts at language reform: the international auxiliary language Esperanto is counted a success among constructed languages because perhaps two million people have learned it to varying degrees, while other, arguably better-designed, languages have languished

301

in still greater obscurity. More than two million people use emoji every single hour.

Emoji didn't succeed because they were a language, they succeeded because they're *not* a language. Rather than try to compete with words on their home turf, emoji added in a whole new system to represent a whole other layer of meaning. We already had a way of representing individual sounds, in the form of letters, and we've been developing the system for representing tone of voice using our existing punctuation and capitalization that we talked about in the previous chapter. So emoji and other pictorial elements are filling the third important pillar of communication: a way of representing our gestures and physical space.

We don't know whether emoji per se will be popular in future centuries or are merely a passing fad. But my prediction is that, having unlocked a way of conveying gesture and intention in writing, we'll continue caring about digital embodiment, even though we may very well change the specific tools we use to project it. To be sure, there are differences between gesture and emoji as well: gestures are good at movement, while emoji are better at detail. Don't ask me how I'd convey a birthday in gesture or the way to throw a frisbee in emoji — I really have no idea. But their core function, the way that they fit into our systems of communication, has too many similarities to be an accident.

Thinking of emoji as gestures helps put things into perspective: if we're tempted to start thinking, "If words were good enough for Shakespeare, why aren't they good enough for us?" we can pause and realize that plain words *weren't* actually good enough for Shakespeare. A lot of what Shakespeare wrote was plays, designed not to be read on a page, but to be performed by people. How many of us have struggled through reading Shakespeare as a disembodied script in school, only to see him come to life in a well-acted production? Or, to take a more contemporary example, when the long-awaited, next-generation story *Harry Potter and the Cursed Child* came out in book form, it got mixed reviews. People who saw the play generally really enjoyed it, but people who just read the script were more polarized. If Shakespeare and J. K. Rowling can't make disembodied dialogue feel natural, what hope is there for J. Q. Notapoet, our average internet user?

Emoji and gesture also share a murky relationship with "universal" meaning. They both cross boundaries that plain words don't: I'd certainly rather be dropped on an island where I didn't share a language with anyone if I could use gesture or emoji. But pantomime and cartoon pictures will only get me so far, and at the same time, there are plenty of things about both that are culturally specific, whether that's different obscene gestures or illustrations of objects that are only common in Japan. Even the idea of pictorial communication is culturally bound: people tend to tell emoji "stories" in left-to-right or right-to-left order depending on the direction of their writing systems, and those who are illiterate have a difficult time with linear picture stories or simplified emoji-like drawings at all. And neither pictures nor gestures are useful for one of the most powerful features of language: its ability to talk about ideas that are hard to visualize. Nuclear scientists, for example, have had an incredibly difficult time communicating the fairly simple concept "Danger: There is nuclear waste here" in a way that will continue to make sense for the next ten thousand years. Circle with a slash? Nope, could be a sideways hamburger. Skull and crossbones? Nope, could refer to the Day of the Dead or pirates. Much as we might wish it to be otherwise, there's just no panacea for universal communication.

This comparison between gesture and

emoji can help us with more immediate decisions, however. Judges and juries are grappling with emoji sensemaking, according to law professor Eric Goldman, in much the same way as they've long had to interpret gestures and punctuation. Courts have already deliberated over whether a raised hand is a threat, or if a particular handshape is a gang sign, or what exactly was meant by a particular comma. It's by similar logic that a court interpreted a smiley emoticon in one context as indicating that something was a joke, not to be taken seriously as evidence, while another court interpreted a smiley emoticon in a different context as merely a symbol of happiness. In a list of emoji examples from court cases compiled by US criminal justice news organization The Marshall Project, emoji are often treated as a clue regarding the intent of the writer, such as whether a gun emoji can indicate a genuine threat, whether a face with tongue stuck out emoji is enough to indicate that a violent post is a joke, or whether sharing a violent video with smile and heart emoji indicates a "twisted delight" in it.

Expanding our tools for conveying our intentions may even make us better at reading other people's mental states by giving us more practice taking them on. If we look at the history of literature, medieval and classical texts simply described what the characters did (wring their hands, tear their hair) rather than their mental states, while early modern stories started incorporating monologues where characters spoke their thought processes out loud (think Hamlet or Juliet wondering about death). With the invention of the novel, omniscient narrators could hint at mental states that even the characters didn't fully understand, while twentieth-century modernist writers tried to evoke the actual experience of a particular mental state in the reader. Sure enough, researchers have found that people who read a lot of fiction are better at understanding mental states than those who read primarily nonfiction or don't read at all. In the twenty-first century, we're going a step further: emoji and the rest make us not just readers of mental states, but writers of them. The younger Internet People who complain that their parents don't understand how their tone comes across in text may be onto something important.

The idea of mental states can reassure anyone who's worried about emoji or textspeak creeping into student essays. Even as mental states have gotten more deep and subtle in literature and informal writing, we've kept essays around as a formal genre for other purposes. No one is writing in a formal context, "omggg wtf the mitochondria is the powerhouse of the cell 😂 😂 😂 😂," any more than a hundred years ago people were writing, "Oh my heavenly stars, the mitochondria is the powerhouse of the cell, isn't that just the bee's knees!!!!" Even if you're the kind of nerdy scientist who's genuinely that excited about basic mitochondria facts, you're still supposed to pretend you're a serious researcher if you want to get published in a serious journal. The convention for formal writing is that it's unemotive and disembodied.

But formality doesn't have to be a requirement for all kinds of writing. Many areas of our lives, like clothing styles and eating styles, run the full gamut from formal to informal with many gradations in between. How marvelous it is that writing styles can do the same! What we're arriving at, between typography and visuals, is a flexible set of ways to communicate our intentions and share space online. Not everyone uses every option: some people love emoji, some people prefer old-school emoticons or abbreviations, some people would rather do it with comedic timing in their vocabulary, linebreaks, and punctuation. But everyone needs something, or you're going to indeed find cyberspace "alienating and unfulfilling." We take the expression of mental states so much for granted in informal speech, that oldest and first-learned form of language, that it takes the dramatic expansion of a new genre, informal writing, to make us pay attention to it again. But now that we've set up our expanded emotional palette, we need to give it a canvas to paint on. Let's expand our focus and have a look at conversations.

CHAPTER 6:
HOW CONVERSATIONS
CHANGE

You probably don't remember learning how to walk, which makes it easy to think that it was obvious. But have you ever seen a computer trying to figure it out? In one video, a blobby computer-simulated humanoid manages to figure out how to walk on two legs, but only by rapidly pumping its fist up and down at the same time. In another, a metallic humanoid exoskeleton sways dangerously to the side with each faltering step, prompting its surrounding humans to hold their open hands a few inches away in case they need to rescue the expensive equipment from falling. The four-legged robots do okay, but the two-legged ones are still not as good at walking as an average human three-year-old is, over twenty years after a computer beat a human grandmaster at chess in the mid-1990s.

When we think about the kind of language that's difficult, we often think of soaring public speeches or a poem that punches us in the feels — the chess of language. We've known how to display this kind of language on screens for a long time, before computers at all: just roll the video, just display some lines of text. What's harder is the walking of language: our ordinary conversations, which we learned and forgot learning at the same time as we were learning and forgetting learning how to walk. Like how we don't pay much attention to our gestures or tone of voice until we need to manage them electronically, the back-and-forth of conversation is surprisingly complex when we try to filter it through a different medium.

But we walk the same way that humans have walked for generations; if you want to know the rules of chess, you can consult a rulebook which simply lists them all. Conversation is different. Its norms are more fluid, emerging from constant negotiation between its participants. And especially when it comes to conversations that happen via technology, its norms are subject to a lot of change.

The telephone was the first major technological rupture for conversation. (Okay, the telegraph was also incredibly weird, but it never made it to mainstream in-home use.) So far, we've gotten away with mostly ignoring phone calls or lumping them into speech in general when talking about styles of communication, but for talking about how conversational norms change, the landline telephone is absolutely critical. The phone was as revolutionary for conversation as the internet was: before the phone, you either had conversations that were spoken and in real time with people right next to you, or written and far away and very slow. When the telephone came, all of a sudden you could have real-time conversations with people who were far away, at any time of the day or night. A whole series of norms, established through centuries of gradual normalization of the written word and millennia of face-to-face conversation, were completely upended. This caused a lot of problems that were similar to the "internet problems" we're encountering now. We have extensive documentation of the rocky moments as the phone spread through society, but they've faded from living memory. Even Non Internet People take phones very much for granted. So the telephone is a useful model to keep in mind as we begin to take the internet for granted as well.

It's easy to celebrate the expansion of the emotional landscape in informal writing — Yay ironic capitals! Yay emoji! Yay gifs! With conversations, there's a tendency to do the opposite: to mythologize a golden age when people had "real" conversations, to wish that telephone calls and emails and Facebook posts were still exciting, rather than tedious games of telephone tag and an overflowing inbox and happy birthday messages from people we've forgotten even existed, to want all our friends to join a new social platform only until people we don't like are there, not recognizing that the people who spoil the network for us are someone else's long-awaited friends.

Let's start with a different thesis: for any type of conversation, people are doing it because it meets a need for them. It might not be a need we remember. It might not be a need we have ourselves. It might not be a need we want to acknowledge. But often, it's a need that we can learn to understand if we start looking for it. When we try to understand the needs that now obsolete communications technologies were meeting, it can help us understand the different stakes of the present. It's too hard to start with current battlegrounds, with questions about the correct email salutation or whether it's rude to answer a text when you're talking with someone else. We've already chosen our sides on those issues. But if we can look at the obsolete controversies of the past, seek to understand what people were aiming for, and realize that the uproar about them seems faintly ridiculous in hindsight, perhaps we can view the controversies of the present with a more compassionate lens. Perhaps we can marvel at how interesting it is when there are several different norms in play, rather than grumbling at how other people are different and wrong. The technologies we now decry as new and inferior are going to be someone else's nostalgia trip; the technologies we now nostalgize were someone else's new and inferior versions.

EMAIL AND PHATIC EXPRESSIONS

When I was in high school, I had a linguistic game I used to play on my unsuspecting schoolmates. Moving through the hallways between classes, we'd normally call out to the people we saw every day, "Hi, how's it going?" or "Hey, what's up?" But I practiced giving the opposite response without skipping a beat. To "What's up?" I'd answer, "Good, how're you?" while to "How's it going?" I'd say, "Not much, what's up with you?" What surprised and delighted me every time is that people never seemed to notice. As long as I could pull it off smoothly, people were perfectly content to accept the "wrong" reply to

313

their greetings — it was only when I faltered that people pulled up short. (Try it yourself sometime!) I didn't understand why, any more than I understood why there were several pairs of greetings that were made out of different words but meant essentially the same thing when taken as a whole, and eventually I chalked it up to one of life's (and my own) little eccentricities.

As I learned more linguistics, I realized two things. First, that this is eminently normal budding linguist behavior, and second, that linguistics had a reason for why my greeting mismatch experiment worked. These social phrases are known as phatic expressions, and their meaning is more about the context you say them in than the sum of their individual words. "How's it going?" and "What's up?" have the same function: they both acknowledge the presence of someone you already know in a way that's slightly more elaborate than a simple greeting ("Hi!") but doesn't go so far as to be an original conversation. So their rote answers are also functionally interchangeable, as long as you say them in the seamless manner of someone following a social script. You can even play around with them still further. I've occasionally, accidentally, replied, "Good, how are you?" to other phatic greetings, such as "Hello" (without being asked how I was), or gone through the exchange an extra time ("Hi, how're you?" "Good, how're you?" "Good, how're you — Wait, um . . ."). If one person falters, the whole thing falls apart and becomes literal again. Otherwise, we're perfectly content to see the meaning behind the social niceties and ignore the actual words.

But phatic expressions are made up of ordinary words. At one point, they did mean what they seem to mean, nothing more and nothing less. Which leaves a person wondering, how does a literal expression become phatic? And can it ever cross back over, from phatic to literal again? The changing norms of technologically mediated conversations allow us to watch these exact shifts happen.

One such shift happened as a result of the telephone. The greetings popular in the 1800s were based on knowing who you were addressing and when you were addressing them: "Good morning, children." "Good afternoon, Doctor." But when you pick up a ringing telephone, you have no idea who's calling (during the many decades before caller ID), and you can't even be sure whether you share a time of day with them. The teleconnected world desperately needed a neutral option. The two most prominent solutions were "Hello," championed by

Thomas Edison, and "Ahoy," championed by Alexander Graham Bell. At the time, both had a similar meaning: they were used to attract attention rather than as a greeting ("hello" has the same origins as "holler"). Why would you need to attract attention? Some early phones were set up as a line that was just open the whole time, with no bell to ring when someone was calling, so "hello" was like calling out to someone in the room next door. Even though we did end up with call bells, early phone books provided model dialogues to new phone customers unsure about proper phone etiquette. One early manual suggested beginning with "a firm and cheery 'hulloa'" or "What is wanted?" and closing with "That is all." Perhaps unsurprisingly, "What is wanted?" and "That is all" didn't catch on, but "hello" did, and quickly spread beyond the phone as an all-purpose greeting.* Vestiges of hello's attention-getting function can still be heard anytime you experience a faulty connection,

*The telephone-answering problem also faced many other languages during the same period. French *allô* and German *Hallo* evoke English "hello," but other languages use variations on "good," "yes," "ready," "please," "who," or the answerer's name.

however; you can say "Hello?" mid-conversation to test the signal, but "Hi?" somehow doesn't sound right there. ("Goodbye," on the other hand, has been around since at least the sixteenth century, but perhaps innovation was less necessary in closing a phone call, since you already knew who you were talking with.)

But there was a period of friction, when "hello" was spreading beyond its summoning origins to become a general-purpose greeting, and not everyone was a fan. I was reminded of this when watching a scene in the BBC television series *Call the Midwife,* set in the late 1950s and early 1960s, where a younger midwife greets an older one with a cheerful "Hello!" "When I was in training," sniffs the older character, "we were always taught to say 'good morning,' 'good afternoon,' or 'good evening.' 'Hello' would not have been permitted." To the younger character, "hello" has firmly crossed the line into a phatic greeting. But to the older character, or perhaps more accurately to her instructors as a young nurse, "hello" still retains an impertinent whiff of summoning. Etiquette books as late as the 1940s were still advising against "hello," but in the mouth of a character from the 1960s, being anti-hello is intended to make her look like a fussbudget, especially playing for an audience of the future who's forgotten that anyone ever objected to "hello."

The "hello" squabble now seems silly, but it's the same thing that's going on in the 2010s with "hey." "Hey" as a summoner, as in "hey you," is a word we've had since at least the 1200s, and "hi" is simply a variant on the vowel, dated back to at least the 1400s. Etymologically speaking, "hey" and "hi" have similar trajectories as "hello," minus the phone part: all three started out as ways of getting attention and have evolved into greetings. But as recently as 1960, researchers for the *Dictionary of American Regional English* found just 60 people who would greet someone they knew well with "hey" — in comparison to 683 who'd say "hi" and 169 who'd say "howdy" — and most of those 60 were in a single region, the South and Lower Mississippi Valley. According to the same survey taken in 2014, "hey" had slightly surpassed "hi" in popularity. Linguist Allan Metcalf reported a recent college graduate explaining to him around the same time: "I almost always say 'hey' in speech but I have free variation between 'hi' and 'hey' in writing. . . . I have a sort of three-way formality distinction for greetings — 'hey' for friends my own age or younger, 'hi' for adults I know well or people my own age I'm just meeting, and 'hello' for adult strangers." Someone born in 2000 could justifiably point out that "hey" has been used as a greeting for their entire life, while someone born in 1950 could, equally justifiably, say, "But I don't feel greeted by 'hey,' I feel summoned!"

Shifts in greetings are especially noticeable in email. When we email, we don't face the total lack of knowledge about who we're communicating with like the telephone users had. Instead, the first time we email a new person, we know just enough about them to be dangerous — we have a name, probably, but very little background information on their desired style of greeting. In speech, it's easier to skip over the details and let our messages be carried by tone of voice. But in writing, you can't get away with answering, "Good, how're you?" to "What's up?" — it's ruined by the other person's ability to reread your message and think about it for an extra half second. Moreover, real-time, embodied communication gives us extra cues for selecting a greeting: to swiftly size up someone's likely attitude towards "hey" based on their age, or adjust our greetings on the fly to mirror the other person's.

The first emails dealt with this lack of cues

by simply not caring. In 1978, said technologists Albert Vezza and J. C. R. Licklider about email, "One could write tersely and type imperfectly, even to an older person in a superior position and even to a person one did not know very well, and the recipient took no offense." Similarly, in an article from 1998, linguist Naomi Baron noted that "most users exercise only a light editorial hand (if any at all) on email messages before they are sent. Many of us chuckle at the error-strewn emails we receive from colleagues otherwise noted for meticulously crafted memoranda." Amid anarchy like this, who had time to care about the niceties of specific greetings? But by 2001, email systems had spellcheck, and linguist David Crystal wrote, "I receive innumerable e-mails which are anything but fragmented sentences."

At the same time, Crystal observed that the most frequent email greeting he received was "Dear David," followed by "David" and then "Hi David." I remember rereading this passage around 2010 and being surprised. I hardly ever saw "Dear Gretchen" in my inbox, and I certainly would never have addressed someone else with it. "Dear" felt both excessively formal and oddly intimate, the kind of thing that I had inscribed in my best grade-school cursive in thank-you notes to my grandmother for the lovely birthday sweater — certainly not the kind of relationship I associated with work or school. "Hi" felt businesslike, breezy, impersonal, like a polite social smile. A few years later, however, as I got more adept at business emails, I did find myself occasionally using "dear," at least enough to switch to it when someone else used it first. According to the research of the linguist Gillian Sankoff, I may not be alone here: although much sociolinguistic research finds that the way you talk is pretty much established by late adolescence, Sankoff finds that some speakers may keep changing well into middle age, especially for formal and prestigious bits of language.

In a historical sense, though, my initial instinct was right on target: we've been following a trend towards shorter and less descriptive greetings for several centuries. "Dear" is our last relic of what used to be an elaborate system of greetings that describe people in flattering terms, which was popular for well over a millennium. Here's a sixteenth-century letter from Edmund Spenser to Walter Raleigh on the publication of *The Faerie Queene,* which is typical of the genre:

To the Right noble, and Valorous, Sir Walter Raleigh, knight, Lo. Wardein of the

Stanneryes, and her Majesties lieftenaunt of the County of Cornewayll.

[text of letter]

> *So humbly craving the continuance of your honorable favour towards me, and th' eternal establishment of your happines [sic], I humbly take leave.*
>
> *23 January. 1589.*
>
> *Your most humbly affectionate. Ed. Spenser.*

But some of these greetings were more rote than sincere. For example, founding fathers Alexander Hamilton and Aaron Burr exchanged a series of letters in 1804 which all closed with "I have the honor to be Your Obedient Servant," but culminated with them fighting a duel. At the time, it was simply a polite, phatic phrase, just as the modern writer of "Sincerely" isn't being especially sincere, simply following a social script. But as "Your Obedient Servant" fell from common usage, its literal meaning recovered. The 2015 musical *Hamilton,* a dramatization of these historic events, highlights this phrase as an ironic juxtaposition by making it the refrain of a song about the origins of the duel. The irony is entirely modern, however: a Founding Father time-traveling to Broadway for opening night wouldn't notice anything amiss.

"The Right Noble and Valorous" and "Your Obedient Servant" are no longer stock, phatic phrases to us — no one in the twenty-first century would employ them in a generic business email. But the same is gradually becoming true for "dear." If you didn't encounter "dear" enough for its meaning to wash out, and the post-letter-writing generations may not have, it feels oddly like calling your boss or your professor your darling. Even if individual people adopt "dear" for older correspondents, as I did, it's doomed in the long run if people aren't using it among their peers, as I would never, never do. Reading through the comments on etiquette posts shows a tendency for younger people to resist advice to use "dear," not through a desire to be rude or informal, but because they simply cannot parse it as anything but intimate. We can only hope that a musical of the 2200s digs up a hostile email thread featuring archival "dears" and writes a song about how dramatically ironic they sound.

It would be easy to attribute the shift in greetings to a broader shift in society: the

323

adjectival greetings could be a bid for affection; the summoning greetings a bid for attention. But such an association is too easy and I think it's simply wrong. It's better to realize that greetings are generally phatic: that we pick a particular greeting because that's what we're used to, and to acknowledge that we've always wanted both affection and attention. (Besides, if the internet is so unaffectionate, why the popularity of the heart-shaped "like" button?) When we zoom out and take a historical perspective, the shift in greetings is simply a change, one that reminds us that language is a thing that lives in the minds of individual humans at individual points in time, a thing that can't be fully encompassed in a static list of rules like a game of chess.

As someone who receives a fair bit of email from people I've never met, I greatly enjoy the chance to treat their various greetings as a game of a different kind, a never-ending multiplayer guessing game of what generation someone's in and what they're trying to signal based on how they address me at the top of their emails. What the random strangers in my inbox have in common is hope. Hope that I'll read their link, hope that I'll reply back with the answer they're looking for — hope, even, unfortunately, that I'll purchase something from their marketing campaign. The solution is less to try to stamp out variation and more to try to exercise the same kind of generosity with each other as my schoolmates unwittingly extended to me in my "How are you?" "Not much" experiments. There's enough genuine malice in the world that we don't need to go hunting for more of it in what is truly a case of harmless difference.

CHAT AND INTERRUPTION

Babies learn the rhythm of having a conversation before they even learn the words to do so. When we talk to them, we tend to ask them questions, leave spaces for them to reply, and react to their cooing and babbling as if they're participating with us. "Are you sleepy?" *baby gurgles and rubs eyes* "Yeahhh, I think you're sleepy."* What we learn, long before we utter any words, is that conversations are made up of turns. A conversation isn't a cacophony of voices all talking at once: it's a smoothly synchronized back-and-forth.

How do we know when it's our turn? It would be easy to assume that we must pause after we're finished saying something, and that other people notice that pause and

*Please read this to yourself in appropriately exaggerated infant-directed intonation.

interpret it as an invitation to speak. But conversation analysts find that actually we don't pause much, any more than we normally pause between each word. If I ask you a question and you don't start answering immediately, I'll probably treat it as a break in communication. Even if just 0.2 seconds go by, I'm likely to repeat the question again, try a different way of phrasing it, or switch languages (to the eternal bane of would-be polyglots). This finely tuned timing is what our caregivers taught us as babies when they treated our gurgling and babbling as conversational turns. (If you've ever found yourself unable to get a word in edgewise, or doing all the talking around someone frustratingly taciturn, it's probably because your cultural timings are ever so slightly miscalibrated for each other, points out the linguist Deborah Tannen.) If you're acting in a play, it's just as important to know when you're supposed to come in as it is to know your actual lines: if you wait for a full pause before every time you start speaking, you'll sound incredibly stilted. While another person is talking, we're not just composing our own reply, we're predicting when they're going to finish, so we can smoothly transition from speaker to speaker.

How do we do this seamless coordination?

It can't be length: a turn can be as short as one word ("Yep") or as long as a whole story. Instead, we listen for signals that someone might be at the end of a turn and, if we're in a group, who they're expecting to speak next. Some of the signals are linguistic, like if someone asks you a direct question with your name in it. Some are gestural: a raised hand is often a signal that you want to get a word in, and people tend to look away during their turn and look back towards the group or the next speaker when they're finishing up. A lot of these signals are about intonation and rhythm: people will speed up if they get to a potential turn end but don't actually want to stop talking, or they'll use a rising intonation to prompt a response.

But none of these cues are a hundred percent reliable, so sometimes we simply guess. Conversation analysts find that "interruptions" aren't randomly distributed in conversation: instead, they're at points when it seems like the main speaker could be finished talking but it turns out they aren't. In face-to-face conversation, a syllable or two of overlap is nothing terrible (humans are good at associating words with the locations of specific people), and we sort out most such confusions without thinking much of it. In conversations mediated by technology, overlaps can be a bigger problem. Walkie-talkies don't allow overlaps at all, so guessing becomes painful and people instead say "over" at the end of a turn. Telegraph operators used to end all their turns with "GA" for "go ahead" for the same reason. Some early chat systems had a similar problem with overlap: the chat feature on a system called TENEX in the early 1970s was a single text file that you and your conversational partner edited together, one keystroke at a time. If you tried to type at the exact same time, you'd end up inter-leaving your letters between each other, so if the letters started jumbling, one person had to stop typing and cede way for the other, or you'd just end up with a horrible mess.

Hey, how's it goignogod how are you?

Some systems tried to prevent jumbling with conventions of their own: users of one text-based chat system developed the habit of typing in two linebreaks between each turn. Other chat systems, such as the Unix talk program, split the screen into several areas and assigned each person their own text box to type in: if I'm typing only in the top box and you're typing only in the bottom one, our letters can't possibly jumble together. You could add more boxes for more people: a chat program created in 1973 called Talkomatic, on a system called PLATO at the University of Illinois, provided five boxes, stacked on top of each other, so it could support up to five participants. One of these boxes was yours to type in, and then you had to keep scanning the others to see what the other people were saying, keystroke by keystroke, each in their own box. Here's a demonstration, because this paradigm is really very different from all the chat systems you're used to.

```
Talky McFirst
hello?
I am demonstrating chat boxes
```

```
Chatter O'Second
hi!
I am a second participant
```

```
Speech Thirdova
I am a third
the responses may look like they're
out of order, because everyone
types in their own box
```

```
Words Fourthescue
I am a fourth
I'm good, how are you number five?
```

```
Typo von Fifth
I am the fifth
how's everyone doing?
```

Scanning between boxes and letters that get jumbled up with each other? Well, we can maybe guess why they didn't catch on. But instantly appearing letters? That sounds fancy! Why did chat systems stop using those after the 1970s and 1980s? Indeed, Google tried to bring instant letters back in 2009 with the short-lived Google Wave, but it never caught on. The problem with keystroke-by-keystroke chat is that it treats conversation as a thing of letters rather than turns. Not only is it painfully slow to watch someone type in a message letter by letter, because we can read faster than we can type, and not only does it make us self-conscious for other people to watch our backspacings, but we also run into the turn-taking problem of radio and telegraph operators. Have I stopped typing because I'm finished, at least for the moment, or just because I'm figuring out how to say something? You have no way of knowing. We could try to impose a convention like "over" or "GA" or a linebreak or some lesser-used punctuation character, but if we've learned one thing from the history of email, it's that people are inconsistent about following etiquette as long as it's a mere suggestion. Far better to hardwire the turn break into the form of the chat interface itself, by letting us send each new message turn by turn, rather than letter by letter.

So where did the upwards-scrolling, dialogic chat interface that we know and love today come from? The oldest example that I've found is from 1980, in the form of a chat program called CB Simulator, which was also the first dedicated, online chatroom to be widely available to the public. It wasn't even called a chatroom yet: instead, it was inspired by shared radio waves. Citizens band, or CB, radio is a kind of radio that doesn't just broadcast out: anyone in the local area can tune in and talk with each other, and enthusiasts do just that. (It's similar to ham radio but even more decentralized.) An employee of CompuServe, an early online service provider, thought CB radio would be a neat thing to emulate in typed form, and CB Simulator was born. But radio conversations are based on a wholly different paradigm than the shared text boxes of early chat systems: instead of people each talking in their own box, radio sees conversation as a single stream of turns that an individual could choose to add to. The multi-box style imposed a hard limit on how many participants could be involved (there's no place for a sixth person in a five-box chat, and it quickly gets difficult to scan back and forth between boxes to follow a lively group conversation). By contrast, the number of participants in stream-style chat was a lot more flexible. CB radio enthusiasts were used to a bit of chaos in their word stream: voices crackling in and out, signals dropping and overlapping. The text format actually made the chaos easier to manage. If several people sent a chat message all at the same time, the system coped gracefully: you simply saw all their messages in a stream rather than hearing their voices talking over each other.

Overlapping letters had been terrible, but a stream of overlapping phrases turned out to be chat's key feature. The multi-box chat style stuck around for a while during the 1980s, but by 1988 the stream-style chat was dominant and here to stay: that's the year Internet Relay Chat (IRC) was created. It was the system that powered the classic public internet chatroom as we know it, and IRC used a stream. These public chatrooms were much analyzed through the 1990s, and one of the things that researchers consistently noticed was how chaotic chatroom conversations were: multiple conversations would happen at once, messages interleaved with each other, and users didn't seem to mind. Here's a nineties example of such overlap:

<ashna> hi jatt

*** Signoff: puja (EOF From client)

<Dave-G> kally i was only joking around

<Jatt> ashna: hello?

<kally> dave-g it was funny

<ashna> how are u jatt

<LUCKMAN> ssa all

<Dave-G> kally you da woman!

<Jatt> ashna: do we know eachother?. I'm ok how are you

*** LUCKMAN has left channel #PUNJAB

*** LUCKMAN has joined channel #punjab

<kally> dave-g good stuff:)

<Jatt> kally: so hows school life, life in geneal, love life, family life?

<ashna> jatt no we don't know each other, i fine

<Jatt> ashna: where r ya from?

The conversation in this chatroom is really two interwoven conversational threads, one between ashna and Jatt ("do we know each other? how are you" "no we don't, i fine") and the other between kally and Dave-G ("only joking" "it was funny" "you da woman"). Public chatrooms had a niche appeal: the average internet user was more likely to encounter chat slightly later and with a person they already knew via instant messaging or chat apps, such as the first wave of ICQ, AOL Instant Messenger (AIM), or MSN Messenger, and the second wave of Gchat (which became Google Hangouts), Facebook Messenger, iMessage, and WhatsApp. But even between the same two people, overlap is common in chat — each person may introduce a topic around the same time, and then since they both hit send at once, they can both start responding to the opposite topic in parallel.

What's curious is that we've retained this essential paradigm of chat for nigh on four decades now, even as many individual chat platforms have come and gone. We've added new features on top (like better graphics support and the "is typing" indicator), but at their core, chat conversations still consistently happen in a stream, and with a high tolerance for multiple, interwoven message threads. Even the "is typing" indicator is a solid couple decades old. This is an eon in computer years: the mouse wasn't even common yet in 1980, let alone laptops or touchscreens! And yet we know from the shared-boxes format of only a decade earlier that the initial format for chat wasn't at all obvious. (Email, by comparison, is older than chat, but it also came with a clear postal analogue from the very beginning.) Chat is a format entirely of and for networked computers, predicated on the idea that you could have a real-time conversation between two or more connected screens. An offline equivalent to chat is barely even sensible, because the circumstances in which you're able to have a real-time conversation with someone on a piece of paper but not able to see or speak to them are so limited. (Passing notes in class or during a meeting might be one exception, but even there you're able to see the other person's raised eyebrow or muffled giggle.)

The chat format's astonishing durability signals the true birth of a new form of communication. Chat is the perfect intersection of written and informal language. Let's consider what we know about these formats.

We can read faster than we can speak, and reading also lets us glance back and check something again, which means that writing naturally supports longer and more complex sentences: if you compare an essay and the transcript of a famous speech, the essay will have more subordinate clauses, while the speech will have more repetition. (If you've ever been forced to listen to a novice public speaker read an essay out loud, it's not your fault you found it hard to follow.) As far as speaking in general goes, the more formal it is, the fewer interruptions it has. A public speaker can reasonably expect to hold the floor for their entire designated period, and anyone else who wishes to talk must either ask permission by raising a hand, or accept the title of "heckler." But you can't heckle a conversation that you're part of already: that's nonsensical, a back-and-forth is expected. Instead, our disparaging vocabulary goes in the other direction: a person who treats a conversation like a speech is long-winded. So when we look at informal writing, we should expect to find both a high information density and a lot of interruptions. Or in other words, exactly what people do in chat. Chat gets bonus extra interruptions in comparison to informal speech, because writing as a medium lets us handle those extra words. What the chatrooms discovered was that overlapping messages weren't a bug, they were a feature.

While emails and social media posts and website text can all lay claim to the title of informal writing by virtue of being unedited, chat is informal writing in its purest form. A post on social media doesn't go through an editor, but when we know that hundreds or thousands of people may see it, it's hard to say that we're not editing ourselves at some level. An email goes to a controllable list of people, but with the amount of digital ink that's been spilled on email etiquette, again, it's hard to say that we're not thinking through (perhaps in fact overthinking) our emails. But with chat, the audience is known and the time horizon is fast. The other person can literally see that you're typing, so it's better to just get something out there than worry about composing the perfect message. Chat isn't as widely studied as those conveniently public tweets, but from what we do know, people use language more informally there than in public posts, using more creative respellings, expressive punctuation, acronyms, emoji, and so on: it's the most hospitable environment for internet slang. It's even still tolerant of typos: if you transpose some letters or your autocorrect fails you,

you can self-correct in the next message and there's not much time for misinterpretation.

So popular is chat that it's also expanded into domains that previously belonged to the email or the phone. Before smartphones, texting had been set up like a miniature email inbox, letting you read one message at a time, with separate screen views for received messages, sent messages, drafts, and composing a new message. When the screens got bigger and became touch-sensitive, the dominant model for texts became the chat stream rather than the email inbox. Reviews of the first-generation iPhone thought it worth noting that "as on many smart phones, a text message thread is displayed as one long conversation — a useful arrangement that allows you to pick which messages you'd like to answer." When texts jumped over into a chat-style interface, chat became thoroughly ubiquitous: you can opt out of social media and use your email inbox purely for auto-generated confirmation emails, but if you use digital technology for communication at all, you'll end up participating in some form of chat. So complete is this shift that a decade later I started hearing people using "text" as a generic term for chat in general, as in "text me on Twitter."

Many popular social apps are simply

variations on a chat app that happened to gain a foothold in a particular area, like WhatsApp in much of the world outside North America, WeChat in China, and Line in Japan and Korea. The biggest change that the chat paradigm developed as smartphones caught on was the integration of multimedia. Snapchat and its imitators let you send a photo with words on top that disappears after a few seconds. WeChat, WhatsApp, and their imitators let you send a short audio clip which is integrated into the back-and-forth chat interface. Both can be more expressive, but can also be hard to use in dark or loud environments.

Chat is also competing with email in professional contexts. For instance, Slack is a chat platform for talking with workplace teams. The first time I got to talk with my internet service provider's tech support via chat rather than on the phone, it was a delight to be able to simply type in the correct spelling of my name and address rather than having to spell out each part aloud. With digital assistants that can set timers or respond to our queries about what the weather's going to be tomorrow, chat is also becoming an interface for us to talk with the machine itself.

The key feature of chat is its real-time

nature, but what it means to be real-time has shifted as our internet norms have shifted. When the internet was a place for die-hard hobbyists to explore new people to talk to, in the days of chatrooms full of strangers, the room would announce your arrival to those who were already there ("_____ has entered the chat") and your departure to those who remained ("_____ has exited the chat"). When chat became a thing of people you already knew, but still tied to computers, the instant messaging would display a "buddy list" of your contacts that told you whether they were online or not: AOL Instant Messenger would play the sound of a door opening or closing whenever someone arrived or left, while later programs like Gchat merely displayed a subtle green dot. When chat became mobile, the relevant information shifted again: we're almost always around a device now, but we're not always free to look at our messages. So chat stopped displaying whether someone was "present" and instead displayed whether someone had seen the latest message. "Read" indicators track smartphones almost exactly, starting with BlackBerry Messenger (BBM) in 2005 for die-hards and Apple's iMessage in 2011 for the mainstream.

Being real-time is also chat's greatest

weakness. You can set aside a time to batch-reply to emails or check social media, but chat requires a certain generic availability in order to be useful. Chats or text messages, which have become pretty much indistinguishable, have the potential to intrude on whatever else you're doing, especially on a mobile device. But this isn't the first time we've faced technological interruption: once again, we can draw insight from the early days of landline telephone use. Before the phone, letters only arrived at designated times of the day, and no one knew if and when you read them; only certain people lived close enough to drop by unexpectedly. But a phone call could arrive from anyone, anywhere, and the only thing you knew about the caller was that someone wanted you — urgently. Perhaps unsurprisingly, then, a 1992 survey found that the overwhelming majority of people would answer a ringing telephone even during a serious argument with their spouse. I tried replicating the survey myself twenty-five years later, and found the exact opposite result: people overwhelmingly wouldn't pick up the phone during a serious discussion with a loved one. Even if nothing particular was going on, people often reported checking to see who was calling before deciding whether to answer. I didn't find the expected age gap, between people who'd acquired their phone norms with landlines and those who oriented towards cellphones: rather, the people who reported a strong inclination to always answer a ringing phone were in their eighties and nineties, not their forties and fifties. Many people evidently adjusted their phone norms in the years after 1992, as caller ID became widely available.

Phone calls have come to represent the halcyon days when people actually talked to each other, but at the time, they had their own communication problems. In the 1970s, 80s, and 90s, a major problem in business communications was that only one in four phone calls resulted in the desired conversation: too often, the person you wanted to reach was out of the office or already on the phone. At first, your only solution was to simply wait a while and try again, or at best, leave a message with another person or on voicemail, hoping that you'd be around when they called back — but if you weren't, now you had to try and call back again. And so on. This "telephone tag" could stretch for days or even weeks. No wonder people picked up every time they heard the phone ring, even if it was just to say, "Sorry, it's not a good time, can

I call you back in an hour?" There was no real way of scheduling a phone call that didn't involve a phone call.

Internet and mobile devices changed this set of norms, not even a full century old itself. If you have a less intrusive way to establish whether someone's available before putting them on the spot with a call, why not take advantage of it? But by the same token, chat has taken on the position that phone calls once had as the most probable way of reaching someone, which in turn means that we must be reachable there instead. (Although sometimes we don't want to be: "butler lies" are the polite social fictions which we use to manage our availability in chat, like "Sorry, just got this" or "Gotta get back to work.") Op-ed articles from the 2010s reveal a generation gap around technological interruptions: younger people find that responding to a text message in the company of others is reasonable, because you can integrate it into the pauses of the conversation, but that unplanned phone calls are a gross interruption because they demand your attention instantly, completely, and unpredictably. Older people are perfectly happy to interrupt or be interrupted by a voice call, because they're unexpected and therefore urgent, but find the sight of someone texting an imposition, precisely because you could have put it off until after the conversation entirely.

This shift in norms is responsible for finally popularizing videocalling. The technology for the videophone has been available since the 1960s — it's just a telephone spliced with a television, after all. Pundits kept predicting it, but it never seemed to catch on. The problem with videocalling was that it faced an insurmountable social obstacle: with a robust norm of always answering a ringing phone and no efficient way to plan a phone call except via the same medium, the risk was too great of catching someone unclothed or with a messy house in the background. Picking up a videocall out of the blue was simply too awkward to contemplate. But since every videochat program includes a text messaging feature, you can plan a videochat before committing to one ("hey, you ready to skype?" "just give me 2 min") and this awkwardness vanishes: you have the option to decline via text where no one can see you, or a minute to scramble into a decent-looking shirt. Paradoxically, having access to the lesser intrusiveness of chat conversations makes it easier to have higher-bandwidth conversations in video.

The lure of cyberspace to its early arrivals wasn't just as an easier way of passing notes, avoiding telephone awkwardness, or sending interoffice memos. It was the promise that somewhere out in the world, you could find other people who matched your unique weirdnesses, or at least understood your niche passions. But to send someone a message, you need to find them first, and for that, you need some sort of shared space that several people can drop in on.

The idea of a third place is often invoked to explain the appeal of Starbucks: the first place is home, the second place is work, but people also need a third place to socialize that's neither home nor work, like a coffeeshop. What Ray Oldenburg, the sociologist who coined the term in a 1989 book called *The Great Good Place,* had in mind was something more specific than just any convenient spot where you might stop by for a cup of joe. Oldenburg's third places are first of all social centers, distinguished by an emphasis on conversation and playfulness, regular attendees who set the tone for newcomers, the freedom to come and go as you please, a lack of formal membership requirements, and a warm, unpretentious feeling of home away from home. Examples include pubs, taverns, and bars, cafés and coffeeshops, barbershops, community centers, markets, malls, churches, libraries, parks, clubs and organizations, main streets, public squares, and neighborhood activities like block parties, town meetings, and bingo.

When I think of where my own third places have been, I keep coming back to hallways. In high school, we'd sit in the halls with our backs against the lockers at lunchtime or recess, certain corners occupied by certain regulars. In dorms, you'd signal your willingness to join into impromptu social activity by whether you left your door open to the hall. At conferences, the talks are merely a pretext for assembling people with shared interests so that we can run into each other in the hallways. In the best third places, it takes me half an hour to travel the length of a single hallway because I run into seventeen people who I absolutely must talk with — and sometimes I even set out for such a walk with no particular destination, because I know I'll run into someone enjoyable.

When I've tried to articulate the appeal of Linguist Twitter to linguists who aren't on it, I've talked in terms of hallways: You know how the best part of a conference is the hallway? Imagine if you could have that hallway available at any time of the day or night! But perhaps I should have talked in terms of third places. The parallel is compelling, and not just for my corner of the internet: the emphasis on conversation and wit describes the memes and hashtag wordplay games, like #RemoveALetterRuinABook, that regularly sweep the trending topics. Unlike an email inbox or a chat with a specific person, you can drop in on a social media feed at any time of the day or night and expect to see both regulars and newcomers. Trying to focus on work with social media available is, alas, like trying to work in a hallway of friends and acquaintances, but you can also credit social media's serendipitous encounters with letting you hear about job opportunities and other useful morsels of news.

When Facebook and Twitter started letting you post status updates, their appeal was explained in terms of ambient awareness of what your friends were doing, which could lead to spontaneous encounters or being able to pick up a conversation later as if no time had passed, without needing to catch up first. Facebook status updates in 2006 came with a few dropdown options meant to reflect typical college activities, like "is sleeping," "is studying," "is in class," or "is at a party." Even when you typed in your

347

own status message, the "is" was obligatory and a period was automatically inserted at the end, clearly trying to push people in the direction of a particular genre of update. While early tweets didn't have the same grammatical constraints, they still tended to be about the here and now, such as "walking on the sunny side of the street," "digesting a burrito," and "just setting up my twttr."

It's true that people did use statuses for mundane daily updates, but ambient posts about what people had for lunch didn't explain why Twitter was such an effective tool for coordination in times of natural disaster and political upheaval. Awareness that your friends were in the library or watching a movie didn't explain why people spent an average of fifty minutes per day on Facebook in 2016, up from forty minutes per day in 2014. Moreover, as connectivity became ever easier and more mobile, it was no longer necessary to explain why you were away from the computer: you weren't. Yet social media posts got more popular, rather than less, joined by mobile-first platforms like Instagram and Snapchat, which required that posts include an image or short video. Snapchat and later Instagram even brought us a new format for posts: the story which vanishes after twenty-four hours, a window into the fun, non-computery things you've been doing. A "normal" profile page gradually changed from being a list of static facts about you to a list of things you've posted recently. What does explain the appeal of posts in their various formats is thinking of them as a third place.

Do you keep refreshing social media at the expense of your bedtime? Oldenburg has an explanation for that: "Third place conversation is typically engrossing. Consciousness of conditions and time often slip away amid its lively flow." What about when a random person goes viral or a celebrity replies to an unsuspecting fan? Third places are a leveler: "the charm and flavor of one's personality, irrespective of his or her station in life, is what counts." Why do games like FarmVille and Pokémon Go periodically sweep social media? In a previous decade, games like gin rummy and pool, which are conducive to lively conversation, were characteristic of third places. Oldenburg also points out how third places have been essential to forming the kinds of large, loose-knit social groups that are the core of new social movements, such as the agora in ancient Greek democracy, taverns around the American Revolution, and coffeeshops during the Age of Enlightenment, which parallels how Twitter was used for the Arab Spring or the Black Lives Matter protests. You can't fit enough dissenters in your living room to make a revolution out of close ties alone: you need the larger, looser network of a third place.

Third places have been hacked into existence from the very early stages of using computers to talk with each other. Pretty much as soon as email became possible — long before the internet as we know it — people started sending messages to multiple people at once. Particular people became known for coordinating lists of email addresses of people interested in particular topics, so if you heard about a list that you wanted to join, you'd send that person an email and they'd add you. Popular email lists that have been documented from ARPANET were called human-nets (the human side of the network), sf-lovers (science fiction fans), network-hackers, and wine-tasters. But adding people manually to email lists got tedious, and the military, understandably, wasn't particularly keen on letting random civilians join their network just so they could talk about wine. So later technology such as Usenet (1980), Listserv (1986), and public chatrooms would let you join as a normal person, browse topics, and add yourself to those that interested you, such as alt.folklore.computers, alt.usage.english, or alt.tv.x-files on Usenet, LINGUIST List (a listserv I'm still on), and #ham-radio or #StarTrek in chatrooms.

Topic-based posting to internet strangers has remained around, in various formats. Blogs are themed around a particular person's life or a more specific topic like cooking, travel, or careers, and sometimes develop community between strangers in the comments section. Multiplayer online games often include a chat function that lets you talk with strangers, or let you import your friends from an existing social network. Reddit, the most popular general-interest forum of the 2010s, has subdivisions for everything from random thoughts that occur to you in the shower to getting famous people to come and answer questions for an hour or two. Other forums are devoted to one topic in particular, whether that's parenting, beer, videogames, knitting, anime, or sharing pictures of cats with writing on top. You've probably read some blog posts and forum posts, when searching for a recipe that fits the ingredients in your fridge or trying to figure out what the error message on your phone means. But how many of us continually maintain a blog ourselves, or are active posters on a forum? Estimates are low: 5 to 8 percent of internet users might be bloggers, and 1 to 10 percent might regularly participate in forums and other online communities. Dropping by a blog or a forum post because it showed up in your search results doesn't make you a regular.

Topic-based internet communities are third places in the way that you can join a pottery class or drop by a networking meetup as a third place. The first few times you show up, you don't know anyone, and you're ostensibly there for the content. But if you keep going back, you start recognizing people, people start recognizing you, and you may gravitate towards some more than others, chat about your lives rather than just the official topic, or make plans to hang out outside the community. The first people to socialize over computer networks were united by their dissatisfaction with the offline social options available to them. They were willing to take the chance that people online might be more congenial, whether they were united by a shared interest in computers in general or a more niche interest (technologist Jess Kimball Leslie describes finding an internet home in the mid-1990s in the Official Bette Midler Online Internet Fan Club). But both online and off, topic-based communities tend to draw people who want to expand their existing friendship circles: there's a reason why joining a club is classic advice for people moving to a new city. It's hard to articulate the third-placean appeal of topic-based internet communities for those who've never been in one. At least with a pottery class or networking event, you can say you're there to make a vase or collect some business cards: tangible outcomes even if you're also searching for intangible community. But for their online versions, the pretexts wear thinner: Why spend so much time talking to strangers about *The X-Files* or wine tasting when you could be actually watching the show or drinking the wine? The social benefits are invisible to people who don't need them.

That's why topic-based forums and messageboards were not how the majority of people discovered that the internet could serve as a third place. Instead, most people discovered internet community by person-based platforms, those that allowed us to import our existing friendships online. The group that discovered this was made up of people who already had friends but lacked the autonomy to spend time with them: teenagers. Teens didn't need a specific topic to find each other: they already knew each other, and just wanted a place to hang out.

In Chapter 3, we noted that suburban isolation and anti-loitering laws discouraged teenagers from hanging out in the offline spaces that had once been theirs. For a while, popular teens hung out on landline telephones, and only misfit teens turned to the internet in search of community. But as the internet became mainstream through the mid- and late 1990s, so did hanging out with your friends there.

The initial way of hanging out with your friends online were the aforementioned late-1990s instant messaging programs, like AIM, MSN, and ICQ. They had a crucial feature besides their ability to chat: the status message. The first status messages, also called away messages and status updates, were intended quite literally to indicate what you were doing while you were away from the computer, such as sleeping, eating dinner, in class, or working. Remembering to accurately update your status quickly became tedious — what if you said you were out at a movie and then you went to bed without turning the computer back on? But status messages were compelling for a different reason: they provided a built-in reason to logon, just to see what your friends had posted, even if you didn't have a specific conversation topic in mind. These IM status messages acquired a sense of aesthetic, containing quotes, song lyrics, ~*~sparkle punctuation~*~, sTudLy cApS, and passive-aggressive notes, sometimes all in one. As *The New York Times* put it in a tweet about AIM closing down for good in 2017, "~* iT's ThE eNd Of An ErA *~."

Status messages made chat more serendipitous, more of a third place: a way of showing up at the school dance to see what everyone was wearing, or leaving your door open to the hallway. They were the precursor to the posts that make social media even more compelling to check: both the tweet and the Facebook post were originally conceived as status updates. It was this overlap between the online and offline third places that eventually got even adults who were already satisfied with their friend networks onto social media — that wave of "my parents got Facebook" that we talked about in Chapter 3.

Oldenburg, writing in the 1980s and 90s, would probably not have agreed with me that the internet could provide a third place, even though he was writing during a period when pretty much every internet community was a third-placean gathering of strangers. He wasn't a fan of technology, criticizing how the television had started occupying the

355

hours that people used to spend hanging out in casual groups of regulars. He especially criticized how suburbs were being built without main streets and town squares and local watering holes to serve as third places. It's often observed that social media is taking on the functions of a hangout place for teenagers. Studies note that post-internet teens aren't drinking as much or having as much sex, because their hangouts happen in virtual space rather than in cars or on street corners. But perhaps it's more that teens across the generations have never stopped prioritizing hanging out with friends, and in truth, all ages are equally in need of the camaraderie of third places.

Oldenburg might be pleased about one thing: the hours that people now spend on social media are often time that would otherwise be spent on television consumption, which he considered an inferior replacement for third places. And the connections forged in online third places might be helping counteract the suburban isolation which he so hated. Moreover, third places, including social media, foster the kinds of repeated, unplanned interactions that sociologists have identified as crucial for the formation of deeper relationships. Casual, third-place acquaintances sometimes become first-place people you'd invite into your home, or second-place people you might end up working with. In fact, we can recast chat and email conversations through the lens of places. While chatrooms of the 1990s were a third place, the one-on-one or small-group chat of the 2010s is more like a first place, people you make a point of talking with, in private. Email listservs were also a third place, but the email inbox has become more of a second place, used for work and official communications. We no longer aimlessly hang out in our email inboxes or chat platforms. The internet platforms that you open up for no particular reason, hoping someone interesting will be around, are the ones with posts. Posting into the ether is like sticking your head out into the hallway to see who you might run into. Many of your Facebook friends, Twitter people, or Instagram folks remain surface-level acquaintances, but adding someone on social media is a way of adding them to the hallway you stroll down, a way of saying, "I might like to have more unplanned interactions with you, and we can see where things go from there."

There's an important difference between physical and virtual third places, however. My local pub or barbershop or park is in principle open to anyone, but in practice circumscribed by both geography and custom: only so many people live nearby or can fit inside, and it's quite clear that I belong neither among the clientele of a barbershop nor (anymore) among the teenagers hanging out in the park. The only things limiting the third places of the internet are customs, and those customs are still evolving. Sometimes, the unbounded geography of the internet is amazing: I can carry friends in my pocket everywhere I go, and there's someone around at every time of the day or night. Airports are no longer impersonal, insomnia is no longer isolating, and the most mundane grocery run can be livened up by a quick exchange with a pocket friend.

Other times, the lack of physical cues is more complicated. I can see the dozen or so people who are sitting around a table or lounging with me in a hallway, but the potential audience for a given post ranges from "zero" to "every single one of the billions of people on the internet," and I can't necessarily tell which one it's going to be until after I've posted it. If I tell a joke at a pub or a coffeeshop, it may fall flat, but at least I know whether I'm being ignored. If I post a clever quip or share an adorable video of frolicking baby animals, I can't tell whether I've caused a hundred people to gasp at their screens or whether no one's seen it at all. That is, unless I can garner a couple likes or comments. Consciously or not, a lot of our social media posts are optimized around getting some kind of interaction: we may fuss over the precise wording for maximum humor, run a draft post by a friend, message specific people to get them to comment, plan the posting time for the most interactions, or simply like others' posts for moral support, so our friends know they aren't shouting into the void.

I did a small-scale analysis of Facebook statuses in early 2009, looking at the ten most recent posts of friends from just before they volunteered for the study. I'd hoped to trace the decline of statuses that began with "is," but I ended up finding clearer patterns in what made for a socially successful post. I found that the statuses that got the most likes and comments weren't necessarily the ones that were universally applicable or made the most sense in isolation: say, a simple announcement of a new phone number, which is relevant to all your friends. Instead, popular posts tended to strike a balance between somewhat obscure but not too cryptic — in-jokes and references that appealed strongly to a distinct subset of people. One of my most popular posts at the time was in a language that only a handful of my Facebook friends even understood — my friends who were taking the same language class. But every single one of them commented on the post, many of them several times. *BuzzFeed,* a few years later, accomplished this on a larger scale, writing highly shareable articles about things particular groups of people understand if they were born in a particular decade or are from a particular place. Memes, which we'll examine closely in the next chapter, capitalize on this tendency because getting the meme automatically makes you part of an in-group.

Trying to prevent certain people from seeing or understanding your posts gets more complicated. Sure, you could just remain completely private by never making an account or posting anything, but that's like saying you could avoid contagious disease by never touching a human, or avoid getting hit by a falling piano by simply never leaving the house. Most of us find that it's worth trading away some privacy for the sake of having a life. Instead of embracing hermithood, we seek a balance: one study found that people differentiated between the kind of information that they'd share in a post versus in a chat message, rating information about their hobbies or favorite TV shows as less intimate and therefore more likely to be shared in a post than their fears, concerns, and personal feelings, which they preferred to share in a private message, if at all. In other areas people disagreed, such as about the privacy of political or religious opinions and life events like births or marriages, which probably explains why it sometimes feels like others are oversharing or overly reticent.

A law paper by Woodrow Hartzog and Frederic D. Stutzman notes that a lot of online information isn't so much completely private but rather obscure, hard enough to access that most people won't bother trying. They describe four factors that can lead to obscurity online: first, whether your post can be found in search or whether a would-be finder needs to click through an obscure trail of links to find it; second, whether your post is restricted to certain people (such as by friendship status or a password); third, whether you're identifiable by name, pseudonym, or not at all; and fourth, how clearly understandable the post is, even if someone comes across it who shouldn't. After all, it doesn't matter so much if a post is technically completely public. If no one knows it's there, that you wrote it, or what it means, it's still effectively private through its obscurity.

In the offline world, a lot of information is technically public but practically obscure, including the messages that we post in spaces where people may pass by, such as graffiti, bulletin boards, and signs on telephone poles advertising yard sales or lost cats. In Montreal, the French-dominant but highly bilingual city where I live, I've always wanted to do a linguistic geography of LOST CAT signs. Unlike posters advertising a concert or a tutoring service, which might justifiably target a particular linguistic demographic, if your cat wanders off, you want to maximize the odds that someone will find it and know how to bring it home. Even if you're not bilingual yourself, you might decide it's worth getting a friend to translate your sign for you. Among the bilingual neighborhoods, I wonder, which ones put French first and which English? Where might people include a third language or only bother with one? By tagging a map of the city's telephone poles with the languages of their LOST CAT signs, you could arrive at a map of what languages people believe their neighbors speak: a folk linguistic cartography of the city.

But while my hypothetical LOST CAT sign is public in some ways, it's obscure in others. Access-wise, it's obscure: I can reasonably expect that it'll be seen by the people on my block, not that it will be reproduced on national television, result in me getting contacted by hundreds of trolls pretending to have found my cat, or end up in a searchable database of LOST CAT signs so that decades hence I'll still be getting served ads for multinational cat-finding services.* But content-wise, a LOST CAT sign must be clear: it must describe the cat in a recognizable way for strangers, rather than as a fuzzy floofball; it must provide accurate contact information, so that anyone who finds my cat can get ahold of me; and it must be in the language or languages that I think my neighbors speak.

With many social media posts, the opposite is true — they're not restricted by location, so people do want to make the message only comprehensible to insiders. Privacy through obscurity is a versatile tool for many social situations. A study of Estonian teens observed the teens doing things like posting song lyrics, quotes, or in-jokes that only made sense to their crush, in the hope that they'd see it and want to respond — which several teens said had worked. A study of queer youth on Facebook found that one way of navigating

*No cats were harmed in the making of this example.

363

how out to be on a platform that contained both family members and potential members of a fellow queer community was to post queer pop culture references that would be easily interpretable by peers and go over the heads of their non-intended audience. Technologist danah boyd observed coded messages in more negative contexts, too: for example, when a teen wanted to indicate bad news of a breakup to friends without worrying her mother, she posted a quote from "Always Look on the Bright Side of Life," a Monty Python song that looks happy but is deeply ironic in context, knowing that she'd recently seen the film with her friends but that her mother wasn't familiar with it.

A less subtle way of navigating the relationship between the public and the obscure is found in subtweeting (subliminal tweets) or vaguebooking (vague facebooking), the art of posting elliptically about a social situation without naming names. Posting a song lyric has plausible deniability: it could just mean you enjoy that song and it's stuck in your head. But if someone posts, "I just don't have time for this nonsense," it's obvious even to the completely uninitiated that some kind of drama is going on; it's just that only certain people are going to already have the right context to interpret it.

Asking what's going on is like interrupting an arguing couple at a restaurant to ask for a detailed relationship history: a definite faux pas. You've got to figure it out for yourself or resign yourself to not knowing. A study of subtweets among college students found indirect posts were indeed considered a more socially acceptable way of conveying negative information than directly mentioning the person in question. (For example, "Thanks to a certain person for backstabbing and completely ruining my day. People like that are pathetic." While people recognized the passive aggression, they preferred it to a version that named and shamed the specific person involved.) The inverse was the case for positive posts — it was considered better to tag someone directly in a post like "Thanks @RyanS for completely making my day. You're awesome."

Gossiping, in-jokes, and hiding messages in plain sight are by no means just a teenage or internet thing. People have long written to advice columnists under pseudonyms, switched languages in front of foreigners, softened swear words (gosh hecking darn it), spelled words in front of children ("Are your kids allowed to have some C-A-K-E?"), and used creative imagery to hide political dissent. Chinese internet dissidents are especially famous for using puns. For example, they might write 河蟹 *héxiè,* "river crab," which sounds like 和谐, *héxié,* the Mandarin word for "harmony," but with different tones. "Harmony" itself is a Chinese euphemism for "censorship," derived from the purported goal of a 2004 internet censorship law to create a "Harmonious Society."

The song lyrics that were ubiquitous in status messages of nineties teens on IM grew directly out of an existing youth cultural practice — teens previously sent hidden messages in yearbook quotes, doodled lyrics onto notebook covers or desks where they might be seen by the relevant person, and graffitied passive-aggressive drama anonymously onto bathroom stalls. Parents of young children often use a nickname or initial to post about their child, so that they can get support from fellow parents while not creating a searchable social media trail for a minor who's not in a position to consent to the sharing of their childish antics. People who already know parent and child can decode the messages, but future employers won't stumble across a twenty-year-old photo of Candidate McJobSearch as a toddler with their face covered in ice cream.

The third places of the internet that are so effective at helping fans of knitting or videogames find each other, and the loose ties that are so effective at mobilizing protests against unjust laws or a beloved TV show being canceled are unfortunately just as effective at enabling hate mobs to assemble. In 2015, Reddit banned several of its subforums that had become strongly associated with hate speech. At the time, there was considerable doubt that it would work: Would the hateful commenters simply invade other subreddits and continue their hateful ways? A study that came out in 2017 suggested they would not. At least on Reddit, users who moved to other communities on the same site reduced their hate speech by at least 80 percent. Other accounts simply became inactive, however, and may have moved to other sites where this behavior was still tolerated.

A German study of hostility in comments on soccer blogs provides a potential reason why the Reddit ban worked. Researchers asked soccer fans to write a comment on a blog post about a controversial soccer issue that already contained six other comments. When the previous comments were hostile and aggressive, so was the new one. When the previous comments were thoughtful and considerate, the new comment again followed suit — and it didn't matter whether such comments were anonymous or linked to real-name Facebook accounts. Thinking about public and semipublic posting on social media sites as third places can provide a way of thinking about the responsibility of a platform to its residents: your local bartenders or baristas don't generally interfere with your conversations, but they do reserve the right to kick people out if they're disturbing other patrons, and this makes the space better as a whole. Every human society has figured out norms and systems for managing group behavior most of the time, and internet groups are no different.

We're used to the idea that language changes, at least somewhat. One generation's new slang is another's tired cliché. We don't talk like Shakespeare. And so on. But what's less apparent is that macro-level conversation norms have changed and will keep changing. Sometimes they change because new technology arises; sometimes the underlying technology is practically unchanged but its social context is different. Telephones changed our greetings, and smartphones changed them again. Business communication spent a whole century getting less ornate, from memos to emails to chat. Posts have a long and complicated relationship with the public sphere. Chat became more intimate and conversational as more people started using it. Videochat may be switching in the opposite direction: becoming more like a third place hangout with the rise of video "chilling" apps like Houseparty, which lets you drop in on a group videochat with whichever of your friends happen to be around. The current configuration of sites that provide us with first and second and third places has changed before and will, in all likelihood, change again, but the appeal of having friends in your pocket is unlikely to go away.

This chapter, more than any other, is a snapshot of a particular moment in time and how we got that way, not a claim to correctness or immortality. What it is instead is a call to humility. To saying, if conversational norms are always in flux, and different at the same time among different people, let's not be over-hasty to judge. Let's ask clarifying questions about what other people mean, rather than rushing to conclusions. Let's assume that communicative practices which baffle us do have genuine, important meaning for the people who use them. We don't create truly successful communication by "winning" at conversational norms, whether that's by convincing someone to omit all periods in text messages for fear of being taken as angry, or to answer all landline telephones after precisely two rings. We create successful communication when all parties help each other win.

CHAPTER 7:
MEMES AND
INTERNET CULTURE

When you say "The City," which city are you referring to?

This is a great way to start an argument. A lot of people will declare for a few classic regional lodestones: London, New York, San Francisco. People already in those metropolitan areas will explain that, actually, the true city is a more specific historic center like Manhattan or the City of London. A smaller number of people will champion a wide array of local centers of gravity, such as Chicago, Toronto, Winnipeg, Norwich, Detroit, New Orleans, Bristol, Seattle, Vancouver, Oklahoma City, Melbourne, Sydney, and Washington, D.C. When I was growing up in Nova Scotia, everyone knew that "I'm going to the city this weekend" clearly meant you were heading to Halifax. People disagree, but everyone who has an answer is really sure about it.

This is not just the narcissism of modern

urbanites. So clear was it to residents of medieval Constantinople that their city was The City that they eventually renamed it as such — *Istanbul* is a variant of Middle Greek *stambóli,* from colloquial Greek *s tan Póli,* "in the City." (The same *pol* as in "acropolis" or at the end of "Constantinople.") Medina, in Saudi Arabia, means "city" in Arabic, and no less than three places in Andhra Pradesh, a state in India, are named *Nagaram,* which is "city" in Telugu.

Even if you don't have your own The City, even if you throw your hands up and say, "I dunno, whatever city's closest?" you notice when visitors say your local landmarks and street names wrong. It's not just that people disagree: after all, you and I presumably also disagree about where "home" is, and this doesn't lead to arguments. But home is naturally personal — to claim otherwise would be like complaining that your "here" is my "there." Cities, landmarks, regions — those are personal and also cultural. How we talk about them is a sign of where we belong.

When it comes to the internet, the question of what truly belongs inside Internet Culture gets people just as passionate as the question of which city is The City. (I have, because I'm fun at parties, verified this through *ahem* extensive personal investigation.) When we write online, we don't do so in a vacuum. We remix. We foster shared cultural references. We draw lines between insiders who get our references and outsiders who don't.

But one thing we know, if we spend more than a minute discussing internet culture, is that it somehow involves a thing called memes.

THE MEME IS DEAD

When Richard Dawkins introduced the idea of memes in 1976, he intended them as an ideological counterpart to genes: like how a gene (such as for brown eyes) spreads through sexual selection and physical fitness, a meme (such as the idea that the earth orbits the sun) spreads through social selection and ideological fitness. He based the word on *mimeme,* from Ancient Greek μίμημα, "imitated thing," and shortened it to pair well with "gene." But Dawkins wasn't making any sort of pronouncement about internet culture: for all he was concerned, memes might have remained a relatively obscure concept in social science research.

The extension of "meme" to the internet definition we're familiar with today was directly related to the question of what should and shouldn't be a part of internet culture. In 1990, a technologist named Mike Godwin was getting annoyed at how every Usenet discussion seemed to eventually devolve into hyperbolic comparisons to Hitler. ("Someone made an extension to change the word 'millennials' to 'snake people'? That's censorship! You know who else was a censor?!?!") Godwin decided to fight back by creating a name for what he was seeing, and trying to make people replicate that idea instead: "I seeded Godwin's Law in any newsgroup or topic where I saw a gratuitous Nazi reference. Soon, to my surprise, other people were citing it — the counter-meme was reproducing on its own!" A few years later, he described his experiment in an article for *Wired,* invoking Dawkins's term to describe what he'd been doing and thereby introducing *Wired*'s readers to the term "meme" in a specifically internet context.

"Meme" was seeded just in time for a major cultural rupture. In the early days of Usenet, September was the worst time of the year. It represented an annual influx of new users — students getting internet access for the first time via their universities — who had to be acculturated into proper Netiquette by the beleaguered old-timers. In September 1993, this changed. AOL began sending out internet connection CDs in the mail and thus, according to the book *Net.wars,* in the space of a single year "unleashed its one million users onto the Net in what was then the largest single block of new users the Net had ever been asked to absorb." Existing netizens were unable to fully acculturate this influx and were Not Pleased by the results, dubbing the period thereafter Eternal September.

Although counter-memetics may not have become quite the noble cause Godwin envisioned, the idea of memes — the meme of memes, if you will — certainly did spread and mutate online. A meme in the internet sense isn't just something popular, a video or image or phrase that goes viral. It's something that's remade and recombined, spreading as an atom of internet culture. I might put the idea of the earth orbiting the sun into my own words to spread it in the Dawkins sense, but for it to be an internet meme, I'd need to be one of many people remaking it. Perhaps I'd invent a solar system dance so hilaribad that people around the world would be unable to resist posting videos of themselves doing it, or riff on some crude art labeling all the planets as kinds of Canada ("Canada Major," "Red Canada," "Not-a-Single-Lady Canada," "Canada

That Is Totally A Planet," and so on).* Once you've seen a few examples, you have a sense of what they have in common and can try your hand at your own version. When you're fluent in meme culture, the logical next step is to mash several well-known memes together.

Weird cultural artifacts spreading through a whole bunch of people deciding to replicate them is older than the internet: in the book *Memes in Digital Culture,* Limor Shifman points to "Kilroy Was Here" (a graffiti sketch of a big-nosed man looking over a wall that became popular during World War II) as an example of a pre-internet meme. The new part is the connection of the name "meme" with the kind of cultural replication that happens on the internet. All the way back to Godwin's Law and Eternal September, making and sharing memes is about policing what's in and what's out of internet culture. This became difficult as aspects of internet culture changed, especially the relationship between cultural and technical fluency. Like how the first wave of Internet

*The dance is not real, to my knowledge, but the Canada planet meme is. Try imgur.com/gallery/gsMqxpq or google "Canada a bit to the left meme."

People conflated knowledge of programming jargon and internet slang, the early waves of meme creators felt that there was a link between knowing the technical tools required to make memes and understanding the subcultures in which they fit. They worried that if meme-making became too easy, the culture itself would get diluted.

One tool for easier meme creation was macros. Although "image macro" has come to be a synonym for "image meme," a macro started as any short command that you could use to make your computer do a larger task, such as renaming a whole series of files at once. On the forum Something Awful in 2004, a macro made it easier to add an image to a comment. Rather than re-uploading the same image each time, you could just type, for example, [img-blownaway] to summon an image containing "I'm blown away!" in pale turquoise all caps. Using macros to make it easier to post images had an insider/outsider dynamic from the very beginning: according to a history of the forum, its moderator had created the image macro feature to prove a point about how annoying repetitive images were. Instead, people loved them. A further macro came with an even more popular meme: lolcats. People started sharing pictures of blissed-out cats with overlaid text on the anonymous forum 4chan starting in 2005, in a Saturday celebration of cats known as "Caturday," and the lolcat phenomenon eventually occasioned articles everywhere from academic journals to *Time* magazine. Like the earlier memes, the first lolcats had their text added manually, using graphics programs like Photoshop and Microsoft Paint.

As lolcats became popular, so did a second kind of timesaving macro, which would place the text automatically on the base image — much faster than downloading it to a separate program. These meme generator sites promoted a consistent meme aesthetic: the all-caps, black-bordered white Impact font (a brilliant innovation in automatic caption generation because it stands out easily no matter what colors or patterns are behind it).

Making lolcat generation easier became controversial. Putting text on top of an image had formerly required a certain amount of technical knowledge of photo-editing software. Now, it was easy. Too easy, according to some "insiders." Technologist Kate Miltner documented this split among two kinds of lolcat fans in the late 2000s. Self-described MemeGeeks had liked the early kind of lolcats on 4chan but had moved on to other memes, like Advice Animals, as

378

I-are serious cat.
This is serious thread.

INVISIBLE BIKE

I CAN HAS
CHEEZBURGER?

I made you a cookie...

but I eated it.

lolcats became more popular and easier to create. Self-described Cheezfriends, on the other hand, tended to reside on the site *I Can Has Cheezburger* and demonstrated their community membership through fluency in the stylized lolspeak itself, rather than technical prowess creating the memes. At peak lolcat, posters on the lolcat forums at *I Can Has Cheezburger* would type entire messages to each other in lolspeak, and it was easy for them to linguistically tell apart the newbs from the true Cheezfriends, even without any cat images to help.

Rather than dive into old Cheezburger forum posts, let's look at the closest thing lolcat has to a peer-reviewed text: a translation of the Bible into lolspeak. It was written collaboratively on a wiki, with multiple authors contributing and voting. I'm going to quote from lolspeak Genesis, which as the beginning of the text received a lot of editing:*

Oh hai. In teh beginnin Ceiling Cat maded teh skiez An da Urfs, but he did not eated dem.

*You can read the whole thing at lolcatbible.com, but for a sense of what it's like, Ceiling Cat is God, Basement Cat is the Devil, Happy Cat is Jesus, and tents are often replaced by sofas.

Da Urfs no had shapez An haded dark face, An Ceiling Cat rode invisible bike over teh waterz.

At start, no has lyte. An Ceiling Cat sayz, i can haz lite? An lite wuz.

An Ceiling Cat sawed teh lite, to seez stuffs, An splitted teh lite from dark but taht wuz ok cuz kittehs can see in teh dark An not tripz over nethin.

An Ceiling Cat sayed light Day An dark no Day. It were FURST!!!1

Practically every single word in this excerpt is a reference to something. "Oh hai" is from one lolcat meme. "Teh" is early internet slang. Ceiling Cat is a specific cat in another meme. "Maded" and "eated" are from the "I made you a cookie but I eated it" meme that we saw above. "FURST" is one bit of internet slang, and "!!!1" is another. Not to mention, of course, all the references to the Bible as a source text. But to have a dense set of references explained to you like this is about as much fun as reading the Wikipedia article for a highly technical field that you know nothing about: by the time you click on all the words you don't know, you've lost the thread of why the original topic was interesting. Creating a dense set of references, on the other hand, or just getting them when you see them, is a sheer delight, like meeting a compatriot when you're far away from home: you get a rush of fellow-feeling simply from swapping familiar landmarks. The appeal of memes is the appeal of belonging to a community of fellow insiders.

This community was about to get a lot bigger. The meme generation websites that had popped up towards the end of the lolcat meme brought in a whole wave of new animal memes from 2008 to 2014. These Advice Animal memes contained a stock character archetype in the center, either a person or an animal, and a two-line narration of either the character's actions or internal monologue, invariably in black-bordered white Impact. Some of the stock images are cut-out faces in the center of a multicolored pinwheel, especially the earlier examples, while later stock images are often full photos. For example, Philosoraptor is a velociraptor drawing in a pinwheel that ponders hypothetical questions, Scumbag Steve is a full photo of a frat bro in a distinctive patterned hat who engages in irresponsible or unethical behavior, and Grumpy Cat is a cat with a characteristically unamused facial expression.

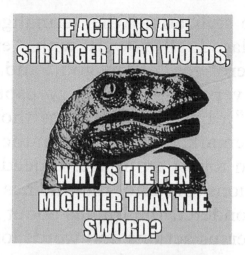

What was interesting about Advice Animals was how they democratized and fragmented the meme space. Lolcat was based around a more or less unified set of linguistic references, a single kitteh grammar of "oh hai" and "I can has" and "k thx bai." Advice Animals were open-ended: they were a meme family that different subgroups engaged with at different levels. Some had linguistic stylization (the "ermahgerd" version replaced all vowels with "er," as in "ermahgerd" for "oh my god," and the Ryan Gosling version began every caption with "hey girl"), but many, such as those above, were unremarkable when not in the two-part format on top of an image. Indeed, some of the captions predate the memes entirely: people pondered the quotes about pens and swords versus actions and words long before the meme was created.

Because of this democratization, Advice Animals ran the gamut from very well-known to very obscure. I picked Philosoraptor and Scumbag Steve above because I'd expect anyone familiar with memes to have heard of them, but others were popular in a single community. For example, Linguist Llama is only (but tremendously) popular among linguists, where it joined a medium-sized trend for Advice Animals themed around academic subjects, such as Art Student Owl and History Major Heraldic Beast ("You aren't a real goth / until you sack Rome"). Still others were popular only within a single friend group, such as the truly obscure Linguist Lingcod, which a group of friends and I made in 2011 based off the fact that there really is a fish by that name. We had a fun time, but it remained obscure even within the linguistics community, and for several very good reasons: few people have heard of the lingcod, they definitely didn't realize that our hideous picture of a fish was supposed to be one, our captions were only funny if you'd been there, and we didn't know enough other linguists to spread the meme very far.

Despite how much our fish meme, uh, flopped, it was an important milestone for me. I'd encountered lolcats and participated in text-based memes before, such as "answer a list of questions and tag some friends to do the same," but if I'd known anyone who was originating image memes, they weren't going to tell me about it. Lolcats were made by people "out there" on the internet, and the most I could do to participate was imitate the language; Advice Animals were the first memes where some were made by people I knew offline. In retrospect, this was part of a broader shift in memes as a thing of Old Internet People, people who went online to interact with strangers, to memes as a thing of Full Internet People, people who went online to interact with people they already knew. ROFLCon, an internet culture conference that started in 2008, also grappled with the changing relationship between online and offline culture. Its organizers

ultimately decided to make the 2012 conference the last: as creators Tim Hwang and
Christina Xu explained, "In 2012 we were
on the phone with Grumpy Cat's agent, and
it was like, 'This cat has an agent.' I think
that fact alone was a really big indication
of how the space of internet culture had
changed in a four-year time period."

My next brush with participatory mem-
edom further blurred the line between internet and non-internet culture. Early in
2012, I'd been active in competitive debate
for a number of years, and late one night I
decided that what the world really needed
was a mashup of debate jargon and the Ryan
Gosling "hey girl" meme. I made a couple examples, sent the link to a few debate friends,
and went to bed. The next morning, I had
dozens of messages and a couple thousand
hits on my fledgling memeblog. People I
didn't even know sent in their own versions!
It was thrilling and short-lived: at the debate
tournament that weekend, I felt like the cool-
est person in the whole (deeply nerdy) place,
and yet ten days later, I'd stopped updating
the blog entirely. But I bring it up because
this is the perfect scale to see the power of an
in-joke: general enough that it spread a step
or two beyond my personal acquaintances,
insidery enough that it stopped there. I went

back and tried to find one of these memes to give here as an example, and I couldn't find a single one that wouldn't require at least a full paragraph of context, but danged if they didn't still make me laugh after all this time. The debate memes were only funny to maybe a few hundred people, half of whom I knew offline, but that handful of people felt purely understood.

A year later, I was spending more and more time on the internet, a necessary diversion from the master's thesis I was supposed to be writing. I started seeing a new style of image meme, one that avoided the one-two setup and payoff in black-bordered white Impact for a series of smaller phrases scattered around the face of a round-faced dog in Comic Sans. One with — joy of joys — a new and peculiar grammar. I started analyzing it in my head, vowing that I'd write up a description of this new meme the moment my thesis was in. This was a meme known as doge, based on a photo by Japanese teacher Atsuko Sato of her shiba inu, and I ultimately wrote a linguistic analysis of it for the eclectic and now sadly departed website *The Toast* in 2014. Doge was one of several memes that sprouted with this scattered interior monologue caption style, which draws

on the minimalist typography that we saw in Chapter 4. A later example was snek, which was based on multiple photos of snakes and often featured softened swear words like "heck" and the phrase "doing you a [verb]."

I spent the entire time writing the doge article in a state of barely contained glee, and again, people shared my joy. Only this time, as it turned out, the group of "people who enjoy academic analyses of internet culture" is rather larger than "people familiar with the in-jokes of the Canadian University Society for Intercollegiate Debate."* A few days later, I was talking about doge on the BBC, and I occasionally hear from fans of the article even years later.

What was the difference between making the Linguist Lingcod, the debate Ryan Gosling, and the grammar of doge? It wasn't my mental state: the experience of making a meme and the experience of analyzing one feel very much the same from the inside, the same fizzing ebullience that I get when any kind of writing is going really, really well. (In many ways, the irresistible lure of analyzing memes is simply a meme itself, one that mashes up the conventions of academic and internet cultures.) The difference also wasn't individual people's reactions to the memes: my short-lived 2012 memeblog is probably one of millions of obscure internet mashups made by individual people aiming to strongly appeal to their particular subcommunity. What was unique about the memes that took off was not the in-jokes, but the scale: in a world where in-jokes

*Notwithstanding the fact that Prime Minister Justin Trudeau was once a member of the latter, and I do not know his status on the former.

happen all the time and distribution costs are zero, a few of them can get really big because their in-groups are actually very large, like "people who use the internet," "people who agree that this particular cat looks very grumpy," or "people who saw the previous very popular in-joke." The beauty of memes that are predicated on internet culture itself is that they can bring the internet together; the hardship of them is that they draw boundaries around who gets to be an insider and who doesn't.

Even as the internet briefly united around doge, the meme space was fragmenting further. Advice Animals had been enabled by meme generation sites, which also hosted the memes once they were made, meaning that you could browse them directly to keep up. Doge and snek lost that consistent aesthetic by virtue of further advantages in custom image labeling, and were no longer spread by meme generation sites. Understandably, this freaked out two then PhD students who were writing dissertations about memes. In their subsequent books, they grappled with the idea that they might be obsolete before they were even published. As Ryan Milner put it, in his book about memes, "My moment of reckoning also came in 2014, when I was discussing my PhD dissertation with a student. 'I remember memes,' the college sophomore said. 'They were really big in high school. Junior year.' The thought that my two-year-old dissertation was now a historical analysis of a dead communicative genre prompted some angst." Whitney Phillips described similar shifts in her book about internet trolls, and stated one of the causes to be the rise of the website Know Your Meme, a sort of Urban Dictionary of memes: "Know Your Meme was written with the novice in mind, with detailed, almost clinical explanations of the Internet's most popular participatory content. [It] helped democratize a space that had previously been restricted to the initiated."

But that's not the end of the meme story. During the 2016 US presidential election, memes became more popular than ever, often as a way of making abhorrent beliefs look appealingly ironic. This phenomenon spawned serious op-eds about political memes from mainstream outlets like *USA Today* and *The Guardian,* a Know Your Meme entry considerably more extensive than the ones for the previous two elections, and even an official HillaryClinton.com meme explainer of why the Pepe the Frog meme was linked to white supremacy. Mike Godwin himself felt the need to clarify that Godwin's Law only applied to frivolous Holocaust comparisons, not to calling out genuine similarities, tweeting, "By all means, compare these shitheads to Nazis. Again and again. I'm with you." Around the same time, "wholesome" memes of cute doggos and puppers rejuvenated social media feeds that seemed daily filled with fresh horrors.

In 2017, an article for the news site Mic reported on a trend in prestigious US college admissions: students were making and sharing memes on college-specific Facebook groups, as a way of bonding with fellow students or making friends before arriving at school. Some prospective students even assessed the quality of a college's memes in deciding whether to go there. As the then eighteen-year-old Brandon Epstein, founder of MIT Memes for Intellectual Beings and Spicy Memelords, put it, "We're the ones that have been most immersed in meme culture. When last year's freshmen became freshmen, memes weren't the cultural monolith they are now. Considering that memes really rose to mainstream prominence during the time when we were in high school, I think there's a bigger focus on memes for people my age."

At first glance, this looks contradictory.

How is it that we have a college student in 2014 claiming that memes are dead and, three meme-filled years later, a different college freshman claiming that the students only a year older don't truly understand memes? (Both students were mere children during Peak Lolcat in 2007, and neither of them was even born when Mike Godwin started seeding counter-Nazi memes on Usenet in 1990, if we want to really put our harrumphing hats on.)

It doesn't make sense if we think of memes as a single, unified phenomenon. True, lolcats and Godwin's Law are now historical memes, but there were certainly remixed images and texts and videos of various kinds that were being shared throughout these years. In fact, a new category of image meme was born during this very time period: where the animal-based memes from lolcat to snek used superimposed text to narrate the interior monologue of the animal, the newer memes used superimposed text to label objects in some sort of relation to each other, such as Distracted Boyfriend, a stock photo showing a boyfriend looking interestedly at another girl while his girlfriend looks on, aghast, with the people labeled, or Galaxy Brain, a series of expanding neon diagrams of the brain, each diagram labeled.

Where, in this hubbub of activity, did the meme have time to die?

If we think of memes as a claim on internet culture, things become clearer. Memes periodically shift away from one of their founder populations. Those particular memes, to that particular group, are indeed dead. But as long as people are creating culture on the internet, a different group will emerge with a different format to take up the mantle of "meme." Memes had shifted yet again, from the Full Internet People to the Post Internet People, the ones who had no recollection of a life without internet.

The meme is not dead: it's reborn.

LONG LIVE THE MEME

On my wall hangs an embroidered meme. It consists of an embroidered peasant with arms outstretched and the stitched, faux-old-timey caption BEHOLD THE FIELD IN WHICH I GROW MY FVCKS. LAY THINE EYES VPON IT AND THOV SHALT SEE THAT IT IS BARREN. It's based off an internet meme which reads the same thing, created with a meme generation site that turns your words into an imitation of the Bayeux Tapestry, placing stitched-looking letters on a fabric-looking background.

The Behold the Field meme is an item

of internet culture, but it's also an item of English culture, dating back nearly a thousand years to the Norman Conquest. The unnamed women who stitched the nearly 230-foot-long Bayeux Tapestry were also combining images and words, dealing in stock characters (mustachioed Anglo-Saxons and clean-shaven Normans), reifying and mythologizing current events of the era (our impression that Harold Godwinson, last king of the Anglo-Saxons, was killed by an arrow to the eye in the Battle of Hastings is based on this tapestry). The tapestry has been remade at other times, often by stitching: a full-sized copy was created by the members of the Leek Embroidery Society during the Victorian era, and a *Game of Thrones* Bayeux Tapestry was unveiled in Northern Ireland in 2017.

The Behold the Field meme even has a stylized sort of language, a creative distortion that draws on, rather than internet slang, our shared understanding as English speakers of what "old-timey English" sounds like, with "thou" and a "u" that looks like "v" and vocabulary like "barren" (even though the original tapestry was in Latin).

I can't claim to be original: I made it because I'd seen other people's embroideries of the same meme, via photos that they put online. I looked at several versions while making mine, but I also changed several features: I used backstitch instead of cross-stitch because it looks smoother, and I made the dude peasant gesturing at the field into a lady peasant who looks kind of like me. After all, this is my personal field in which to grow my fucks, and this is my personal claim on internet culture.

But what exactly am I claiming? I reproduced this particular meme in this particular format, rather than, say, painting a lolcat, because it fascinates me in its juxtaposition of old and new, of oral culture and digital culture, of domestic and profane, of the aspiration to give fewer fucks and the reality that delicate stitchwork requires many fucks indeed. Even the circumstances under which I made it were a juxtaposition: at a gathering of crafty internet people who I knew because I'd written those *Toast* articles on meme linguistics, who gave me advice on how many strands of floss to use and how to avoid lumps on the back of the fabric (I also snuck out my phone and googled diagrams of how to do a French knot).

Embroidering the meme was the most digital kind of art I've ever done in physical form. The canvas of the fabric is a grid of small threads going sideways and down, a grid of pixels that you can count and balance much like you'd do in Photoshop. I later learned that Susan Kare, who designed most of the original Apple computer icons, cited her experience with needlepoint and mosaics as preparation for creating icons from small arrays of pixels. The thread was surprisingly friendly to my novice embroidery skills: if I didn't like a stitch, I could just unpick it and start again. The fabric would retain just a couple small pinprick holes, which closed up again as I kept handling it — more like the endless "undo" of a computer program than a canvas that gets stained or a sheet of paper that retains smudges and dents after being erased.

Both memes and needlework are collective folk texts that spread because people remix and remake them. The words "text" and "textile" have a common origin, from a Proto-Indo-European root *teks,* "to weave." Writing and weaving are both acts of creation by bringing together. A storyteller is a spinner of yarns, and the internet's founding metaphor is of a web. If we go far enough back, before printing presses and cameras and photocopiers introduced the notion of faithful reproduction, all transmission is re-creation. *Teks* is also the root in the word "technology," which at one point meant a systematic treatise on an art or craft, or even a grammar, before it referred to a study of mechanical or industrial arts (a 1902 dictionary gives the examples of "spinning, metal-working, or brewing") and then to digital tech.

Memes have coexisted with and been made possible by technology for a long time. Physically mailed chain letters such as the Send-a-Dime "Prosperity Club," which made headlines in 1935, and chain emails ("Every time this email is forwarded, Bill Gates will donate a dollar to cure cancer") are fairly well known. Less well known is a precursor that came in between chain letters and emails, known as "faxlore" or "Xeroxlore": jokes, stories, and warnings that circulated via email, fax, and photocopy. The most famous of these was Blinkenlights, a mock-German warning to stick on the wall above any fancy equipment saying that it "ist nicht für der gefingerpoken und mittengraben. . . . Das rubbernecken sichtseeren keepen das cotten-pickenen hans in das pockets muss; relaxen und watchen das blinkenlichten." As Michael J. Preston described in his article coining the term "Xeroxlore" in 1974, this genre tended to feature mock memos and other workplace humor, since most people didn't have access to a photocopier at home.

But while the photocopier and fax machine enabled these stories to spread, it was harder to remix them when copy-pasting involved literal photocopiers and jars of paste.

Like how expressive typography and co-text doodles predate the internet, in-joke replication has a multigenerational cultural history. I, as a Full Internet Person, remember Blinkenlights as a chain email that my dad (Semi Internet) forwarded me in the early 2000s, but the Jargon File dates it back to 1955 at IBM, from the days when computers really did blink rows of LEDs rather than have a screen. The Jargon File also points to further roots in mock-German signs common in Allied machine shops during and after the Second World War. One such sign, although lacking the titular word "blinkenlights," has several familiar phrases: "Das Machinen ist nodt for gefingerpoken und mittengrabben. . . . Das rubbernekken sightseeren und stupidisch volk bast relaxen." My dad was definitely not around for World War II, but I mentioned Xeroxlore to him anyway. "Oh yeah," he said, "your grandfather was really into photocopied jokes. Even after he retired, he kept a fax machine at home for years so his buddies could send him the latest jokes. He had a folder an inch thick with the best of them." My grandfather couldn't be said to have been an internet person: he had email for a while, but he never had a smartphone or a social media account anywhere, and yet there was an extended period when he was as into curating his own meme collection as any teenage denizen of Tumblr or Imgur.

The next time I visited, my dad produced a nondescript brown manila file folder stuffed with loose papers. "I found this while clearing out Granddad's office. I thought you might be interested."

My grandfather's meme stash? Of course I was.

Looking through the papers, the first thing that jumped out at me was how large the letters were. If I'd had any doubts that there were truly senior citizen memes, the font size — double or triple what I would use — would have confirmed it. These documents were produced by and for people who needed reading glasses. Alas, it appeared that the folder I held in my hands was merely a portion of my grandfather's meme collection — no nineties faxlore was to be found. (My father pointed out that most of the fax memes would have been printed on rolls of shiny thermal paper, like many receipts still are, which is not at all durable.) Instead, the collection consisted entirely of oft-forwarded emails, printed out from Microsoft Outlook between about 2004 and 2011. It was clear, however, that "an inch thick" had been an underestimate.

Only slightly daunted, I started reading anyway. But here I was disappointed. The jokes were unoriginal and repetitive — lots of professions and nationalities and public figures walking into bars and arriving at pearly gates, precocious children and human-acting pets making jokes that belied their innocence, stock figures like blondes and country bumpkins and old married couples playing to and occasionally subverting their trope. Experimentally, I googled "classic jokes." Yep, here was the same genre, misattributed to the same few legendary wits or lacking attribution at all, listed by the hundreds on websites with bad graphic design, replete with groan-worthy puns and cringe-worthy stereotypes. If this was the legacy of my grandfather as memelord, I wasn't sure I wanted to inherit it.

But where's the enjoyment in a meme if not from repetition? The first time I see a cat or dog with peculiar grammar, I'm somewhere between mildly tickled and simply confused. It's around the third or fifth version that the humor kicks in, and it's around the twentieth incarnation, when I think I've gotten tired of it but someone comes up with a truly spectacular reimagining, that I laugh the hardest. Memes are full of stock characters. That's the entire conceit of the Advice Animals: they started with thematic animal mashups, like Philosoraptor and Socially Awkward Penguin, and expanded to humanoid stereotypes that come with just as much gendered and racial baggage as the "classic" jokes, like Overly Attached Girlfriend or High Expectations Asian Father.

Stock figures and caricatures go a lot further back than classic jokes. Public figures and archetypes are found in political cartoons through the eighteenth and nineteenth centuries, such as the donkey and elephant of American political parties, which are found in cartoons of the 1870s. Martin Luther, in a pamphlet from 1521 designed to drum up populist support against the Catholic Church, commissioned cartoons which remixed iconic biblical scenes to comment on then current ecclesiastical politics. (Religious stock figures retain their appeal in meme form: in one repeated image, a Jesus painting photoshopped with hipster glasses contains the caption "I had followers before Twitter.") Personifications of places and abstract ideas, like Liberty and Britannia, go back to Roman goddesses, while ancient

402

Greek vases and theatrical masks also contained caricatures. Animal stories that make a point about the human world are perhaps the oldest of all. They're found in Aesop's fables, nursery rhymes, and all sorts of ancient myths and legends.

What's unique about memes, then, isn't that they're participatory, or that they remix visuals and stock figures. What makes a meme a meme instead of a cartoon, a joke, or a fad is the same thing that lends a frisson of irony to the claim that my grandfather had a meme stash: a meme is an atom of internet culture, and my grandfather was never really an internet person. Creating, sharing, or laughing at a meme is staking a claim to being an insider: I am a member of internet culture, it says, and if you don't get this, then you aren't.

Like how typographical irony creates space for sincerity, jokes are also claims to cultural space. Laughing at an in-joke says, "I too was here when this happened." Laughing at a joke about shared struggles says, "We're all in this together." Laughing at a racist or sexist joke says, "I accept these stereotypes." Memes can be a linguistic recruitment tool: observers want to be part of the in-group that gets the memes, whether benignly (I've seen linguistics memes encourage people to

403

read the linguistics articles on Wikipedia) or for more nefarious purposes (far-right discussion forums use memes and irony strategically to promote extreme ideology with a veneer of plausible deniability). Explaining a joke and explaining a meme fall flat for the same reasons, because "getting it" without explanation is kind of the point.

If a meme is an atom of internet culture, then as internet culture becomes simply popular culture, memes spread with it. The linguist Erin McKean tweeted a dialogue with her teenage son that illustrates this point:

KID: fidget spinners are, like, a physical meme
ME: THAT'S A FAD

The comparison between meme and fad is not entirely off base. Technologist An Xiao Mina has written about how the internet, and especially manufacturing-on-demand services in Shenzhen, China, has made it possible for physical objects to go viral and be remixed in much the same way as memes. It's never been easier to get a custom design printed on a t-shirt or to collectively brainstorm protest slogans, which then spread and replicate again via photos on social media. When I decided to embroider the

Behold the Field meme because I've seen photos of other people's embroideries, was I participating in internet culture or material culture? At this point, is there even a difference?

Any community that talks with each other via the internet now has its own set of memes. There are memes about videogames and parenting and anime. There are political memes for any persuasion. There are linguistics memes, which I'm partial to for obvious reasons.* (I conscientiously procrastinated on this book by making a linguistics version for every meme that crossed my Twitter feed while I was supposed to be writing.) The Library of Congress archives memes now, preserving things like the Lolcat Bible, Urban Dictionary, and Know Your Meme. It calls them, charmingly and also not entirely inaccurately, "folklore." There are people with full-time jobs in advanced memology, like the academics I've mentioned already, the staff of Know Your Meme, and Amanda Brennan, Tumblr's "meme librarian."

Our meme dissertators from 2014, Whitney Phillips and Ryan Milner, wrote a later book together about memes as a kind of internet

*Linguist Llama says, "I wanna be a schwa. It's never stressed."

folklore, drawing parallels to dirty limericks, ghost stories, and pranks. If a meme can refer to anything that's popular, we've almost come full circle, back to Dawkins's original definition of a meme as an idea that spreads through cultural replication.

But there's still something that makes a meme distinct from an idea that remains obscure or merely becomes popular without spawning imitations. Often, it's that memes are *weird*. Why do memes look like they do? In particular, why do they often involve distinctive and weird linguistic styles? Limor Shifman provides a tantalizing clue: she did a study of YouTube videos that spawned many imitations compared with videos that had the same number of views but few or no imitations. Surprisingly, she found that the more professional-looking videos were less likely to be memed. In Shifman's words: " 'Bad' texts make 'good' memes." Or in other words, since memes are based on active involvement, "The ostensibly unfinished, unpolished, amateur-looking, and even weird video invites people to fill in the gaps, address the puzzles, or mock its creator."

Incoherent language or bad photoshop accomplishes the same thing. Just as slang or minimalist typography can convey that you're approachable or invite people to understand your layers of irony, the playful language of many memes provides a clear route to participation. Formally constructed cultural items hide the patchwork and edits and labor that go into them, making the aspiring author or artist intimidated by the roughness of their first drafts in comparison to the polish of others' final versions. Incoherence does the opposite: the meme as internet folklore is imperfect, constantly under construction, and something you could write, too. Release the meme into the world anonymously or from behind a pseudonym, as many people do, and it matters even less if it's a flop. The stylized language signals their genre, the same way as "once upon a time" or "knock knock" signals a fairy tale or a knock-knock joke.

Writing that builds on the universe of other writing is among our oldest forms of storytelling: the *Iliad* is attributed to Homer but started out as oral literature; Virgil's *Aeneid* borrows a minor character from the *Iliad,* Aeneas, and makes him into a hero of Rome; Dante's *Divine Comedy* then borrows the historical personage of Virgil and makes him into Dante's guide to Purgatory and Hell. But building on another universe requires making assumptions about what your audience already knows, and that's tricky.

In a world of only print, I have to decide exactly how much of a source to quote, and as a reader you can't see anything more than that without a lot of effort. If you're lucky, you might have the original book on your shelf, and you can go look up a reference — as long as I've provided a page number, and as long as it's the same edition. Otherwise, you're making a trip to the library, and who knows if they even have a copy? With the internet, we often have access to the full text of the original source at the twitch of a finger. When I'm writing something online, I can use a potentially obscure term or a reference by just linking to an explanation or source, letting a text serve multiple audiences. People who already get the reference won't bother to click, while people who don't can click through for a fuller explanation than I could possibly provide by interrupting myself to explain. Even when I haven't provided a link, people can discover the context by searching. Without hypertext and search, I have to consider my audience more narrowly, deciding at every stage whether to risk boring some readers with a definition or confusing others without one.

The internet has been very good for shared

authorship, and not just of the memeish kind. Take Wikipedia, which has used volunteer editing and the collaborative wiki format to create an English-language encyclopedia sixty times larger than any that's ever been printed — plus a couple hundred encyclopedias of varying sizes in other languages. Take fanfiction: communities of people forming around a particular source text and rewriting it in conversation with each other. Though fanfiction existed before the internet (Sherlock Holmes and *Star Trek* being notable examples), the interest-based discussion-board structure of the early internet encouraged fans to find each other, especially fans of *The X-Files* and *Buffy the Vampire Slayer.* Later waves of fans showed no signs of slowing down. They've gathered on blogs like LiveJournal and later Tumblr, and fic-hosting websites like Fanfiction.net, Archive of Our Own, and Wattpad, writing about Harry Potter, One Direction, and the trifecta of Superwholock (*Supernatural, Doctor Who,* and BBC *Sherlock*), at a volume of posts at least double that of Wikipedia.

Our modern, Western notion that authorship should be solo and original is comparatively young and culturally bound, dating back only to after we had the ability to make faithful and exact copies at a mass scale.

Copyright started evolving into its modern form in the centuries after the invention of the printing press made copying easy. In other words, we've had the right to adapt longer than we've had the right to prevent copying. I'm grateful for copyright and solo authorship: it's what allows me, and all the other authors I've loved, to make any kind of living. But let's not pretend that professionalized creativity is the only kind of creativity. There's a joy in a joke well told, a wicked delight in a delicately stitched swear word, a burning curiosity that can only be quenched by rewriting one's favorite characters in a new environment — and yes, an exhilaration in riffing together in perfect synchro-meme.

Whether the memeish subculture is large or small, creating and sharing memes is an act of claiming space as an internet person, of saying that people like you deserve to be on the internet. Perhaps the final stage of meme maturity will be when we stop asserting that other groups are Doing Memes Wrong and instead recognize them as cultural objects that come in multiple and evolving genres.

In the meantime, though, we're still bridging the gap between people raised on internet culture and people trying to understand how the internet can even have a culture, so here's an analogy. When I was a kid, I just couldn't wrap my head around the crossword puzzles they printed in the newspaper. Sure, I understood how a crossword puzzle might be fun in theory, but in practice, I could just never get the clues. How was I supposed to know about events and celebrities from before I was even born? How was anyone?? Where was the hidden list of cultural references that everyone was cribbing from???

I never found such a list. But when I happen across a crossword puzzle now, in an airplane magazine or a relative's morning paper, something curious has happened. Somehow, now, I can solve most of the clues. Movies? I remember when they came out, even if I didn't see them. Politicians? I remember them being elected, even when I wish I didn't. As for the references from before I was born, they're getting fewer and fewer, but the ones that remain have come up in conversation enough over the years that I somehow know which ones are fair game for the puzzling public.

I couldn't make a list of these references and how I know them all, but they're there, waiting to be pulled out of me by a well-placed clue or a few key letters. I can now tap into the cultural conversation that crossword puzzles assume, in a way that was

411

completely baffling to me as a child outside it.

It's the same thing with internet culture. I can't make an exhaustive list of all the memes that I know, and I definitely can't explain why a given meme tickles me in exactly the right place, any more than my grandfather could articulate to me what it felt like for his joke collection to feel new and exciting and worth preserving. We're used to in-jokes and shared jargon out of the mouths of families, longtime friends, workplace buddies, even entire industries and geographical regions. It's the written part that throws us off, because we're used to written things being formal, and part of that formality is a cultural flattening to appeal to a general audience: a newspaper crossword puzzle is created for a mass-market newspaper reader. Informal writing is different, and the meme is the cultural atom of this difference. We're still so delighted when we come across something that seems to have been written exactly for our own tastes. (Anyone who's confused can google it.)

Like all cultures, internet culture is referential, baffling to outsiders, relying more on shared history than explicit instruction. Like all cultures, it's not truly a single culture: it has some parts that are widely shared and others that occupy tiny niches. Like all cultures, importantly, it's in flux, however neatly we archive our favorite parts and attempt to pass them down to our offspring.

So where else might this state of flux be taking us?

CHAPTER 8:
A NEW METAPHOR

When you think about the English language, what do you picture?

I decided to consult the oracle of the contemporary human id to find out. In other words, I searched for "English language" in Google Images and twenty other stock photo sites.

What I found was books. There were other motifs, too, such as chalkboards, speech bubbles, wooden letter blocks, and a couple inexplicably disturbing tongues with flags painted on them, but mostly, there were books. Books all alone, books with apples and pencils, books with people reading them, books with "English" on the front cover, books piled up in stacks with "English" and "Grammar" and "Spelling" on the spines, and especially books open to a dictionary entry for the word "English." So very many photographs of dictionary entries.

To dictionary editors, this is not surprising.

Many will tell you that people think of "the" dictionary as the English language itself, as if there weren't even multiple dictionaries, as if they weren't made by fallible humans. Lexicographer Kory Stamper kept a record of the emails she received from Merriam-Webster's Ask an Editor service, and many of them consisted of people wanting their favorite words added or most hated words removed, in the belief that a sanction by Merriam-Webster is what makes a word "real" or not.

Even those of us who know that a single book isn't the sole repository of a language and that dictionaries are records of how people are already using the language, not providers of words for us to start using — we still often think of the English language as contained within a sufficiently large quantity of books. We think of it as "the language of Shakespeare," or the twenty volumes of the second edition of the *Oxford English Dictionary,* or the entire Library of Congress, or the millions of books scanned and made searchable by Google Books.

This association isn't accidental.

If we look at how frequently people wrote the phrase "English language" across all the books scanned by Google, from 1500 to 2000, we see a major upswing between 1750 and 1800. It's consistently low beforehand,

and consistently high thereafter. "English" and "language" by themselves are pretty much steady — it's just the two words together that go up.

What happened in that period? Well, in 1755, Samuel Johnson published *A Dictionary of the English Language,* the first major English print dictionary. Johnson's dictionary became widely cited, and Johnson was interested in defining exactly what the English language consisted of. As he put it in the dictionary's preface: "I found our speech copious without order, and energetick without rules: wherever I turned my view, there was perplexity to be disentangled, and confusion to be regulated."

We can't just blame Sam — he was part of a movement. The late 1700s and early 1800s saw the beginnings of a massive trend in publishing dictionaries and grammars and books about "the English language." On the one hand, this period brought us the first incredibly cool dialect maps that we saw in Chapter 2. On the other, this detailed record-making was a way of constructing what it meant to be the English language, or even a language at all. And what it meant to be a language was to be a book. As late as 1977, a Merriam-Webster ad campaign proclaimed, "Webster's New Collegiate Dictionary: it's where the words live."

But the book metaphor has run its course. Just as early analogies of the brain compared it to a steam engine or hydraulic pump, while many modern neuroscientists invoke computers as metaphor, our language metaphors, too, need to evolve with the times. Here, perhaps, is the greatest impact that the internet can have on the English language: as a new metaphor.

Like the big collaborative projects of the internet, such as Wikipedia and Firefox, like the decentralized network of websites and machines that make up the internet itself, language is a network, a web. Language is the ultimate participatory democracy. To put it in technological terms, language is humanity's most spectacular open source project.

Just as we find things on the internet by following links from one place to another, language spreads and disseminates through our conversations and interactions. We each inhabit our own idiosyncratic corner of the internet, a weird mix of friends, acquaintances, people we haven't talked with in ages, and people we secretly think are way too cool for us. Likewise, we each speak a slightly different idiolect informed by our entire unique linguistic history.

When we thought of language as a book,

we thought of it as static and authoritative, a thing which would be better if we returned to a pristine first edition and erased all the messy new words that people had scribbled into the margins. But there is no pristine first edition of a network. A network is not debased as it changes; its flexibility is a key part of its strength. So, too, is language enriched and made alive again for each subsequent generation as new connections grow and old ones wither away.

When we thought of language like a book, we thought of it as an unruly mess of words that had to be kept in order, like a Victorian gardener constantly retrimming the hedges into spirals and globes. When we think of language like a network, we can see order as a thing that emerges out of the natural tendencies of the individuals, the way that a forest keeps itself in order even though it doesn't get pruned and weeded.

When we thought of language as a book, we thought of it as linear and finite. A book can only have so many pages, so you have to decide what to keep in, what to fence out, and how to order what remains. If you and I buy the same dictionary, we read the same exact words, making it seem like there is a single, finite English language that everyone agrees upon, which can be contained between two covers. But the internet has no beginning or end, and it's growing faster than any one person can follow. Sure, it does technically take up space, in the form of fiber-optic cables running under oceans and chilled rows of hard drives in data centers, but while a book is always telling your hands how many pages it has left, an internet device is a portal to a universe bigger than you can fathom.

A single human mind can come up with a sentence that's never been said before in human history, and it's not even hard. Here's one: "The hesitant otters enjoyed the moon floating above the purple forest." In fact, even "The otters enjoyed the moon" was enough to get me zero Google hits at time of writing. You can do it yourself: make a sentence containing an animal that would be unwise to keep as a pet, a verb with at least two syllables, a color or texture that you're wearing, and something nonwearable in your immediate environment. Your odds are really good that no one's ever said it before. But you don't even have to go surreal: try googling in quotation marks the last message you texted that was longer than ten words. You'll probably get zero hits.

When we know language as a network, we realize that any portrait of it is incomplete, and that's a marvelous thing. Many web-pages are dynamic, generated only as we reach for them by searching for or posting something brand-new. So, too, is the creative capacity of language greater than its entire recorded history. Any one of us can coin a word or compose a sentence that has never been said before, and it now exists in the language as soon as we utter it, whether it winks in and out for a single moment or whether it catches on and endures in the minds of people yet unborn. When you lay a book down and come back to it, you expect all its ink to stay where you left it, but the only languages that stay unchanging are the dead ones. When you step away from a living language, or a network made of human beings, you don't expect it to fall silent and still without you.

A language with people but no books is a living language that can always create books, but a language with books and no people exists only in pale, shadowed, ghostly form. Johnson and his contemporaries found English "energetick without rules" by the standards of Latin because they were comparing a living language with a fossil. Fossils can teach us a lot of things, but that doesn't mean that living animals are only worthy of study once they've been stripped down to their bones and footprints. Rather than thinking of books as a way of embalming language, of rendering it fixed and dead for eternity (or at least of trapping and caging it so it doesn't move around quite so much), we can think of them as maps and guidebooks to help people navigate language's living, moving splendor. Every atlas eventually becomes a history book, but a globe is still a glorious thing to feel spinning under your hands with potential.

It's always tempting to apologize, when writing about technology, for how out of date this book is going to be at some point and all the areas that I inevitably haven't covered. But that would be missing the point. The purpose of this book isn't to enshrine internet language, like an unlucky dinosaur caught in quicksand, as if it's a thing that I can capture and preserve. Rather, it's to provide a snapshot of a particular era and a lens that we can use to look at future changes. When we study only formal language, we see through this tiny pinhole into what English can do. When we study informal language, we open our minds wide. We step out of the library and see the complexity of the wide world that surrounds us.

So if you're wondering why this book hasn't talked about something you're interested in, consider this an invitation to draw your own map of another portion of the territory, to conduct your own internet linguistic research. The future of research on internet language lies with you, the reader, just as much as the future of language itself lies with you, the speaker. In particular, here are a few areas that I think may be fruitful for future research. For one thing, this has been a book primarily about English, and in particular American English, simply because a lot of dialect maps are drawn of the United States. But there are other Englishes and other languages, especially as the second half of the world's population comes online.

Around 7,000 languages are spoken in the world today, and the vast majority of them have only a tiny amount of representation on the internet. Wikipedia only has articles in 293 languages, and half of those languages have less than ten thousand articles. Google Translate supports 103 languages, but many of the language pairs are translated via English. Major social networks support even fewer: Facebook's interface is available in about 100, Twitter's in about 50, and new social networks tend to launch exclusively in one language. Even relatively substantial national languages, like Icelandic, are becoming displaced by English and a handful of other languages with big internet presences, and those that don't have government funding behind them are doing even worse. Unfortunately, the versions of these statistics that I included in the first draft of this chapter in 2016 had barely changed when I updated them in early 2019. The momentum for making the internet hospitable to every language is slowing where it should be increasing. Nonetheless, users are still figuring out ways to communicate online: people who are illiterate or who speak languages that don't have well-established writing systems or autocomplete tools are among the highest users of voice texting, or sending five- to thirty-second audio clips through chat apps.

A second broad domain for continued investigation is technological changes. Just as digital tone of voice developed in all caps and all lowercase, with emoticons and emoji, further changes in how we convey the intentions behind our words will also develop as technology evolves. We'll undoubtedly come up with new ways to express our intentions as voice, image, and video tools become easier to integrate into our conversations. Normal people don't talk in the vanilla standardized language of books and television, and we'll hack at our communicative tools until they let us reflect that, or else relegate them to information or entertainment rather than communication.

Our collective societal relationship to technologically mediated communication is also changing. At the moment, there's still a generation gap. But the gap isn't really about whether you know what the acronyms stand for or which buttons to press: it's about whether you dismiss the expressive capacity of informal writing or whether you assume it. As an older person who'd recently been told that ending a text with a period made them sound annoyed told me, "They know I'm old! Why would anyone assume I know how to communicate something that subtle in a text?" All three generations of Internet People assume that everyone is constantly communicating subtle emotional signals in text, even if there's some minor disagreement about exactly which subtleties mean what. Getting an Internet Person to stop overthinking a text message is just as impossible as getting people of any age to stop reading emotional nuances from tone of voice. We can't help it.

But relatively soon, there will no longer be any people left who aren't internet people, at least not at a generational level, not in major world languages. The internet will be like prior technologies that no one could escape: the radio or the telephone or the book. An individual person can still refuse to use social media or have a smartphone, just like a person in the 1980s could refuse to own a television set or have a phone line, but you'll still know a lot about it regardless. The internet has become ambient, an inescapable part of the broader culture.

That's why I've avoided referring to things that aren't online as "real life." The internet has become real life. Popular culture and internet culture overlap more often than they diverge. True, "irl" and "real life" are common expressions, and it's quite possible that they may stick around with their original connotation washed out through continued use. But that hasn't happened quite yet, and in the meantime there are real harms to not recognizing the common humanity of the real people who are touched or harmed at the other end of our digital messages.

Similarly, it's easy to assume that all new words in the twenty-first century are internet words, because we may notice them first online. But Future English was *always* going to be different from Present English, just like Present English is different from the English spoken a hundred or a thousand years ago. While the internet is often a means for spreading new words, that doesn't mean it's always the cause of them. It's important to recall that while the *linguistic* features of teenagers are a harbinger of the future — the vowels, the words, the inflections — we shouldn't confuse them with the *social* features of teenagers — the cliques, the social drama, who's a jock or a nerd, and so on. Kids eventually grow up and get jobs and find social niches that more or less suit them, and take it in their own turn to complain about the next generation — middle school is an aberration for all of us. Interviewing a couple teenagers about what's cool on social media may tell us which linguistic features and technological platforms we'll all be using in a couple years, but it won't tell us what our social lives will feel like from the inside. (Thank goodness.)

We know that language as a human ability is so very old — some hundred thousand years older than any form of writing — and what that means is that language is incredibly durable. We know that we've met many societies without any form of writing system, but we've never met any without spoken or signed language at all. Furthermore, linguistic complexity is unrelated to the complexity of the material culture it comes from. Language has existed with or without all kinds of technology — writing, agriculture, aqueducts, electricity, industrialization, automobiles, airplanes, cameras, photocopiers, televisions — and the internet is no exception. In fact, language's only known predator is other people: many languages have been stamped out or imposed on others through war or conquest.

The changeability of language is its strength: if children had to copy exactly how their parents spoke in order for language to be transmitted, language would be brittle and fragile. It would be losable, the way that ancient techniques for art or architecture can be lost. But because we remake language at every generation, because we learn it from our peers, not just our elders, because we can make ourselves understood even though we all speak subtly different personal varieties, language is flexible and strong.

When we thought of language like a book, perhaps it was natural that we were worried and careful about what we enshrined in it. But now that we can think of language like the internet, it's clear that there is space for innovation, space for many Englishes and many other languages besides, space for linguistic playfulness and creativity. There's space, in this glorious linguistic web, for you.

ACKNOWLEDGMENTS

The best part about writing a book about the internet is that when you inevitably get distracted by the internet, it often ends up sparking something to write about. Thanks to internet people in general.

A big problem in internet research is that half the links you cite will stop working in just two years. To mitigate link rot, every link in this book has been saved in the Internet Archive's Wayback Machine, and I've made a donation to help it stay in operation. Enter any broken urls at archive.org for a backed-up copy.

I'd like to thank my editor, Courtney Young, for understanding the spirit of the book better than I did myself at times. Thank you also to the rest of the team at Riverhead Books, especially Kevin Murphy, and the copyediting team for gracefully handling a style guide founded on internet style; jacket designer Grace Han for landing on a

429

brilliant representation of internet writing; and my publicist, Shailyn Tavella, for her energy and enthusiasm. I'd also like to thank my agent, Howard Yoon, for all his support behind the scenes, Dara Kaye for her sense of humor and advice on multilingualism, and the rest of the team at Ross Yoon.

Massive thanks to Nicole Cliffe at *The Toast* for responding to my most ridiculous pitches with unmitigated enthusiasm, and to the Toasties for making me write better just to imagine you reading me. Huge thanks also to *Wired* and Alexis Sobel Fitts, Andrea Valdez, and Emily Dreyfuss, for creating such a fantastic new home for the Resident Linguist series. I'd also like to thank for their mentorship Mignon Fogarty, Arika Okrent, Clive Thompson, Emily Gref, Jennifer Kutz, Erin McKean, and Ben Zimmer. Special thanks to Laura Bailey, Megan Garber, Molly Atlas, and the American Dialect Society for the title, and to A.E. Prevost for their attention to detail and highly articulate cat.

I'm greatly indebted to previous scholars of the internet, whose vivid descriptions and archives helped me get a feeling for the early days of networked computers. I'm equally indebted to junior internet researchers working on emerging internet communication styles beyond my experience. Special thanks to everyone who sent me student papers, conference presentations, master's theses, PhD dissertations, and other cutting-edge internet linguistics.

Thank you to my educational institutions: King's-Edgehill School, the International Baccalaureate, Queen's University, McGill University, and my advisors, especially Jessica Coon and Janine Metallic. Many thanks also to the readers, listeners, and patrons of my blog and podcast, whose enthusiasm was a vital counterbalance to the solitude of book writing.

I'd like to thank my family, my first and longest-running test audience for articulating why I find linguistics so exciting. In particular, I appreciate my sister Janis for answering questions on whether things were still cool, my brother Malcolm for thoughts on breaking down massive goals, and my parents for their complete trust that I was doing what I needed to do and that somehow it would work out, even when they didn't understand any of it.

A big thank you to the ling-friends who encouraged my first forays into pop linguistics, Leland Paul Kusmer and Caroline Anderson; to the ling-friends who came along a little later, Moti Lieberman, A.E. Prevost,

Jane Solomon, Jeffrey Lamontagne, Emily Gref, Sunny Ananth, and Linguist Twitter; and to non-ling friends including Sabina, Jenny, and the groupchat. Special thanks to Alex and family for letting me stay with them in NYC, and to the coffeeshops of Montreal, especially the ones that stay open late.

Perhaps the biggest thanks of all to Lauren Gawne, my cohost on *Lingthusiasm*. Not just for cracking the emoji chapter by introducing me to gesture research, but also for countless helpful comments, both in the manuscript and when I couldn't look at the manuscript anymore. I never expected to find myself in one of those fabled business partnerships one reads about and I'm so grateful to have ended up there with you.

NOTES

Chapter 1. Informal Writing

In the year 800: James Westfall Thompson. 1960. *The Literacy of the Laity in the Middle Ages.* Burt Franklin.

informal survey: Gretchen McCulloch. November 24, 2015. twitter.com/Gretchen AMcC/status/669255229729341441.

the word "rhinoceros": Douglas Harper. 2001–2018. "Rhino." *Online Etymological Dictionary.* www.etymonline.com/word /rhino.

One study showed: T. Florian Jaeger and Celeste Kidd. 2008. "Toward a Unified Model of Redundancy Avoidance and Strategic Lengthening." Presented at the 21st Annual CUNY Conference on Human Sentence Processing, March 2008, Chapel Hill, North Carolina.

new symbols such as & and %: Keith Houston. June 26, 2011. "The Ampersand," part 2 of 2. *Shady Characters.*

www.shadycharacters.co.uk/2011/06/the
-ampersand-part-2-of-2/. Keith Houston.
March 17, 2015. "Miscellany No. 59: The
Percent Sign." *Shady Characters.* www
.shadycharacters.co.uk/2015/03/percent
-sign/.

The word "acronym" itself entered English: S. V. Baum. 1955. "From 'Awol' to 'Veep': The Growth and Specialization of the Acronym." *American Speech* 30(2). pp. 103–110.

After the war, acronyms just kept proliferating: Ben Zimmer. December 16, 2010. "Acronym." *The New York Times Magazine.* www.nytimes.com/2010/12/19/magazine/19FOB-onlanguage-t.html.

Roman orator Quintilian: Adam Kendon. 2004. *Gesture: Visible Action as Utterance.* Cambridge University Press. Quintilian. 1922. *Institutio Oratoria,* trans. H. E. Butler (Loeb Classical Library). Heinemann.

Chapter 2. Language and Society

A German dialectologist named Georg Wenker: Stefan Dollinger. 2015. *The Written Questionnaire in Social Dialectology: History, Theory, Practice.* John Benjamins.

if one teacher wrote "Affe": Charles Boberg. 2013. "Surveys: The Use of Written Questionnaires." In Christine Mallinson,

Becky Childs, and Gerard Van Herk, eds., *Data Collection in Sociolinguistics: Methods and Applications.* Routledge.

The fieldworker he selected was a grocer: J. K. Chambers and Peter Trudgill. 1998. *Dialectology,* 2nd ed. Cambridge University Press.

In each village, he interviewed: Jules Gilliéron and Edmond Edmont. 2017. Atlas Linguistique de la France. GIPSA-Lab and CLLE-UMR 5263. cartodialect .imag.fr/cartoDialect/.

Both Wenker's and Gilliéron's dialect maps: Taylor Jones. September 28, 2014. "Big Data and Black Twitter." *Language Jones.* www.languagejones.com/blog-1/2014 /9/26/big-data-and-black-twitter.

Or you can read Wenker's hand-drawn map: Lisa Minnick. January 10, 2012. "From Marburg to Miami: Putting Language Variation on the Map." *Functional Shift.* functionalshift.wordpress .com/2012/01/10/miami/.

44,000 completed surveys: Stefan Dollinger. 2015. *The Written Questionnaire in Social Dialectology: History, Theory, Practice.* John Benjamins.

sent out fieldworkers: August Rubrecht. 2005. "Life in a DARE Word Wagon. Do You Speak American?" www.pbs.org

435

/speak/seatosea/americanvarieties/DARE
/wordwagon. Jesse Sheidlower. September 22,
2017. "The Closing of a Great American Dialect Project." *The New Yorker.* www.newyorker.
com/culture/cultural-comment/the-closing-
of-a-great-american-dialect-project.

The Atlas of North American English: Wil-
liam Labov, Sharon Ash, and Charles
Boberg. 2005. *The Atlas of North American
English: Phonetics, Phonology and Sound
Change.* Walter de Gruyter. www.atlas
.mouton-content.com/.

In 2002, the Harvard Dialect Survey: Bert
Vaux and Scott Golder. 2003. *The Harvard
Dialect Survey.* Harvard University Lin-
guistics Department. dialect.redlog.net/.

**massively popular *New York Times* dia-
lect quiz:** Josh Katz and Wilson An-
drews. December 21, 2013. "How Y'all,
Youse and You Guys Talk." *The New York
Times.* www.nytimes.com/interactive/2014
/upshot/dialect-quiz-map.html.

**Regardless of who technically has ac-
cess:** Alice E. Marwick and danah boyd.
2011. "I Tweet Honestly, I Tweet Passion-
ately: Twitter Users, Context Collapse,
and the Imagined Audience." *New Media
& Society* 13(1). pp. 114–133.

**When the Library of Congress an-
nounced:** Matt Raymond. April 14, 2010.

"How Tweet It Is! Library Acquires Entire Twitter Archive." *Library of Congress Blog.* blogs.loc.gov/loc/2010/04/how-tweet-it-is-library-acquires-entire-twitter-archive/.

"What's up, posterity?": Alex Baze. April 16, 2010. twitter.com/bazecraze/status/12308452064.

"Please index all my kitten pictures": understandblue. April 15, 2010. twitter.com/understandblue/status/12247489441.

The personal data derived: Jamie Doward, Carole Cadwalladr, and Alice Gibbs. March 4, 2017. "Watchdog to Launch Inquiry into Misuse of Data in Politics." *The Guardian.* www.theguardian.com/technology/2017/mar/04/cambridge-analytics-data-brexit-trump

Both of these findings: Jacob Eisenstein. 2014. "Identifying Regional Dialects in Online Social Media." www.cc.gatech.edu/~jeisenst/papers/dialectology-chapter.pdf. Kelly Servick. February 15, 2015. "Are yinz frfr? What Your Twitter Dialect Says About Where You Live." *Science.* news.sciencemag.org/social-sciences/2015/02/are-yinz-frfr-what-your-twitter-dialect-says-about-where-you-live.

Other features he found on Twitter: Jacob Eisenstein, Brendan O'Connor, Noah A. Smith, and Eric P. Xing. 2014.

"Diffusion of Lexical Change in Social Media." *PLOS ONE* 9(11). Public Library of Science. e113114. doi.org/10.1371/journal.pone.0113114.

Beyond just reinforcing the informal intuition: Jack Grieve, Andrea Nini, Diansheng Guo, and Alice Kasakoff. 2015. "Using Social Media to Map Double Modals in Modern American English." Presented at New Ways of Analyzing Variation 44, October 22–25, 2015, Toronto.

somewhat milder terms: Jack Grieve. July 16, 2015. "A Few Swear Word Maps." *Research Blog.* sites.google.com/site/jackgrieveaston/treesandtweets.

The example quotations for "mafted": Katherine Connor Martin. 2017. "New Words Notes September 2017." *The Oxford English Dictionary Today.* public.oed.com/the-oed-today/recent-updates-to-the-oed/september-2017-update/new-words-notes-september-2017/.

It's a little bit harder: Rachael Tatman. 2015. "# go awn: Sociophonetic Variation in Variant Spellings on Twitter." *Working Papers of the Linguistics Circle of the University of Victoria* 25(2). p. 97.

sound, and this particular spelling: Jane Stuart-Smith. 2004. "Scottish English: Phonology." In Bernd Kortmann and Edgar W. Schneider, eds., *A Handbook of Varieties of English* 1. De Gruyter. pp. 47–67.

"the private and personal word-creations": David Crystal. December 1, 2008. "On *Kitchen Table Lingo*." *DCBLOG*. david-crystal.blogspot.ca/2008/12/on-kitchen-table-lingo.html.

Queen Elizabeth II: Richard Kay. July 17, 2015. "Think George Is a Little Monkey? You Were WORSE, Wills: The Pictures That Show How Little Terror Prince Is Taking After His Naughty Daddy." *Daily Mail.* www.dailymail.co.uk/news/article-3165864/Think-George-little-monkey-WORSE-Wills-pictures-little-terror-prince-taking-naughty-daddy.html.

language and high school cliques: Penelope Eckert. 1989. *Jocks and Burnouts: Social Categories and Identity in the High School.* Teachers College Press. Penelope Eckert. 2004. "Adolescent Language." In Edward Finegan and John Rickford, eds., *Language in the USA.* Cambridge University Press. pp. 361–374.

vowel change going on: William Labov. 2011. *Principles of Linguistic Change,* vol. 3: *Cognitive and Cultural Factors.* John Wiley & Sons. p. 65. See also www.npr.org/templates/story/story.php?storyId=5220090.

features linked to intellectualism: Mary Bucholtz. 1996. "Geek the Girl: Language, Femininity, and Female Nerds." In Natasha Warner, Jocelyn Ahlers, Leela Bilmes, Monica Oliver, Suzanne Wertheim, and Melinda Chen, eds., *Gender and Belief Systems.* Berkeley Women and Language Group. pp. 119–131.

A study of Latinas: Norma Mendoza-Denton. 1996. "Language Attitudes and Gang Affiliation Among California Latina Girls." In Natasha Warner, Jocelyn Ahlers, Leela Bilmes, Monica Oliver, Suzanne Wertheim, and Melindwileya Chen, eds., *Gender and Belief Systems.* Berkeley: Berkeley Women and Language Group. pp. 478–486.

study in Panama City: Henrietta Cedergren. 1988. "The Spread of Language Change: Verifying Inferences of Linguistic Diffusion." In Peter H. Lowenberg, ed., *Language Spread and Language Policy: Issues, Implications, and Case Studies.* Georgetown University Press. pp. 45–60. Sali A. Tagliamonte and Alexandra D'Arcy. 2009. "Peaks Beyond Phonology: Adolescence, Incrementation, and Language Change." *Language* 85(1). pp. 58–108.

It's been peaking in adolescence:

440

Timothy Jay. 1992. *Cursing in America: A Psycholinguistic Study of Dirty Language in the Courts, in the Movies, in the Schoolyards, and on the Streets.* John Benjamins. Mike Thelwall. 2008. "Fk yea I swear: Cursing and Gender in MySpace." *Corpora* 3(1). pp. 83–107.

Researchers from Georgia Tech, Columbia, and Microsoft: Rahul Goel, Sandeep Soni, Naman Goyal, John Paparrizos, Hanna Wallach, Fernando Diaz, and Jacob Eisenstein. 2016. "The Social Dynamics of Language Change in Online Networks." *Proceedings of the International Conference on Social Informatics* (SocInfo16). Springer International. pp. 41–57.

the abbreviation "af": Jacob Eisenstein, Brendan O'Connor, Noah A. Smith, and Eric P. Xing. 2014. "Diffusion of Lexical Change in Social Media." *PLOS ONE* 9(11). Public Library of Science. e113114. doi.org/10.1371/journal.pone.0113114, journals.plos.org/plosone/article?id=10.1371/journal.pone.0113114#s1.

in 2014 and 2015, "af": "AF" appeared in an end-of-year 2014 post, "20 Young Celebs That Were 2014 AF," www.buzzfeed.com/christineolivo/2014

441

-supernovas, in the list "Here's What These Popular Dating Terms Really Mean" in July 2015, www.buzzfeed.com/kirstenking/single-as-fuq, and by late 2015 in "17 Dads Who Are Dad AF" www.buzzfeed.com/awesomer/dad-to-the-bone (October 2015), whereas earlier headlines contained F**k, "27 Animals Who Don't Give a F**k," www.buzzfeed.com/chelseamarshall/animals-who-dont-give-a-fk (2014), and F#@k, "30 Easy Steps to Not Give a F#@k," www.buzzfeed.com/daves4/easy-steps-to-start-not-giving-a-f (2013).

beer jargon: Cristian Danescu-Niculescu-Mizil, Robert West, Dan Jurafsky, Jure Leskovec, and Christopher Potts. 2013. "No Country for Old Members: User Lifecycle and Linguistic Change in Online Communities." *Proceedings of the 22nd International Conference on World Wide Web Pages*. pp. 307–318.

Adults periodically move: Jennifer Nycz. 2016. "Awareness and Acquisition of New Dialect Features." In Anna M. Babel, ed., *Awareness and Control in Sociolinguistic Research*. Cambridge University Press. pp. 62–79.

Framingham where researchers have followed: James H. Fowler and Nicholas A. Christakis. 2008. "Dynamic Spread of Happiness in a Large Social Network: Longitudinal Analysis over 20 Years in the Framingham Heart Study." *The BMJ* 337: a2338.

The traditional finding for gender: Suzanne Grégoire. 2006. "Gender and Language Change: The Case of Early Modern Women." Unpublished manuscript, University of Toronto. Retrieved from homes.chass.utoronto.ca/~cpercy/courses/6362-gregoire.htm.

Research in other centuries: William Labov. 1990. "The Intersection of Sex and Social Class in the Course of Linguistic Change." *Language Variation and Change* 2(2). pp. 205–254.

Young women are also consistently: Alexandra D'Arcy. 2017. *Discourse-Pragmatic Variation in Context: Eight Hundred Years of LIKE.* John Benjamins.

in a paper he wrote in 1990: William Labov. 1990. "The Intersection of Sex and Social Class in the Course of Linguistic Change." *Language Variation and Change* 2(2). pp. 205–254.

Lots of reasons: Suzanne Romaine. 2005. "Variation in Language and Gender." In Janet Holmes and Miriam Meyerhoff, eds., *The Handbook of Language and Gender.* Blackwell.

linguists Susan Herring and John Paolillo: Susan C. Herring and John C. Paolillo. 2006. "Gender and Genre Variation in Weblogs." *Journal of Sociolinguistics* 10(4). pp. 439–459.

looking at a corpus of 14,000 Twitter users: David Bamman, Jacob Eisenstein, and Tyler Schnoebelen. 2014. "Gender Identity and Lexical Variation in Social Media." *Journal of Sociolinguistics* 18(2). pp. 135–160.

changing the vowel in "car": Lesley Milroy. 1980. *Language and Social Networks.* Blackwell.

strong and weak ties: James Milroy and Lesley Milroy. 1985. "Linguistic Change, Social Network and Speaker Innovation." *Journal of Linguistics* 21(2). pp. 339–384.

Strong ties are people: Mark S. Granovetter. 1973. "The Strength of Weak Ties." *American Journal of Sociology* 78(6). pp. 1360–1380.

English and Icelandic: Magnús Fjalldal. 2005. *Anglo-Saxon England in Icelandic Medieval Texts.* University of Toronto Press.

Fagyal and colleagues: Zsuzsanna Fagyal, Samarth Swarup, Anna María Escobar, Les Gasser, and Kiran Lakkaraju. 2010. "Centers and Peripheries: Network Roles in Language Change." *Lingua* 120(8). pp. 2061–2079.

between four and twenty-six: *Economist* Staff. February 26, 2009. "Primates on Facebook." *The Economist.* www .economist.com/node/13176775.

titles of three books: Kevin Major. 2001. *Eh? to Zed: A Canadian Abecedarium.* Illustrator: Alan Daniel. Red Deer Press. Anne Chisholm. 1993. *From Eh to Zed: Cookbook of Canadian Culinary Heritage.* Food Lovers' Canada. David DeRocco and John Sivell. 1996. *Canada from Eh to Zed.* Illustrator: Christine Porter. Full Blast Productions.

Indeed, noted Chambers, "zed": J. K. Chambers. 2002. *Sociolinguistic Theory: Linguistic Variation and Its Social Significance,* 2nd ed. Blackwell.

"in middle-class style": William Labov. 1972. "The Social Stratification of (r) in New York City Department Stores." *Sociolinguistic Patterns.* University of Pennsylvania Press. pp. 43–54.

R-ful varieties are found: Peter Trudgill. 1984. *Language in the British Isles.* Cambridge University Press.

It's like how blue: Penelope Eckert. 2008. "Variation and the Indexical Field." *Journal of Sociolinguistics* 12(4). pp. 453–476.

"was quite insistent": James Milroy. 1992.

Linguistic Variation and Change: On the Historical Sociolinguistics of English. Blackwell. H. C. Wyld. 1927. *A Short History of English*. John Murray.

"This is an Idiom which": Robert Lowth. 1762. *A Short Introduction to English Grammar*. Digitized in 2006 via Oxford University.

Communication tools that expose: Tim McGee and Patricia Ericsson. 2002. "The Politics of the Program: MS WORD as the Invisible Grammarian." *Computers and Composition* 19. pp. 453–470.

But spellchecks have tried: Lynne Murphy. 2018. *The Prodigal Tongue: The Love-Hate Relationship between American and British English*. Penguin. pp. 148–152.

What I've seen from several editors: Anne Curzan. April 10, 2015. "Singular 'They,' Again." *The Chronicle of Higher Education: Lingua Franca*. www.chronicle.com/blogs/linguafranca/2015/04/10/singular-they-again. John E. McIntyre. April 10, 2015. "Singular "They": The Editors' Decision." *The Baltimore Sun*. www.baltimoresun.com/news/language-blog/bal-singular-they-the-editors-decision-20150410-story.html. Personal communication with Benjamin Dreyer, chief copy editor, Random House; Peter Sokolowski, lexicographer, Merriam-Webster.

subtle problems of bias: (No author cited.) (No date cited.) "Wikipedia: Systemic Bias." Wikipedia. en.wikipedia.org/wiki /Wikipedia:Systemic_bias.

Google Docs: Yew Jin Lim. March 21, 2012. "Spell Checking Powered by the Web." *Google Drive Blog.* drive.googleblog.com /2012/03/spell-checking-powered-by-web .html.

Textio: Kieran Snyder. November 11, 2016. "Want to Hire Faster? Write about 'Learning,' Not 'Brilliance.'" *Textio* blog. textio. ai/growth-mindset-language-41d51c91432. Marissa Coughlin. October 18, 2017. "20 Benefits That Speed Up Hiring and 5 That Slow It Down." *Textio* blog. textio.ai/20 -benefits-that-speed-up-hiring-and-5-that -slow-it-down-af266ce72ee8. Kieran Snyder. August 9, 2017. "Why AI Is Already Dead (and What's Coming Next)." *Textio* blog.textio .ai/ai-and-ml-in-job-posts-67b24b2033f8.

William Labov studied residents: William Labov. 1963. "The Social Motivation of a Sound Change." *Word* 18. pp. 1–42.

young men in Washington: Nicole R. Holliday. 2016. "Intonational Variation, Linguistic Style and the Black/Biracial Experience." PhD dissertation, New York University.

the speech patterns: Paul E. Reed. 2016. "Sounding Appalachian: /ai/ Monophthongization, Rising Pitch Accents, and Rootedness." PhD dissertation, University of South Carolina.

the speech of Jewish women: Rachel Burdin. 2016. "Variation in Form and Function in Jewish English Intonation." PhD dissertation, Ohio State University.

Research on youth language: Penelope Eckert. 2003. "Language and Adolescent Peer Groups." *Journal of Language and Social Psychology* 22(1). pp. 112–118. Jennifer Florence Roth-Gordon. 2003. "Slang and the Struggle over Meaning: Race, Language, and Power in Brazil." PhD dissertation, Stanford University. Vivienne Méla. 1997. "Verlan 2000." *Langue Française* 114. pp. 16–34. Mary Bucholtz. 1999. "You Da Man: Narrating the Racial Other in the Production of White Masculinity." *Journal of Sociolinguistics* 3(4). pp. 443–460. Cecilia A. Cutler. 1999. "Yorkville Crossing: White Teens, Hip Hop and African American English." *Journal of Sociolinguistics* 3(4). pp. 428–441. Jane H. Hill. 1993. "Hasta la Vista, Baby: Anglo Spanish in the American Southwest." *Critique of Anthropology* 13(2). pp. 145–176.

"lit" or "bae" . . . "on fleek": Renée

Blake and Mia Matthias. 2015. "'Black Twitter': AAE Lexical Innovation, Appropriation, and Change in Computer-Mediated Discourse." Presented at New Ways of Analyzing Variation 44, October 22–25, 2015, Toronto.

columbusing: CollegeHumor. July 7, 2014. "Columbusing: Discovering Things for White People." YouTube. www.youtube.com/watch?v=BWeFHddWL1Y. Rebecca Hotchen. October 12, 2015. "Update: What Happened to 'Columbusing'?" *Oxford Dictionaries* blog. blog.oxforddictionaries.com/2015/10/columbusing-update/.

participants in the study commented: David Palfreyman and Muhamed Al Khalil. 2007. "'A Funky Language for Teenzz to Use': Representing Gulf Arabic in Instant Messaging." In Brenda Danet and Susan C. Herring, eds., *The Multilingual Internet: Language, Culture, and Communication Online.* Oxford University Press. pp. 43–64.

Egyptian Twitter users: Zoë Kosoff. 2014. "Code-Switching in Egyptian Arabic: A Sociolinguistic Analysis of Twitter." *Al-'Arabiyya: Journal of the American Association of Teachers of Arabic* 47. Georgetown University Press. pp. 83–99.

Our @mentions: Jacob Eisenstein. 2018.

"Identifying Regional Dialects in Online Social Media." In Charles Boberg, John Nerbonne, and Dominic Watt, eds., *The Handbook of Dialectology*. John Wiley & Sons. Kelly Servick. February 15, 2015. "Are yinz frfr? What Your Twitter Dialect Says about Where You Live." *Science*. news .sciencemag.org/social-sciences/2015/02 /are-yinz-frfr-what-your-twitter-dialect -says-about-where-you-live. Umashanthi Pavalanathan and Jacob Eisenstein. 2015. "Audience Modulated Variation in Online Social Media." *American Speech* 90(2). pp. 187–213.

The inverse was less common: Dong-Phuong Nguyen, Rudolf Berend Trieschnigg, and Leonie Cornips. 2015. "Audience and the Use of Minority Languages on Twitter." *Proceedings of the Ninth International AAAI Conference on Web and Social Media*. AAAI Press. pp. 666–669.

informal language in Indonesian: Claudia Brugman and Thomas Conners. 2016. "Comparative Study of Register Specific Properties of Indonesian SMS and Twitter: Implications for NLP." Presented at the 20th International Symposium on Malay/ Indonesian Linguistics, July 14–16, 2016, Melbourne, Australia. Claudia Brugman and Thomas Conners. 2017. "Querying the Spoken/Written Register Continuum through Indonesian Electronic Communications." Presented at the 21st International Symposium on Malay/Indonesian Linguistics, May 4–6, 2017, Langkawi, Malaysia. Moti Lieberman. January 26, 2016. "Writing in Texts vs. Twitter." *The Ling Space* blog. thelingspace.tumblr.com/post /138053815679/writing-in-texts-vs-twitter.

favors a few elite languages and dialects: François Grosjean. 2010. *Bilingual.* Harvard University Press.

One method of bridging: Su Lin Blodgett, Lisa Green, and Brendan O'Connor. 2016. "Demographic Dialectal Variation in Social Media: A Case Study of African-American English." *Proceedings of the 2016 Conference on Empirical Methods in Natural Language Processing.* pp. 1119–1130. arxiv.org/pdf/1608.08868v1.pdf.

"15-year-old users": Ivan Smirnov. 2017. "The Digital Flynn Effect: Complexity of Posts on Social Media Increases over Time." Presented at the International Conference on Social Informatics, September 13–15, 2017, Oxford, UK. arxiv .org/abs/1707.057555.

textisms might interfere: Michelle Drouin and Claire Davis. 2009. "R u txting?

Is the Use of Text Speak Hurting Your Literacy?" *Journal of Literacy Research* 41. Routledge. pp. 46–67.

Several studies show that people: Jannis Androutsopoulos. 2011. "Language Change and Digital Media: A Review of Conceptions and Evidence." In Nikolas Coupland and Tore Kristiansen, eds., *Standard Languages and Language Standards in a Changing Europe.* Novus Forlag. pp. 145–160. Christa Dürscheid, Franc Wagner, and Sarah Brommer. 2010. *Wie Jugendliche schreiben: Schreibkompetenz und neue Medien.* Walter de Gruyter.

only 2.4 percent: Crispin Thurlow. 2006. "From Statistical Panic to Moral Panic: The Metadiscursive Construction and Popular Exaggeration of New Media Language in the Print Media." *Journal of Computer-Mediated Communication* 11(3). pp. 667–701.

What the teens were doing: Sali Tagliamonte and Derek Denis. 2008. "Linguistic Ruin? LOL! Instant Messaging and Teen Language." *American Speech* 83(1). pp. 3–34.

A paper analyzing the effects: Tim McGee and Patricia Ericsson. 2002. "The Politics of the Program: MS WORD as the Invisible Grammarian." *Computers and*

Composition 19. Elsevier. pp. 453–470.

I'm also not alone: Lauren Dugan. November 11, 2011. "Twitter Basics: Why 140-Characters, and How to Write More." *Adweek.* www.adweek.com/digital/twitter-basics-why-140-characters-and-how-to-write-more/. Patrick Iber. October 19, 2016. "A Defense of Academic Twitter." *Inside Higher Ed.* www.insidehighered.com/advice/2016/10/19/how-academics-can-use-twitter-most-effectively-essay.

Chapter 3. Internet People

In 1984, a researcher: Naomi S. Baron. 1984. "Computer-Mediated Communication as a Force in Language Change." *Visible Language* 18(2). University of Cincinnati Press. pp. 118–141.

"basically alienating and unfulfilling": James E. Katz and Ronald E. Rice. 2008. "Syntopia: Access, Civic Involvement, and Social Interaction on the Net." In Barry Wellman and Caroline Haythornthwaite, eds., *The Internet in Everyday Life.* John Wiley & Sons.

over a third of couples: John T. Cacioppo, Stephanie Cacioppo, Gian Gonzaga, Elizabeth L. Ogburn, and Tyler J. VanderWeele. 2013. "Marital Satisfaction and Break-ups Differ across On-Line and

Off-Line Meeting Venues." *Proceedings of the National Academy of Sciences* 110 (25). pp. 10135–10140.

15 percent of American adults: Aaron Smith. February 11, 2016. "15% of American Adults Have Used Online Dating Sites or Mobile Dating Apps." Pew Research Center. www.pewinternet .org/2016/02/11/15-percent-of-american -adults-have-used-online-dating-sites-or -mobile-dating-apps.

The first year that marriages: Michael J. Rosenfeld. September 18, 2017. "Marriage, Choice, and Couplehood in the Age of the Internet." *Sociological Science.* www .sociologicalscience.com/download/vol-4 /september/SocSci_v4_490to510.pdf.

But a whole lot of people: Simon Kemp. January 30, 2018. "Digital in 2018: World's Internet Users Pass the 4 Billion Mark." *We Are Social.* wearesocial.com/blog/2018/01 /global-digital-report-2018.

Linguists call this "the founder effect": Salikoko S. Mufwene. 2001. *The Ecology of Language Evolution.* Cambridge University Press.

Most families who immigrate: U.S. Census Bureau, Population Division. 2000. "Ancestry." Chapter 9 of *Census Atlas of the United States.* www.census.gov

/population/www/cen2000/censusatlas/pdf/9_Ancestry.pdf.

The distinctive accents: Walt Wolfram and Natalie Schilling. 2015. *American English: Dialects and Variation,* 3rd ed. Language and Society, vol. 25. John Wiley & Sons.

The vowels of Raleigh: Robin Dodsworth and Mary Kohn. July 2012. "Urban Rejection of the Vernacular: The SVS Undone." *Language Variation and Change* 24(2). pp. 221–245.

Cockney has been replaced: Jenny Cheshire, Paul Kerswill, Sue Fox, and Eivind Torgersen. 2011. "Contact, the Feature Pool and the Speech Community: The Emergence of Multicultural London English." *Journal of Sociolinguistics* 15(2). pp. 151–196.

writing yourself into existence: Jenny Sundén. 2003. *Material Virtualities.* Peter Lang.

"some explanations": DFWX and Guardian of Eden. 2006. About DFWX.com. *DFWX: Dallas - Fort Worth Exchange.* www.dfwx.com/about_us.htm.

"us old Internet people need": User DirigoDev. June 13, 2011. Reply to thread titled "Facebook Still Growing but Losing Users in Countries It Was First Established." Webmaster World forum. www.webmasterworld.com/facebook/4325404.htm.

"Looks like it's really hitting": Dave Delaney. May 15, 2018. twitter.com /davedelaney/status/996241627717959680.

A website version of the Jargon File: Eric S. Raymond, ed. December 29, 2003. "Chapter 3. Revision History." The on-line hacker Jargon File, version 4.4.7. catb.org /jargon/html/revision-history.html.

The oldest version of the Jargon File: Steven Ehrbar (archivist). August 12, 1976. The Jargon File Text Archive: A large collection of historical versions of the Jargon File, version 1.0.0.01. jargon-file .org/archive/jargon-1.0.0.01.dos.txt.

Other terms in the file: Steven Ehrbar (archivist). (No date cited.) The Jargon File Text Archive: A large collection of historical versions of the Jargon File, versions 1.0.0.01 to 4.4.7. jargon-file.org/.

between March and April 1977 . . . This version: Steven Ehrbar (archivist). March 11, 1977, and April 24, 1977. The Jargon File Text Archive: A large collection of historical versions of the Jargon File, versions 1.0.0.9 and 1.0.0.10. jargon-file.org/archive /jargon-1.0.0.09.dos.txt and jargon-file.org /archive/jargon-1.0.0.10.dos.txt.

a version in December 1977: Steven Ehrbar (archivist). December 29, 1977. The Jargon File Text Archive: A large collection of historical versions of the Jargon File, version 1.0.0.16. jargon-file.org/archive /jargon-1.0.0.16.dos.txt.

When the Jargon File resumed: Emoticons and "lol" first added in: Guy L. Steele and Eric S. Raymond, eds. June 12, 1990. The Jargon File, version 2.1.1. jargon-file .org/archive/jargon-2.1.1.dos.txt. All caps as shouting first added in: Guy L. Steele and Eric S. Raymond, eds. December 15, 1990. The Jargon File, version 2.2.1. jargon-file.org/archive/jargon-2.2.1.dos.txt.

"these are not used at universities": Guy L. Steele and Eric S. Raymond, eds. June 12, 1990. The Jargon File, version 2.1.1. jargon-file.org/archive/jargon-2.1.1.dos.txt.

"IMHO, ROTF, and TTFN": Eric S. Raymond, ed. March 22, 1991. The Jargon File, version 2.8.1. jargon-file.org/archive /jargon-2.8.1.dos.txt.

the acronym UTSL: Eric S. Raymond, ed. December 29, 2003. "UTSL." The on-line hacker Jargon File, version 4.4.7. www.catb.org/jargon/html/U/UTSL.html.

online role-playing games in Germany: Sonja Utz. 2000. "Social Information Processing in MUDs: The Development of Friendships in Virtual Worlds." *Journal of Online Behavior* 1(1). psycnet.apa.org /record/2002-14046-001.

"A friend of mine who went": Wayne Pearson. 2002. "The Origin of LOL." University of Calgary webpage. pages.cpsc .ucalgary.ca/~crwth/LOL.html.

The first known citation: Vince Periello, ed. May 8, 1989. *International FidoNet Association Newsletter* 6(19). www.textfiles.com /fidonet-on-the-internet/878889/fido0619 .txt. John Brandon. November 7, 2008. "Opinion: FWIW — The Origins of 'Net Shorthand." *PCWorld.* www.pcworld.com/ article/153504/net_shorthand_origins.html.

The first year that over half: Andrew Perrin and Maeve Duggan. June 26, 2015. "Americans' Internet Access: 2000–2015." Pew Research Center. www.pewinternet .org/2015/06/26/americans-internet-access -2000-2015/.

In 1995, a mere 3 percent: (No author cited.) October 16, 1995. "Americans Going Online . . . Explosive Growth, Uncertain Destinations." Pew Research Center. www.people-press.org/1995/10/16 /americans-going-online-explosive-growth -uncertain-destinations/.

"What a difference a year makes": Rob Spiegel. November 12, 1999. "When Did the Internet Become Mainstream?" *Ecommerce Times.* www.ecommercetimes.com /story/1731.html?wlc=1226697731.

The dominant narrative: Marc Prenksy. 2001. "Digital Natives, Digital Immigrants." *On the Horizon* 9(5). pp. 1–6. Don Tapscott. 1998. *Growing up Digital: The Rise of the Net Generation.* McGraw-Hill.

Even as this narrative was being proposed: Ruth Xiaoqing Guo, Teresa Dobson, and Stephen Petrina. 2008. "Digital Natives, Digital Immigrants: An Analysis of Age and ICT Competency in Teacher Education." *Journal of Educational Computing Research* 38(3). pp. 235–254.

"the academic equivalent of a 'moral panic' ": Sue Bennett, Karl Maton, and Lisa Kervin. 2008. "The 'Digital Natives' Debate: A Critical Review of the Evidence." *British Journal of Educational Technology* 39(5). pp. 775–786.

An article reminiscing: Melissa McEwen. November 13, 2017. "The Teenage Girl's Internet of the Early 2000s." Medium. medium.com/@melissamcewen /the-teenage-girls-internet-of-the-early -2000s-ffa05702a9aa.

virtual-pet websites: Melissa McEwen. May 14, 2016. "Petz: A Lost Community of Mostly Female Coders/Gamers." Medium. medium.com/@melissamcewen /petz-a-lost-community-of-mostly-female -coders-gamers-2eb0e1a73f42.

"a mix between Tamagotchi": Nicole Carpenter. October 23, 2017. "'Neopets': Inside Look at Early 2000s Internet Girl Culture." *Rolling Stone.* www.rollingstone .com/glixel/features/neopets-a-look-into -early-2000s-girl-culture-w509885.

There were waves: (No author cited.) October 7, 2017. "AOL Is Shutting Down Its Instant Messenger and 90s Kids Are Reminiscing." *The Irish Examiner.* www.irish examiner.com/breakingnews/technow/aol -is-shutting-down-its-instant-messenger -and-90s-kids-are-reminiscing-808938 .html. Madeleine Buxton. October 6, 2017. "AIM Is Coming to an End & 90s Kids Everywhere Can't Deal." *Refinery 29.* www.refinery29.com/2017/10/175504 /aol-instant-messenger-discontinued. Adrian Covert and Sam Biddle. May 16, 2011. "Remember When AOL Instant Messenger Was Our Facebook?" *Gizmodo.* gizmodo.com/5800437/remember-when -aol-instant-messenger-was-our-facebook.

archivists scrambled: Olia and Dragan. (No date cited.) *One Terabyte of Kilobyte Age.* blog.geocities.institute/. (No author cited.) December 4, 2017. "GeoCities." Archive Team. www.archiveteam.org /index.php?title=GeoCities. Dan Fletcher. November 9, 2009. "Internet Atrocity!

GeoCities' Demise Erases Web History." *Time.* content.time.com/time/business/article/0,8599,1936645,00.html. Dan Grabham. November 26, 2009. "Geo-Cities Closes: Fond Memories of Free Sites and Terrible Web Design." *Techradar.* www.techradar.com/news/internet/web/geocities-closes-fond-memories-of-free-sites-and-terrible-web-design-644763.

When AIM shut down: Taylor Lorenz. March 1, 2017. twitter.com/TaylorLorenz/status/837032527219068928.

Similarly, a 2000 survey: Elisheva F. Gross. 2004. "Adolescent Internet Use: What We Expect, What Teens Report." *Applied Developmental Psychology* 25. pp. 633–649.

A study of myths: R. Kvavik, J. B. Ca-ruso, and G. Morgan. 2004. *ECAR Study of Students and Information Technology 2004: Convenience, Connection, and Control.* EDUCAUSE Center for Applied Research. Sue Bennett, Karl Maton, and Lisa Kervin. 2008. "The 'Digital Natives' De-bate: A Critical Review of the Evidence." *British Journal of Educational Technology* 39(5). pp. 775–786.

Later surveys: Anoush Margaryan, Alli-son Littlejohn, and Gabrielle Vojt. 2011. "Are Digital Natives a Myth or Reality?

461

University Students' Use of Digital Technologies." *Computers & Education* 56(2). pp. 429–440. Gregor E. Kennedy, Terry S. Judd, Anna Churchward, Kathleen Gray, and Kerri-Lee Krause. 2008. "First Year Students' Experiences with Technology: Are They Really Digital Natives?" *Australasian Journal of Educational Technology* 24(1). ASCILITE. pp. 108–122. Hannah Thinyane. 2010. "Are Digital Natives a World-Wide Phenomenon? An Investigation into South African First Year Students' Use and Experience with Technology." *Computers & Education* 55. pp. 406–414.

A 2007 survey of internet users: Ellen Helsper and Rebecca Eynon. 2009. "Digital Natives: Where Is the Evidence?" *British Educational Research Journal* 36(3). pp. 1–18.

In the years after 2007: Michelle Slatalla. June 7, 2007. " 'omg my mom joined facebook!!' " *The New York Times.* www.nytimes.com/2007/06/07/fashion/07Cyber.html. Hadley Freeman. January 19, 2009. "Oh No! My Parents Have Joined Facebook." *The Guardian.* www.theguardian.com/media/2009/jan/19/facebook-social-networking-parents.

In 2017, Pew Research: (No author cited.)

January 11, 2017. "Who Uses Social Media." Pew Research Center. www.pewinternet .org/chart/who-uses-social-media/.

xkcd comic: Randall Munroe. August 24, 2009. "Tech Support Cheat Sheet." *xkcd.* xkcd.com/627/.

In 1995, Pew found: (No author cited.) December 16, 1996. "News Attracts Most Internet Users: Online Use." Pew Research Center. www.people-press.org/1996/12/16 /online-use/.

email use remained saturated: Kristen Purcell. August 9, 2011. "Search and Email Still Top the List of Most Popular Online Activities." Pew Research Center. www.pewinternet.org/2011/08/09/search -and-email-still-top-the-list-of-most -popular-online-activities/.

As early as 2001: David Crystal. 2001. *Language and the Internet.* Cambridge University Press.

"We should change 'lol'": ThatGuy-Ponna. September 9, 2015. "We should change 'Lol' to 'Ne' (Nose Exhale) because that's all we really do when we see something funny online." Reddit. www .reddit.com/r/Showerthoughts/comments /3ka70x/we_should_change_lol_to_ne _nose_exhale_because/.

Old, Full, and Semi Internet People: In

1995, Pew reported that only 20 percent of American internet users had ever visited a website but that 53 percent sent or received email at least once a week. (For younger folks, this was in an era before "webmail" existed, when you would check your email by opening a specific email program, not by going to, say, the Gmail website.) (No author cited.) October 16, 1995. "Americans Going Online . . . Explosive Growth, Uncertain Destinations." Pew Research Center. www.people-press.org/1995/10/16/americans-going-online-explosive-growth-uncertain-destinations/.

But that number rose: Andrew Perrin and Maeve Duggan. June 26, 2015. "Americans' Internet Access: 2000–2015." Pew Research Center. www.pewinternet.org/2015/06/26/americans-internet-access-2000-2015/.

Pew also found: Aaron Smith. January 12, 2017. "Record Shares of Americans Now Own Smartphones, Have Home Broadband." Pew Research Center. www.pewresearch.org/fact-tank/2017/01/12/evolution-of-technology/.

They might only use: Gretchen McCulloch. February 6, 2017. twitter.com/GretchenAMcC/status/828809327540654083.

West periodically documents: Jessamyn West. November 2, 2016. storify.com /jessamyn/highlights-from-drop-in-time.

between 2015 and 2018: Monica Anderson, Andrew Perrin, and Jingjing Jiang. March 5, 2018. "11% of Americans Don't Use the Internet. Who Are They?" Pew Research Center. http://www.pewresearch .org/fact-tank/2018/03/05/some-americans -dont-use-the-internet-who-are-they/.

more common among older people: Jessamyn West. 2016. "Solve the Digital Divide with One Neat Trick!" Presented at the New Hampshire 2016 Fall Conference and Business Meeting, November 3, 2016, Hooksett, New Hampshire. www .librarian.net/talks/nhla16/nhla16.pdf.

Her role becomes as much: Jessamyn West. October 16, 2015. "Transcription: Jessamyn West, Technology Lady." Medium. medium.com/tilty/transcription-jessamyn -west-technology-lady-6c6f5fefa507.

By nature, these are the kind: Gretchen McCulloch. November 2, 2017. twitter.com/GretchenAMcC/status /935506746222759937.

"i just had to beat": Paris Martineau. February 8, 2018. "Why... Do Old People... Text... Like This... ? An Investigation..." *The Outline.* theoutline.com/post/3333

/why-do-old-people-text-like-this-an-investigation.

"thank you all for the birthday wishes": Minisixxx. July 26, 2017. Posted to a group exclusively for old photos of a town. Reddit. www.reddit.com/r/oldpeoplefacebook/comments/6p29xj/posted_to_a_group_exclusively_for_old_photos_of_a/?st=j775761s&sh=6eb68538. PeriodStain. August 6, 2016. "Old People vs Clickbait." Reddit. www.reddit.com/r/oldpeoplefacebook/comments/4whj2u/old_people_vs_clickbait/?st=j7752f4k&sh=5b833dcc. Noheifers. August 6, 2017. "Good question." Reddit. www.reddit.com/r/oldpeoplefacebook/comments/6rvtwf/good_question/?st=j775amjd&sh=03c72ac6.

When West says it is: Jessamyn West. July 9, 2007. "Me at Work, Seniors Learning Computers." *Librarian.net.* www.librarian.net/stax/2083/me-at-work-seniors-learning-computers/. iamthebest artist. July 8, 2006. "Computer Class in Vermont." YouTube. www.youtube.com/watch?v=3A4R38VOgdw.

John Lennon and Paul McCartney: Ringo Starr. 2004. *Postcards from the Boys: Featuring Postcards Sent by John Lennon, Paul McCartney, and George Harrison.* Cassell Illustrated.

"Hi Dad": (No author cited.) January 15, 2008. Lot 468: A POSTCARD FROM GEORGE HARRISON. *Bonhams Auctions.* www.bonhams.com/auctions/15765 /lot/468/.

corpus study of over five hundred Swiss postcards: Kyoko Sugisaki. 2017. "Word and Sentence Segmentation in German: Overcoming Idiosyncrasies in the Use of Punctuation in Private Communication." Unpublished manuscript. sugisaki.ch /assets/papers/sugisaki2017b.pdf.

Finnish teenagers: Jan-Ola Östman. 2003. "The Postcard as Media." In Srikant Sarangi, ed., *Text and Talk* 24(3). pp. 423–442.

small-scale efforts to teach older folks: Tara Bahrampour. July 13, 2013. "Successful Program to Help D.C. Senior Citizens Use iPads to Prevent Isolation Will Expand." *The Washington Post.* www .washingtonpost.com/local/dc-senior -citizens-use-ipads-to-expand-social -interactions/2013/07/13/491fdb72 -ea7a-11e2-aa9f-c03a72e2d342_story .html?hpid=z5.

mediated by their caregivers: Loren Cheng. December 4, 2017. "Introducing Messenger Kids, a New App for Families to Connect." *Facebook Newsroom.* newsroom.fb.com/news/2017/12/

introducing-messenger-kids-a-new-app
-for-families-to-connect/. Josh Constine.
December 4, 2017. "Facebook 'Messenger
Kids' Lets Under-13s Chat with Whom
Parents Approve." *Techcrunch.* techcrunch
.com/2017/12/04/facebook-messenger-kids/.
certain genre of trendy article: Crispin
Thurlow. 2006. "From Statistical Panic
to Moral Panic: The Metadiscursive Construction and Popular Exaggeration of
New Media Language in the Print Media."
*Journal of Computer-Mediated Communica-
tion* 11. International Communication Association. pp. 67–701. Ben Rosen. February
8, 2016. "My Little Sister Taught Me How
to 'Snapchat Like the Teens.'" *BuzzFeed.*
www.buzzfeed.com/benrosen/how-to
-snapchat-like-the-teens. Mary H.K. Choi.
August 25, 2016. "Like. Flirt. Ghost. A
Journey into the Social Media Lives of
Teens." *Wired.* www.wired.com/2016/08
/how-teens-use-social-media/. Andrew
Watts. January 3, 2015. "A Teenager's View
on Social Media." *Wired.* backchannel
.com/a-teenagers-view-on-social-media
-1df945c09ac6. Josh Miller. December 29,
2012. "Tenth Grade Tech Trends." Medium. medium.com/@joshm/tenth-grade
-tech-trends-d8d4f2300cf3.
Susan Herring points out: Susan Herring.

2008. "Questioning the Generational Divide: Technological Exoticism and Adult Constructions of Online Youth Identity." In David Buckingham, ed., *Youth, Identity, and Digital Media.* MIT Press. pp. 71–94.

French sociology study: Michel Forsé. 1981. "La Sociabilité." *Economie et Statistique* 132. pp. 39–48. www.persee .fr/docAsPDF/estat_0336-1454_1981 _num_132_1_4476.pdf.

"All else being equal": Susan Herring. 2008. "Questioning the Generational Divide: Technological Exoticism and Adult Constructions of Online Youth Identity." In David Buckingham, ed., *Youth, Identity, and Digital Media.* MIT Press. pp. 71–94.

Studies consistently show: Sarah Holloway and Gill Valentine. 2003. *Cyberkids: Children in the Information Age.* Psychology Press. Sonia Livingstone and Moira Bovill. 1999. *Young People, New Media: Summary Report of the Research Project Children, Young People and the Changing Media Environment.* Media@LSE. eprints .lse.ac.uk/21177/. Keri Facer, John Furlong, Ruth Furlong, and Rosamund Sutherland. 2003. *Screenplay: Children and Computing in the Home.* Psychology Press.

"more fun" . . . "can understand": Victoria Rideout. 2006. "Social Media,

Social Life." Common Sense Media. www
.commonsensemedia.org/sites/default/files
/research/socialmediasociallife-final-061812
.pdf.

in-person hangouts difficult . . . "Most teens": danah boyd. 2015. *It's Complicated: The Social Lives of Networked Teens.* Yale University Press.

"context collapse": danah boyd. December 8, 2013. "How 'Context Collapse' Was Coined: My Recollection." *Apophenia.* www.zephoria.org/thoughts/archives /2013/12/08/coining-context-collapse .html.

linguist Michelle McSweeney: Note that some of McSweeney's examples are partially in Spanish because it was a bilingual corpus. I am presenting English translations as they appear in the paper itself. Michelle McSweeney. January 6, 2017. "lol i didn't mean it! Lol as a Marker of Illocutionary Force." Presented at the Annual Meeting of the Linguistics Society of America, January 4–7, 2018, Salt Lake City.

study of natural conversations: Robert R. Provine. 1993. "Laughter Punctuates Speech: Linguistic, Social and Gender Contexts of Laughter." *Ethology* 95(4). pp. 291–298.

470

Chapter 4. Typographical Tone of Voice

less stereotypically robotic: Jacob Kastrenakes. March 30, 2016. "Google Now's Voice Is Starting to Sound Way More Natural." *The Verge.* www.theverge.com/2016/3/30/11333524/google-now-voice-improved-smoother-sound.

Jane Austen: Kathryn Sutherland, ed. July 31, 2012. Jane Austen's Fiction Manuscripts Digital Edition. janeausten.ac.uk/index.html.

Emily Dickinson's poetry: Edith Wylder. 2004. "Emily Dickinson's Punctuation: The Controversy Revisited." *American Literary Realism* 36(3). pp. 6–24.

thinkpieces in 2013: Jeff Wilser. June 18, 2013. "10 Ways That Men Text Women." *The Cut.* nymag.com/thecut/2013/06/10-ways-that-men-text-women.html. Ben Crair. November 25, 2013. "The Period Is Pissed." *New Republic.* newrepublic.com/article/115726/period-our-simplest-punctuation-mark-has-become-sign-anger.

handful of other publications: *Jezebel, The Washington Post,* the *Toronto Star, Salon, The Telegraph* (UK), *Yahoo! News, The Harvard Crimson.*

thinkpiece in 2018: Paris Martineau. February 8, 2018. "Why . . . Do Old

People . . . Text . . . Like This . . . ? An Investigation . . ." *The Outline.* theoutline .com/post/3333/why-do-old-people-text -like-this-an-investigation.

since at least 2006: The Bishop of Turkey. December 13, 2006. "Why Are People Using Ellipses instead of a Period?" *Ask Metafilter.* ask.metafilter.com/53094/Why -are-people-using-ellipses-instead-of-a -period.

hyphen and string of commas: Infovore. May 3, 2011. "Using Commas as Ellipses." *The Straight Dope.* boards.straightdope .com/sdmb/showthread.php?t=607076. Bfactor. January 3, 2011. "Why do some people do this,,, instead of this..." *PocketFives.* www.pocketfives.com/f13 /why-do-some-people-do-instead-614200/. Starwed. February 24, 2015. "Origin of the 'Triple Comma' or 'Comma Ellipsis.'" *Stackexchange, English Language & Usage.* english.stackexchange.com/questions /230189/origin-of-the-triple-comma-or -comma-ellipsis.

fears mongered by headlines: Mark Liberman. November 26, 2013. "Aggressive Periods and the Popularity of Linguistics." *Language Log.* languagelog.ldc .upenn.edu/nll/?p=8667.

a study of periods: Katy Steinmetz.

September 24, 2016. "Why Technology Has Not Killed the Period. Period." *Time.* time.com/4504994/period-dying-death-puncuation-day/.

punctus: Stephen R. Reimer. 1998. *Paleography: Punctuation.* University of Alberta. sites.ualberta.ca/~sreimer/ms-course/course/punc.htm.

ancient Greek and Roman writing: Daniel Zalewski. 1998. "No Word Unspoken." *Lingua Franca.* linguafranca.mirror.theinfo.org/9804/ip.html.

rise of the printing press and dictionaries: Edmund Weiner. (No date cited.) "Early Modern English Pronunciation and Spelling." *Oxford English Dictionary* blog.public.oed.com/aspects-of-english/english-in-time/early-modern-english-pronunciation-and-spelling/. John Simpson. (No date cited.) "The First Dictionaries of English." *Oxford English Dictionary* blog. public.oed.com/aspects-of-english/english-in-time/the-first-dictionaries-of-english/.

Linguist Maria Heath: Maria Heath. January 6, 2018. "Orthography in Social Media: Pragmatic and Prosodic Interpretations of Caps Lock." Presented at the Annual Meeting of the Linguistic Society of America, January 4–7, 2018, Salt Lake City.

473

Usenet groups . . . Philippa Schuyler: Alice Robb. April 17, 2014. "How Capital Letters Became Internet Code for Yelling." *New Republic.* newrepublic.com /article/117390/netiquette-capitalization -how-caps-became-code-yelling.

author L. M. Montgomery: Lucy Maud Montgomery. 1925. *Emily Climbs.* Frederick A. Stokes. Lucy Maud Montgomery. 1927. *Emily's Quest.* Frederick A. Stokes.

a newspaper in 1856: (No author cited.) April 17, 1856. "The Dutchman Who Had the Small Pox." *The Yorkville Enquirer* (South Carolina). In Library of Congress, ed., *Chronicling America: Historic American Newspapers.* chroniclingamerica.loc.gov /lccn/sn84026925/1856-04-17/ed-1/seq-4/.

at one point it did: Thanks to Guy English (personal communication) for confirming that this was the case for FORTRAN and COBOL.

millions of books scanned: Search for block capitals, block letters, all caps, all uppercase, caps lock in *Google Books Ngram Viewer* with date parameter 1800 to 2000. books.google.com/ngrams/graph ?content=block+capitals%2Cblock+letters %2Call+caps%2Call+uppercase%2Ccaps +lock&year_start=1800&year_end=2000 &corpus=15&smoothing=3. Jean-Baptiste

Michel, Yuan Kui Shen, Aviva Presser Aiden, Adrian Veres, Matthew K. Gray, The Google Books Team, Joseph P. Pickett, Dale Hoiberg, Dan Clancy, Peter Norvig, Jon Orwant, Steven Pinker, Martin A. Nowak, and Erez Lieberman Aiden. 2010. "Quantitative Analysis of Culture Using Millions of Digitized Books." *Science.* American Association for the Advancement of Science.

Corpus of Historical American English: Mark Davies. 2010. *Corpus of Historical American English: 400 Million Words, 1810–2009.* Brigham Young University. corpus .byu.edu/coha/.

"'Confectionary, confectionary'": Maturin Murray Ballou. 1848. *The Duke's Prize; a Story of Art and Heart in Florence.* (No publisher cited.) www.gutenberg.org /ebooks/4956.

top twenty most lengthened words: Samuel Brody and Nicholas Diakopoulos. 2011. "Cooooooooooooooooollllllllllllllll!!!!!!!!!!!!!!! Using Word Lengthening to Detect Sentiment in Microblogs." *Proceedings of the 2011 Conference on Empirical Methods in Natural Language Processing.* Association for Computational Linguistics. pp. 562–570.

expressive lengthening: Tyler Schnoebelen.

January 8, 2013. "Aww, hmmm, ohh heyyy nooo omggg!" *Corpus Linguistics.* corplinguistics.wordpress.com/2013/01/08/aww-hmmm-ohh-heyyy-nooo-omggg/. Jen Doll. 2016. "Why Drag It Out?" *The Atlantic.* www.theatlantic.com/magazine/archive/2013/03/dragging-it-out/309220/. Jen Doll. February 1, 2013. "Why Twitter Makes Us Want to Add Extra Letterssss." *The Atlantic.* www.thewire.com/entertainment/2013/02/why-twitter-makes-us-want-add-extra-letterssss/62348/.

people lengthen more in private texts: Claudia Brugman and Thomas Conners. 2016. "Comparative Study of Register Specific Properties of Indonesian SMS and Twitter: Implications for NLP." Presented at the 20th International Symposium on Malay/Indonesian Linguistics, July 14–16, 2016, Melbourne, Australia. Claudia Brugman and Thomas Conners. 2017. "Querying the Spoken/Written Register Continuum through Indonesian Electronic Communications." Presented at the 21st International Symposium on Malay/Indonesian Linguistics, May 4–6, 2017, Langkawi, Malaysia. Moti Lieberman. January 26, 2016. "Writing in Texts vs. Twitter." *The Ling Space* blog. thelingspace.tumblr.com/post/13805381

5679/writing-in-texts-vs-twitter.
flamewars, shouty caps, and misunderstood sarcasm: Lori Foster Thompson and Michael D. Coovert. 2003. "Teamwork Online: The Effects of Computer Conferencing on Perceived Confusion, Satisfaction and Postdiscussion Accuracy." *Group Dynamics: Theory, Research, and Practice* 7(2). pp. 135–151. Caroline Cornelius and Margarete Boos. 2003. "Enhancing Mutual Understanding in Synchronous Computer-Mediated Communication by Training: Trade-offs in Judgmental Tasks." *Communication Research* 30(2). pp. 147–177. Radostina K. Purvanova and Joyce E. Bono. 2009. "Transformational Leadership in Context: Face-to-Face and Virtual Teams." *The Leadership Quarterly* 20(3). pp. 343–357. Erika Darics. 2014. "The Blurring Boundaries between Synchronicity and Asynchronicity: New Communicative Situations in Work-Related Instant Messaging." *International Journal of Business Communication* 51(4). pp. 337–358.

A study from 1999: Susan E. Brennan and Justina O. Ohaeri. 1999. "Why Do Electronic Conversations Seem Less Polite? The Costs and Benefits of Hedging." *Proceedings of the International Joint Conference on Work Activities, Coordination,* *and Collaboration (WACC'99)*. pp. 227–235. www.psychology.stonybrook.edu/sbrennan -/papers/brenwacc.pdf.

Wikipedia administrators: Cristian Danescu-Niculescu-Mizil, Moritz Sudhof, Dan Jurafsky, Jure Leskovec, and Christopher Potts. 2013. "A Computational Approach to Politeness with Application to Social Factors." Presented at 51st Annual Meeting of the Association for Computational Linguistics. arxiv.org/abs /1306.6078.

study by Carol Waseleski: Carol Waseleski. 2006. "Gender and the Use of Exclamation Points in Computer-Mediated Communication: An Analysis of Exclamations Posted to Two Electronic Discussion Lists." *Journal of Computer-Mediated Communication* 11(4). pp. 1012–1024.

"In a diabolical omission": (No author cited.) May 12, 2014. "Stone-Hearted Ice Witch Forgoes Exclamation Point." *The Onion.* www.theonion.com/article/stone -hearted-ice-witch-forgoes-exclamation -point-36005.

Emotional Labor: emotional-labor.email/. Reviewed in Jessica Lachenal. February 17, 2017. "Emotional Labor Is a Pain in the Butt, so This Gmail Add-On Does It for You on Your E-Mails." *The*

Mary Sue. www.themarysue.com/gmail
-emotional-labor-add-on/.

leetspeak: Anthony Mitchell. December 6,
2005. "A Leet Primer." *E-commerce Times.*
www.technewsworld.com/story/47607.html.

A 2005 paper about leetspeak: Katherine Blashki and Sophie Nichol. 2005.
"Game Geek's Goss: Linguistic Creativity in Young Males Within an Online
University Forum (94/\/\3 933k'5 9055
oneone)." *Australian Journal of Emerging
Technologies and Society* 3(22). pp. 77–
86. With thanks to Sophie Nichol (personal communication) for confirming
this translation.

a trend piece from 2018: Julie Beck.
June 27, 2018. "Read This Article!!!" *The
Atlantic.* www.theatlantic.com/technology
/archive/2018/06/exclamation-point
-inflation/563774/.

hypothetical deadline reminder: Erika
Darics. 2010. "Politeness in Computer-
Mediated Discourse of a Virtual Team."
Journal of Politeness Research 6(1). De
Gruyter. pp. 129–150.

"even if you are on very good terms":
Erika Darics. February 6, 2014. "Watch
Where You Put That Emoticon AND
KEEP YOUR VOICE DOWN." *The
Conversation.* theconversation.com/watch

-where-you-put-that-emoticon-and-keep -your-voice-down-22512.

"Split-p soup?": Eric S. Raymond, ed. December 29, 2003. "The -P Convention." The on-line hacker Jargon File, version 4.4.7. catb.org/jargon/html/p-convention .html.

"registering for a conference": Byron Ahn. April 10, 2017. twitter.com/lingulate /status/851576612927803392.

Chris Messina reached for the #: Chris Messina. August 23, 2007. twitter.com /chrismessina/status/223115412.

officially support hashtags: Lexi Pandell. May 19, 2017. "An Oral History of the #Hashtag." *Wired.* www.wired .com/2017/05/oral-history-hashtag/.

#sarcasm and other joke hashtags: Gretchen McCulloch. April 5, 2017. twitter. com/GretchenAMcC/status/849745 556188672000.

"When hanging out": Ben Zimmer. November 21, 2009. "Social Media Dialects: I Speak Twitter . . . You?" Archived at Internet Archive Wayback Machine. web.archive.org/web/20140423112918 /mykwblog.wordpress.com/2009/11/21 /social-media-dialects-i-speak-twitter-you/.

parents reporting: Gretchen McCulloch. March 25, 2017. twitter.com

/GretchenAMcC/status/84584424504
7070720.

"hashtag mom joke": Alexandra D'Arcy.
March 26, 2017. twitter.com/LangMaverick
/status/845863180534349824.

"My daughter just finished": Lady_Gar-
dener. March 25, 2017. twitter.com/daisy
_and_me/status/845597012071669978.

"one comma of the law": Richard Hovey.
1898. *Launcelot and Guenevere.* Small,
Maynard.

"a very big question mark": Paul Leices-
ter Ford. 1894. *The Honorable Peter Stirling
and What People Thought of Him.* Grosset
& Dunlap.

Exclamation!compounds: nentuaby.
July 7, 2014. allthingslinguistic.com/post
/95133324733/hey-whats-up-with-the
-in-fandoms-ie. (No author cited.) June
18, 2017. "!." Fanlore wiki. fanlore.org
/wiki/!. robert_columbia. January 17, 2011.
Can You Still Send an Email Using a
"Bang Path"? *The Straight Dope* message
board. boards.straightdope.com/sdmb/
showthread.php?t=593495. Robert L.
Krawitz. February 15, 1985. "Symphony
for the Devil (sic)." *Ask Mr. Protocol.* www
.textfiles.com/humor/COMPUTER/mr
.prtocl.

predated the internet: (No author cited.)

Draft additions September 2004. scare quotes. OED Online. Oxford University Press. Citing Gertrude Elizabeth Margaret Anscombe. 1956. *Mr. Truman's Degree.* Oxonian Press. Greg Hill. 1963. *Principia Discordia.*

may be Very Old Indeed: A connection first proposed by Tumblr user uglyfun: uglyfun. May 10, 2017. uglyfun.tumblr.com/post/160525273744/hi-im-here-to-propose-that-aa-milnes, quoting chapter 4 of A. A. Milne. 1926. *Winnie-the-Pooh.* Methuen.

Two LiveJournal threads: Anonymous. August 7, 2012. "Leading tilde?" *Fail. Fandom. Anon.* fail-fandomanon.livejournal.com/38277.html?thread=173014917#t173014917. Wayback Machine / archive.org and Google Search are blocked by the site's robots.txt, but a searchable archive of this forum is available on Google Groups at groups.google.com/forum/#!topic/sock_gryphon_group/c0juZF--BL8%5B551-575%5D.

"It seems to designate": Seasontoseason. July 12, 2010. "Tilde in Internet Slang." Linguaphiles LiveJournal group. linguaphiles.livejournal.com/5169778.html.

"what I am guessing": Anonymous. August

7, 2012. "Leading tilde?" *Fail. Fandom. Anon.*
fail-fandomanon.livejournal.com/38277
.html?thread=173014917#t173014917.
Wayback Machine / archive.org and Google
Search blocked by site's robots.txt, but a
searchable archive of this forum is available on Google Groups at groups.google
.com/forum/#!topic/sock_gryphon_group
/c0juZF--BL8%5B551-575%5D.

2010 LiveJournal thread: Seasontoseason. July 12, 2010. "Tilde in Internet
Slang." Linguaphiles LiveJournal group.
linguaphiles.livejournal.com/5169778
.html.

"somewhere between sarcasm": Joseph
Bernstein. January 5, 2015. "The Hidden Language of the ~Tilde~." *BuzzFeed.*
www.buzzfeed.com/josephbernstein
/the-hidden-language-of-the-tilde#
.ut0PpRAL3.

**popular computer operating system
Unix:** The Open Group. (No date cited.)
"History and Timeline." Unix.org. www
.unix.org/what_is_unix/history_timeline
.html.

actually *crackers*: Eric S. Raymond, ed.
December 29, 2003. "Hacker Writing
Style." The on-line hacker Jargon File,
version 4.4.7. www.catb.org/jargon/html
/writing-style.html.

"Netiquette" guides: Chris Pirillo. 1999. "E-mail Etiquette (Netiquette)." *The Internet Writing Journal.* www.writerswrite .com/journal/dec99/e-mail-etiquette -netiquette-12995.

forum posts into the mid-2000s: Damian. May 4, 2000. "People Who Don't Capitalize Their I's." *Everything2.* everything2 .com/title/People+who+don%2527t +capitalize+their+I%2527s.

terms of ease of use: Norm De Plume. September 26, 2004. "Why do some people write entirely in lowercase?" *DVD Talk.* forum.dvdtalk.com/archive/t-387605. html. Postroad. August 4, 2006. "Why do so many people always use lower case letters when using the net?" *Ask Metafilter.* ask.metafilter.com/43656/Why-do -so-many-people-always-use-lower-case -letters-when-using-the-net.

Trend pieces about passive-aggressive texting: Ben Crair. November 25, 2013. "The Period Is Pissed." *New Republic.* newrepublic.com/article/115726/period -our-simplest-punctuation-mark-has -become-sign-anger. Brittany Taylor. March 4, 2015. "8 Passive Aggressive Texts Everybody Sends (and What to Type Instead!)." *Teen Vogue.* www.teenvogue.com /story/passive-aggressive-texts-everyone

-sends. Dan Bilefsky. June 9, 2016. "Period. Full Stop. Point. Whatever It's Called, It's Going out of Style." *The New York Times.* www.nytimes.com/2016/06/10/world/europe/period-full-stop-point-whatever-its-called-millennials-arent-using-it.html?_r=0. Jeff Guo. June 13, 2016. "Stop Using Periods. Period." *The Washington Post.* medium.com/the washingtonpost/stop-using-periods-period-93a6bb357ed0#.fqi6as3ly.

surpassed sales of non-smart cellphones: Peter Svensson. April 28, 2013. "Smartphones Now Outsell 'Dumb' Phones." *Newshub.* www.newshub.co.nz/technology/smartphones-now-outsell-dumb-phones-2013042912.

informal poll on Twitter in 2016: Gretchen McCulloch. December 9, 2016. twitter.com/GretchenAMcC/status/807321178713059328.

involving their undergraduate students: Anne Curzan. April 24, 2013. "Slash: Not Just a Punctuation Mark Anymore." *The Chronicle of Higher Education, Lingua Franca* blog. www.chronicle.com/blogs/linguafranca/2013/04/24/slash-not-just-a-punctuation-mark-anymore/.

partnering with local schools: Sali Tagliamonte. 2011. *Variationist Sociolinguistics:*

Change, Observation, Interpretation. John Wiley & Sons.

thesis by Harley Grant: Harley Grant. 2015. "Tumblinguistics: Innovation and Variation in New Forms of Written CMC." Master's thesis, University of Glasgow.

thesis by Molly Ruhl: Molly Ruhl. 2016. "Welcome to My Twisted Thesis: An Analysis of Orthographic Conventions on Tumblr." Master's thesis, San Francisco State University.

You either need to be: Grant and Ruhl are examples of the former; for an example of the latter about a different topic see: Elli E. Bourlai. 2017. "'Comments in Tags, Please!' Tagging Practices on Tumblr." *Discourse Context Media.*

between ages sixteen and twenty-four: Cooper Smith. December 13, 2013. "Tumblr Offers Advertisers a Major Advantage: Young Users, Who Spend Tons of Time on the Site." *Business Insider.* www.businessinsider.com/tumblr-and-social-media-demographics-2013-12.

most popular such post: copperbooms. July 30. 2012. "when did tumblr collectively decide not to use punctuation like when did this happen why is this a thing." *Copperbooms.* copperbooms.tumblr.com

/post/28333799478/when-did-tumblr
-collectively-decide-not-to-use.

"when did tumbler" . . . this and similar posts: Archived version of whole post and a few similar ones by tumblinguistics. tumblinguistics.tumblr.com /post/113810945986/tumblinguistics -apocalypsecanceled-sunfell.

"i think it's really Cool": Original post by user eternalgirlscout. May 20, 2016. eternalgirlscout.tumblr.com/post/14466 1931903/i-think-its-really-cool-how -there-are-so-many. First reply by user takethebulletsoutyourson. July 25, 2016. takethebulletsoutyourson.tumblr.com/ post/147975549371/eternalgirlscout -i-think-its-really-cool-how. Second reply by user eternalgirlscout. July 25, 2016. eternalgirlscout.tumblr.com/post /147978362708/takethebulletsoutyour- son-eternalgirlscout-i. Archive by Molly Ruhl: amollyakatrina.tumblr.com/post /150704937613/eternalgirlscout -takethebulletsoutyourson.

"i just want": Jonny Sun. October 1, 2014. twitter.com/jonnysun/status /517461703630794752.

fifty original paintings: Jerome Tomasini. October 22, 2016. "How a Tweet by @jonnysun Resonated with

487

People & Inspired More Art." twitter.com/i /moments/789936594480427008.

Sun cited instead a soft/weird: Sophie Chou. September 27, 2017. "How to Speak Like an aliebn — No, That's Not a Typo." *The World in Words.* www.pri.org /stories/2017-09-27/How-Speak-Aliebn -No-Thats-Not-Typo.

If polite typography: Jeffrey T. Hancock. 2004. "Verbal Irony Use in Face-to-Face and Computer-Mediated Conversations." *Journal of Language and Social Psychology* 23(4). pp. 447–463.

Any variation from an expected baseline: Molly Ruhl. 2016. "Welcome to My Twisted Thesis: An Analysis of Orthographic Conventions on Tumblr." Master's thesis, San Francisco State University.

one much-reblogged post: tangleofrainbows. August 17, 2015. "re: how teens and adults text, I would be super interested for you to explain your theory!" *Tangleofrainbows.* tangleofrainbows.tumblr.com /post/126889100409/re-how-teens-and -adults-text-i-would-be-super.

psychologist Jeffrey Hancock: Jeffrey T. Hancock. 2004. "Verbal Irony Use in Face-to-Face and Computer-Mediated Conversations." *Journal of Language and Social Psychology* 23(4). pp. 447–463.

IBM experimented: Alexis C. Madrigal. January 10, 2013. "IBM's Watson Memorized the Entire 'Urban Dictionary,' Then His Overlords Had to Delete It." *The Atlantic.* www.theatlantic.com/technology /archive/2013/01/ibms-watson-memorized -the-entire-urban-dictionary-then-his -overlords-had-to-delete-it/267047/.

Chapter 5. Emoji and Other Internet Gestures

Second Life made: The most recent statistic that Linden Lab provides is from 2013 and consists of 36 million accounts created in total, with a million monthly active users. (No author cited.) June 20, 2013. "Infographic: 10 Years of Second Life." Linden Lab. www.lindenlab .com/releases/infographic-10-years-of -second-life. This 2017 article estimated 600,000 regular users: Leslie Jamison. November 11, 2017. "The Digital Ruins of a Forgotten Future." *The Atlantic.* www .theatlantic.com/magazine/archive/2017/12 /second-life-leslie-jamison/544149/.

over six thousand articles: Mark Davis and Peter Edberg, eds. May 18, 2017. "Unicode® Technical Standard #51 UNICODE EMOJI." *The Unicode Consortium.* www .unicode.org/reports/tr51/#Introduction.

489

newspapers in six countries: Ben Medlock and Gretchen McCulloch. 2016. "The Linguistic Secrets Found in Billions of Emoji." Presented at SXSW, March 11–20, 2016, Austin, Texas. www .slideshare.net/SwiftKey/the-linguistic -secrets-found-in-billions-of-emoji-sxsw -2016-presentation-59956212.

So she started in on: Lauren Gawne and Gretchen McCulloch. 2019. "Emoji Are Digital Gesture." *Language@Internet.*

Many theorists call them emblems: Paul Ekman and Wallace V. Friesen. 1969. "The Repertoire of Nonverbal Behavior: Categories, Origins, Usage, and Coding." *Semiotica* 1. pp. 49–98.

the middle finger: Lauren Gawne. October 8, 2015. "Up Yours: The Gesture That Divides America and the UK." *Strong Language.* stronglang.wordpress .com/2015/10/08/up-yours-the-gesture -that-divides-america-and-the-uk/.

obscene emblems: Desmond Morris, Peter Collett, Peter Marsh, and Marie O'Shaughnessy. 1979. *Gestures, Their Origin and Distribution.* Jonathan Cape.

The eggplant emoji: Regan Hoffman. June 3, 2015. "The Complete (and Sometimes Sordid) History of the Eggplant Emoji." *First We Feast.* firstwefeast.com

/features/2015/06/eggplant-emoji-history.

"It says 'I don't like that'": Lauren Schwartzberg. November 18, 2014. "The Oral History of the Poop Emoji (Or, How Google Brought Poop to America)." *Fast Company.* www.fastcompany .com/3037803/the-oral-history-of-the -poop-emoji-or-how-google-brought-poop -to-america.

different app or device manufacturers: Jason Snell. January 16, 2017. "More Emoji Fragmentation." *Six Colors.* sixcolors.com /link/2017/01/more-emoji-fragmentation/.

"The Year of Emoji Convergence": "2018: The Year of Emoji Convergence." February 13, 2018. Emojipedia. https:// blog.emojipedia.org/2018-the-year-of -emoji-convergence/.

"like texting, but you get": Mary Madden, Amanda Lenhart, Sandra Cortesi, Urs Gasser, Maeve Duggan, Aaron Smith, and Meredith Beaton. May 21, 2013. "Teens, Social Media, and Privacy." Pew Research Center. www.pewinternet.org/2013/05/21 /teens-social-media-and-privacy/.

The most engaging gifs: Saeideh Bakhshi, David A. Shamma, Lyndon Kennedy, Yale Song, Paloma de Juan, and Joseph Kaye. 2016. "Fast, Cheap, and Good: Why Animated GIFs Engage Us." *Proceedings of* the *2016 CHI Conference on Human Factors in Computing Systems.* pp. 575–586.

Certain gifs are so emblematic: Tomberry. January 12, 2015. "Popcorn GIFs." Know Your Meme. knowyourmeme.com /memes/popcorn-gifs.

appropriation from African American culture: Geneva Smitherman. 2006. *Word from the Mother: Language and African Americans.* Taylor & Francis.

spread via sports teams: John Mooallem. April 12, 2013. "History of the High Five." ESPN.com. www.espn.com/espn /story/_/page/Mag15historyofthehighfive /who-invented-high-five.

the fistbump: LaMont Hamilton. September 22, 2014. "Five on the Black Hand Side: Origins and Evolutions of the Dap." *Folklife.* folklife.si.edu/talkstory /2014/five-on-the-black-hand-sideorigins -and-evolutions-of-the-dap.

painting fingernails emoji: Alexander Abad-Santos and Allie Jones. March 26, 2014. "The Five Non-Negotiable Best Emojis in the Land." *The Atlantic.* www.theatlantic.com/entertainment /archive/2014/03/the-only-five-emojis-you -need/359646/. www.merriam-webster.com /words-at-play/shade.

She linked this stereotype: Sianne Ngai.

2005. *Ugly Feelings.* Harvard University Press.

when you can't gesture: Frances H. Rauscher, Robert M. Krauss, and Yihsiu Chen. 1996. "Gesture, Speech, and Lexical Access: The Role of Lexical Movements in Speech Production." *Psychological Science* 7(4). pp. 226–231.

Every culture: Pierre Feyereisen and Jacques-Dominique De Lannoy. 1991. *Gestures and Speech: Psychological Investigations.* Cambridge University Press. David McNeill. 1992. *Hand and Mind: What Gestures Reveal About Thought.* University of Chicago Press.

we gesture along with our speech: Akiba A. Cohen and Randall P. Harrison. 1973. "Intentionality in the Use of Hand Illustrators in Face-to-Face Communication Situations." *Journal of Personality and Social Psychology* 28(2). pp. 276–279.

people who have been blind: Jana M. Iverson and Susan Goldin-Meadow. 1997. "What's Communication Got to Do with It? Gesture in Children Blind from Birth." *Developmental Psychology* 33(3). pp. 453–467. Jana M. Iverson and Susan Goldin-Meadow. 1998. "Why People Gesture When They Speak." *Nature* 396(6708). p. 228.

co-speech or illustrative gesture: Pierre Feyereisen and Jacques-Dominique De Lannoy. 1991. *Gestures and Speech: Psychological Investigations.* Cambridge University Press. David McNeill. 1992. *Hand and Mind: What Gestures Reveal about Thought.* University of Chicago Press.

about the thinking of the speaker: Robert M. Krauss, Yihsiu Chen, and Rebecca F. Gottesman. 2000. "Lexical Gestures and Lexical Access: A Process Model." In D. McNeill, ed., *Language and Gesture: Window into Thought and Action.* Cambridge University Press. pp. 261–283.

better at solving math problems: Mingyuan Chu and Sotaro Kita. 2011. "The Nature of Gestures' Beneficial Role in Spatial Problem Solving." *Journal of Experimental Psychology: General* 140(1). pp. 102–116. Sara C. Broaders, Susan Wagner Cook, Zachary Mitchell, and Susan Goldin-Meadow. 2007. "Making Children Gesture Brings Out Implicit Knowledge and Leads to Learning." *Journal of Experimental Psychology: General* 136(4). pp. 539–550. Susan Wagner Cook, Zachary Mitchell, and Susan Goldin-Meadow. 2008. "Gesturing Makes Learning Last." *Cognition* 106(2). pp. 1047–1058.

"up there": David McNeill. 2006. "Gesture

and Communication." In J. L. Mey, ed., *Concise Encyclopedia of Pragmatics.* Elsevier. pp. 299–307.

Less than one in a thousand: Ben Medlock and Gretchen McCulloch. 2016. "The Linguistic Secrets Found in Billions of Emoji." Presented at SXSW, March 11–20, 2016, Austin, Texas. www.slideshare .net/SwiftKey/the-linguistic-secrets -found-in-billions-of-emoji-sxsw-2016 -presentation-59956212.

enjoy texting them messages: Gretchen McCulloch. January 1, 2019. "Children Are Using Emoji for Digital-Age Language Learning." *Wired.* https://www.wired.com /story/children-emoji-language-learning/.

These repetitive gestures: David McNeill. 2006. "Gesture and Communication." In J. L. Mey, ed., *Concise Encyclopedia of Pragmatics.* Elsevier. pp. 299–307.

Emoji have the same rhythmic: Gretchen McCulloch and Lauren Gawne. 2018. "Emoji Grammar as Beat Gestures." Presented at Emoji 2018: 1st International Workshop on Emoji Understanding and Applications in Social Media, co-located with the 12th International AAAI Conference on Web and Social Media (ICWSM-18), June 25, 2018, Palo Alto, California.

Comedian Robin Thede: Robin Thede.

March 17, 2016. "Women's History Month Report: Black Lady Sign Language." *The Nightly Show with Larry Wilmore.* www.youtube.com/watch?v=34PjKtcVhVE.

writer Kara Brown: Kara Brown. April 6, 2016. "Your Twitter Trend Analysis Is Not Deep, and It's Probably Wrong." *Jezebel.* jezebel.com/your-twitter-trend-analysis-is-not-deep-and-it-s-proba-1769411909.

spreading to mainstream Twitter: Chaédria LaBouvier. May 16, 2017. "The Clap and the Clap Back: How Twitter Erased Black Culture from an Emoji." *Motherboard.* motherboard.vice.com/en_us/article/jpyajg/the-clap-and-the-clap-back-how-twitter-erased-black-culture-from-an-emoji.

Medieval scribes illustrated: (No author cited.) September 26, 2013. "Knight v Snail." *British Library Medieval Manuscripts Blog.* britishlibrary.typepad.co.uk/digitisedmanuscripts/2013/09/knight-v-snail.html.

the first English printers: D. G. Scragg. 1974. *A History of English Spelling.* Manchester University Press.

It was in widespread use: William H. Sherman. 2005. "Toward a History of the Manicule." In Robin Myers, Michael Harris, and Gile Mandebrote, eds., *Owners,*

Annotators and the Signs of Reading. Oak Knoll Press and The British Library. pp. 19–48. William H. Sherman. 2010. *Used Books: Marking Readers in Renaissance England.* University of Pennsylvania Press.

stylized arrow shape: Robert J. Finkel. April 1, 2015. "History of the Arrow." American Printing History Association. printinghistory.org/arrow/. Robert J. Finkel. 2011. "Up Down Left Right." Master's thesis, University of Florida.

doodles were popular: (No author cited.) (No date cited.) Lewis Carroll's *Alice's Adventures Under Ground* - Introduction. British Library Online Gallery. www.bl.uk/onlinegallery/ttp/alice/accessible/introduction.html.

Sylvia Plath: Maria Popova. November 6, 2013. "Sylvia Plath's Unseen Drawings, Edited by Her Daughter and Illuminated in Her Private Letters." *Brain Pickings.* www.brainpickings.org/2013/11/06/sylvia-plath-drawings-2/. Richard Watts. October 27, 2016. "UVic Purchases Rare Volume of Plath Novel, plus Doodles for $8,500 US." *Times Colonist* (Victoria, BC, Canada). www.timescolonist.com/news/local/uvic-purchases-rare-volume-of-plath-novel-plus-doodles-for-8-500-us-1.2374834.

The ASCII art: Patrick Gillespie. Text to ASCII Art Generator. patorjk.com. patorjk.com/software/taag/#p=display&h=2&f=Standard&t=ASCII%20art.

professor named Scott Fahlman: Scott E. Fahlman. September 19, 1982. "Original Bboard Thread in which :-) was proposed." Carnegie Mellon University messageboards. www.cs.cmu.edu/~sef /Orig-Smiley.htm.

The idea of a simplified smiling face: The first round black-on-yellow smiley face is generally attributed to a graphic artist named Harvey Ross Ball, who created it for an employee morale-boosting campaign at an insurance company in 1963. But other simplified smiling faces are found even earlier. Jimmy Stamp. March 13, 2013. "Who Really Invented the Smiley Face?" *Smithsonian.* www.smithsonian mag.com/arts-culture/who-really-invented -the-smiley-face-2058483/. Luke Stark and Kate Crawford. 2015. "The Conservatism of Emoji: Work, Affect, and Communication." *Social Media + Society* 1(11).

in 2011, a study of emoticons: Tyler Schnoebelen. 2012. "Do You Smile with Your Nose? Stylistic Variation in Twitter Emoticons." *University of Pennsylvania Working Papers in Linguistics* 18(2).

Penn Graduate Linguistics Society. repository.upenn.edu/cgi/viewcontent .cgi?article=1242&context=pwpl. The paper was published in 2012, but the data was collected in 2011.

Classic kaomoji: Kenji Rikitake. February 25, 1993. "The History of Smiley Marks." Archived at Internet Archive Wayback Machine. web.archive.org/web /20121203061906/staff.aist.go.jp:80/k .harigaya/doc/kao_his.html. Ken Y-N. September 19, 2007. ":-) Turns 25, but How Old Are Japanese Emoticons (?_?)." *What Japan Thinks.* whatjapanthinks .com/2007/09/19/turns-25-but-how -old-are-japanese-emoticons/.

When researchers show: Masaki Yuki, William W. Maddux, and Takahiko Masuda. 2007. "Are the Windows to the Soul the Same in the East and West? Cultural Differences in Using the Eyes and Mouth as Cues to Recognize Emotions in Japan and the United States." *Journal of Experimental Social Psychology* 43(2). pp. 303–311.

Some kaomoji have caught on: Amanda Brennan. April 24, 2013. "Hold My Flower." Know Your Meme. knowyourmeme.com /memes/hold-my-flower.

table flip: nycto. July 8, 2011. "Flipping

Tables / (╯°□°)╯︵┻━┻ ." Know Your Meme. knowyourmeme.com/memes /flipping-tables.

designers at SoftBank: Jeremy Burge. March 8, 2019. "Correcting the Record on the First Emoji Set." *Emojipedia.* https://blog.emojipedia.org/correcting-the -record-on-the-first-emoji-set/.

picture of a normal cow: Sam Byford. April 24, 2012. "Emoji Harmonization: Japanese Carriers Unite to Standardize Picture Characters." *The Verge.* www .theverge.com/2012/4/24/2971039/emoji -standardization-japan-kddi-docomo -eaccess.

Japanese *mojibake*: Ritchie S. King. July 2012. "Will Unicode Soon Be the Universal Code?" *IEEE Spectrum* 49(7). p. 60. ieeexplore.ieee.org/document/6221090/.

Russian *krakozyabry*: Jonathon Keats. 2007. *Control + Alt + Delete: A Dictionary of Cyberslang.* Globe Pequot.

German *Zeichensalat*: "Harte Nuß im Zeichensalat." *Der Spiegel.* June 8, 1998. www.spiegel.de/spiegel/print/d-7907491 .html.

Bulgarian *majmunica*: Ilian Minchev. July 2, 2015. "Как субтитрите, да не ми излизат на маймуница?" (How do the subtitles do not go to a monkey?).

Блогът на Илиян Минчев (The blog of Ilian Minchev). iliqnktz.blogspot.com /2015/07/blog-post.htm. (With thanks to Google Translate.) vik-45. April 21, 2009. "Надписи с 'маймуница'" (Captions with "monkey"). *SETCOMBG forum.* forum.setcombg.com/windows/30330 -%D0%BD%D0%B0%D0%B4%D0%B F%D0%B8%D1%81%D0%B8-%D1%81 -%D0%BC%D0%B0%D0%B9%D0%BC %D1%83%D0%BD%D0%B8%D1%86% D0%B0.html. (With thanks to Google Translate.)

Multiply that by all: According to this link, there are 615 Unicode arrows as of 2017: (No author cited.) (No date cited.) "Unicode Utilities: UnicodeSet." *The Unicode Consortium.* unicode.org /cldr/utility/list-unicodeset.jsp?a=%5Cp%7 Bname=/%5CbARROW/%7D&g=gc.

Apple wanted people in Japan: Mark Davis and Peter Edberg, eds. May 18, 2017. "Unicode® Technical Standard #51 UNICODE EMOJI." *The Unicode Consortium.* www.unicode.org/reports/tr51/.

contained 608 symbols: (No author cited.) (No date cited.) "Emoji and Pictographs." *The Unicode Consortium.* www.unicode .org/faq/emoji_dingbats.html.

Just five years after emoji: Ben Medlock

and Gretchen McCulloch. 2016. "The Linguistic Secrets Found in Billions of Emoji." Presented at SXSW, March 11–20, 2016, Austin, Texas. www.slideshare.net /SwiftKey/the-linguistic-secrets-found-in -billions-of-emoji-sxsw-2016-presentation -59956212.

list of words people also use: Thomas Dimson. May 1, 2015. "Emojineering Part 1: Machine Learning for Emoji Trends." Medium. engineering.instagram.com /emojineering-part-1-machine-learning -for-emoji-trendsmachine-learning-for -emoji-trends-7f5f9cb979ad.

rely less on other expressive resources: Umashanthi Pavalanathan and Jacob Eisenstein. 2016. "More Emojis, Less :) The Competition for Paralinguistic Function in Microblog Writing." *First Monday* 1(1).

most trustworthy kind: Erving Goffman. 1959. *The Presentation of Self in Everyday Life.* Doubleday/Anchor.

deliberate cues to the intention: Eli Dresner and Susan C. Herring. "Functions of the Non-Verbal in CMC: Emoticons and Illocutionary Force." *Communication Theory* 20. pp. 249–268.

the smiley changes the intention: Monica Ann Riordan. 2011. "The Use of Verbal and

Nonverbal Cues in Computer-Mediated Communication: When and Why?" PhD dissertation, University of Memphis.

One teen explained: Mary H.K. Choi. August 25, 2016. "Like. Flirt. Ghost. A Journey into the Social Media Lives of Teens." *Wired.* www.wired.com/2016/08 /how-teens-use-social-media/.

invoked Austin's idea: Adam Kendon. 1995. "Gestures as Illocutionary and Discourse Markers in Southern Italian Conversation." *Journal of Pragmatics* 23(3). pp. 249–279.

Liking can also backfire: Deborah Cicurel. October 27, 2014. "Deep-Liking: What Do You Make of the New Instagram Trend?" *Glamour.* www.glamourmagazine .co.uk/article/deep-liking-instagram -dating-trend.

"Ugh, I got a flat": Carl Rogers and Richard E. Farson. 1957. *Active Listening.* University of Chicago Industrial Relations Center. www.gordontraining.com /free-workplace-articles/active-listening/.

how they used emoji: Ryan Kelly and Leon Watts. 2015. "Characterising the Inventive Appropriation of Emoji as Relationally Meaningful in Mediated Close Personal Relationships." Presented at Experiences of Technology Appropriation: Unanticipated

Users, Usage, Circumstances, and Design, September 20, 2015, Oslo. projects.hci .sbg.ac.at/ecscw2015/wp-content/uploads /sites/31/2015/08/Kelly_Watts.pdf.

looking at cute cat videos: Jessica Gall Myrick. 2015. "Emotion Regulation, Procrastination, and Watching Cat Videos Online: Who Watches Internet Cats, Why, and to What Effect?" *Computers in Human Behavior* 52. pp. 168–176.

cute puppy photos: Jessika Golle, Stephanie Lisibach, Fred W. Mast, and Janek S. Lobmaier. March 13, 2013. "Sweet Puppies and Cute Babies: Perceptual Adaptation to Babyfacedness Transfers across Species." *PLOS ONE.* journals.plos .org/plosone/article?id=10.1371/journal .pone.0058248.

Esperanto: Arika Okrent. 2010. *In the Land of Invented Languages.* Spiegel & Grau.

More than two million: CMO.com Staff. November 22, 2016. "Infographic: 92% of World's Online Population Use Emojis." CMO.com. www.cmo.com/features /articles/2016/11/21/report-emoji-used-by -92-of-worlds-online-population.html#gs .X8X1e_g.

People who saw the play: Sarah Begley. August 12, 2016. "The Magic Is Gone but Harry Potter Will Never Die." *Time.*

504

time.com/4445149/harry-potter-cursed
-child-jk-rowling/.

idea of pictorial communication: Lauren
Gawne. October 5, 2015. "Emoji Deixis:
When Emoji Don't Face the Way You Want
Them To." *Superlinguo*. www.superlinguo
.com/post/130501329351/emoji-deixis
-when-emoji-dont-face-the-way-you.

those who are illiterate: Diana Fussell
and Ane Haaland. 1978. "Communicating
with Pictures in Nepal: Results of Practical Study Used in Visual Education." *Educational Broadcasting International* 11(1).
pp. 25–31.

neither pictures nor gestures: Gretchen
McCulloch. June 29, 2016. "A Linguist Explains Emoji and What Language Death Actually Looks Like." *The
Toast*. the-toast.net/2016/06/29/a-linguist
-explains-emoji-and-what-language-death
-actually-looks-like/.

Nuclear scientists, for example: Juliet
Lapidos. November 16, 2009. "Atomic
Priesthoods, Thorn Landscapes, and
Munchian Pictograms." *Slate*. www.slate
.com/articles/health_and_science/green
_room/2009/11/atomic_priesthoods_thorn
_landscapes_and_munchian_pictograms
.html.

Judges and juries: Eric Goldman. 2018.

"Emojis and the Law." Santa Clara University Legal Studies Research Paper 2018(06).

court interpreted a smiley emoticon: Eric Goldman. 2017. "Surveying the Law of Emojis." Santa Clara University Legal Studies Research Paper 2017(08).

In a list of emoji examples: Eli Hager. February 2, 2015. "Is an Emoji Worth a Thousand Words?" The Marshall Project. www.themarshallproject.org/2015/02/02/is-an-emoji-worth-1-000-words.

people who read a lot of fiction: Julie Sedivy. April 27, 2017. "Why Doesn't Ancient Fiction Talk About Feelings?" *Nautilus.* nautil.us/issue/47/consciousness/why-doesnt-ancient-fiction-talk-about-feelings.

Chapter 6. How Conversations Change

In one video: (No author cited.) July 12, 2017. "Google's DeepMind AI Just Taught Itself to Walk." *Tech Insider* YouTube channel. www.youtube.com/watch?v=gn4nRCC9TwQ.

In another, a metallic: (No author cited.) (No date cited.) "How to Teach a Robot to Walk." *Smithsonian Channel.* www.smithsonianmag.com/videos/category/innovation/how-to-teach-a-robot-to-walk/.

The two most prominent solutions: Ammon Shea. 2010. *The Phone Book: The Curious History of the Book That Everybody Uses but No One Reads.* Perigee/Penguin. Robert Krulwich. February 17, 2011. "A (Shockingly) Short History of 'Hello.'" NPR. www.npr.org /sections/krulwich/2011/02/17/133785829 /a-shockingly-short-history-of-hello.

Some early phones . . . "That is all": William Grimes. March 5, 1992. "Great 'Hello' Mystery Is Solved." *The New York Times.* www.nytimes.com/1992/03/05 /garden/great-hello-mystery-is-solved .html.

"Goodbye": Douglas Harper. 2001–2018. "Good-bye." *Online Etymology Dictionary.* www.etymonline.com/word/good-bye.

"When I was in training": BBC One. January 25, 2015. twitter.com/bbcone /status/559443111936798721.

Etiquette books: Claude S. Fischer. 1994. *America Calling: A Social History of the Telephone to 1940.* University of California Press.

According to the same survey: (No author cited.) (No date cited.) "Expressions (Such as 'Hello') Used When You Meet Somebody You Know Quite Well." *Dictionary of American Regional English.*

507

dare.wisc.edu/survey-results/1965-1970
/exclamations/nn10a.

"I almost always say 'hey' ": Allan Metcalf. November 7, 2013. "Making Hey." *The Chronicle of Higher Education.* chronicle .com/blogs/linguafranca/2013/11/07 /making-hey/.

"One could write tersely": J. C. R. Licklider and Albert Vezza. 1978. "Applications of Information Networks." *Proceedings of the IEEE* (Institute of Electrical and Electronics Engineers) 66(11). archive .org/stream/ApplicationsOfInformation Networks/AIN.txt.

"most users exercise": Naomi S. Baron. 1998. "Letters by Phone or Speech by Other Means: The Linguistics of Email." *Language & Communication* 18. pp. 156–157.

"I receive innumerable e-mails": David Crystal. 2006. *Language and the Internet.* Cambridge University Press.

the research of the linguist Gillian Sankoff: Gillian Sankoff and Hélène Blondeau. 2007. "Language Change across the Lifespan: /r/ in Montreal French." *Language* 83(3). pp. 560–588. Gillian Sankoff and Hélène Blondeau. 2010. "Instability of the [r] ~ [R] Alternation in Montreal French: The Conditioning of a Sound Change in Progress." In Hans van de

Velde, Roeland van Hout, Didier Demolin, and Wim Zonneveld, eds., *VaRiation: Sociogeographic, Phonetic and Phonological Characterics of /r/*. John Benjamins.

"To the Right noble": Edmund Spenser. 1590. "A Letter of the Authors expounding his whole Intention in the course of this Worke." *The Faerie Queene. Disposed into Twelve Books, fashioning XII Morall Vertues.* spenserians.cath.vt.edu/TextRecord .php?textsid=102.

"I have the honor": Alexander Hamilton and Aaron Burr. 1804. Hamilton–Burr duel correspondences. Wikisource. en .wikisource.org/wiki/Hamilton%E2% 80%93Burr_duel_correspondences.

Reading through the comments: Maeve Maddox. January 27, 2015. "Starting a Business Letter with Dear Mr." *Daily Writing Tips.* www.dailywritingtips.com/ starting-a-business-letter-with-dear-mr/. Lynn Gaertner-Johnson. August 16, 2005. "Do I Have to Call You 'Dear'?" *Business Writing.* www.businesswritingblog.com/ business_writing/2005/08/do_i_have_to _ca.html. Susan Adams. August 8, 2012. "Hi? Dear? The State of the E-Mail Salutation." *Forbes.* www.forbes.com/sites /susanadams/2012/08/08/hi-dear-the-state -of-the-e-mail-salutation/.

Even if just 0.2 seconds go by: Antony J. Liddicoat. 2007. *An Introduction to Conversation Analysis*. Continuum.

ever so slightly miscalibrated: Deborah Tannen. 1992. *That's Not What I Meant! How Conversational Style Makes or Breaks Your Relations with Others*. Virago.

Conversation analysts find: Antony J. Liddicoat. 2007. *An Introduction to Conversation Analysis*. Continuum.

Some early chat systems: Brian Dear. 2002. "Origin of 'Talk' Command." *OSDIR.com Forums*. web.archive.org/web /20160304060338/osdir.com/ml/culture .internet.history/2002-12/msg00026.html.

Some systems tried: Paul Dourish. (No date cited.) "The Original Hacker's Dictionary." Dourish.com. www.dourish.com /goodies/jargon.html.

Other chat systems: (No author cited.) (No date cited.) Unix talk screenshot. Wikipedia. en.wikipedia.org/wiki/File:Unix_talk _screenshot_01.png.

You could add more boxes: Brian Dear. 2017. *The Friendly Orange Glow: The Untold Story of the PLATO System and the Dawn of Cyberculture*. Pantheon. David R. Wooley. 1994. "PLATO: The Emergence of Online Community." *Matrix News*. A re-created modern web version of Talkomatic that

you can try out yourself is here: talko.cc
/talko.html.

Indeed, Google tried: Ben Parr. May 28,
2009. "Google Wave: A Complete Guide."
Mashable. mashable.com/2009/05/28
/google-wave-guide/#sHbYql_QFqq4.

read faster than we can type: Keith
Rayner, Timothy J. Slattery, and Nathalie
N. Bélanger. 2010. "Eye Movements, the
Perceptual Span, and Reading Speed."
Psychonomic Bulletin & Review 17(6). pp.
834–839. Teresia R. Ostrach. 1997. *Typing
Speed: How Fast Is Average: 4,000 Typ-
ing Scores Statistically Analyzed and Inter-
preted.* Five Star Staffing. dev.blueorb
.me/wp-content/uploads/2012/03/Average
-OrbiTouch-Typing-Speed.pdf.

The oldest example: Dylan Tweney. September 24, 2009. "September 24, 1979:
First Online Service for Consumers De-
buts." *Wired.* www.wired.com/2009
/09/0924compuserve-launches/.

An employee of CompuServe: Michael
Banks. 2012. *On the Way to the Web: The
Secret History of the Internet and Its Found-
ers.* Apress.

Internet Relay Chat (IRC): Jarkko Oikar-
inen. (No date cited.) Founding IRC.
mIRC website. www.mirc.com/jarkko
.html.

These public chatrooms: John C. Paolillo and Asta Zelenkauskaite. 2013. "Real-Time Chat." In Susan C. Herring, Dieter Stein, and Tuija Virtanen, eds., *Pragmatics of Computer-Mediated Communication.* Mouton de Gruyter. pp. 109–133. Susan Herring. 1999. "Interactional Coherence in CMC." *Journal of Computer-Mediated Communication* 4(4).

Here's a nineties example of such overlap: John C. Paolillo. "'Conversational' Codeswitching on Usenet and Internet Relay Chat." *Language@Internet* Volume 8 (2011). http://www.languageatinternet.org /articles/2011/Paolillo.

Even the "is typing": David Auerbach. February 12, 2014. "I Built That 'So-and-So Is Typing' Feature in Chat and I'm Not Sorry." *Slate.* www.slate.com/articles/ technology/bitwise/2014/02/typing _indicator_in_chat_i_built_it_and_i_m _not_sorry.html.

Reviews of the first-generation: Kent German and Donald Bell. June 30, 2007. Apple iPhone review. CNET. www.cnet .com/products/apple-iphone/review/. Sam Costello. October 19, 2016. First-generation iPhone review. Lifewire. www.lifewire.com /first-generation-iphone-review-2000196.

starting with BlackBerry: Jesse Ariss.

July 27, 2015. "10 Years of BBM." *IN-SIDE BlackBerry*. blogs.blackberry.com/2015/07/10-years-of-bbm/.

Apple's iMessage: Adam Howorth. June 6, 2011. "New Version of iOS Includes Notification Center, iMessage, Newsstand, Twitter Integration Among 200 New Features." *Apple Newsroom*. www.apple.com/uk/newsroom/2011/06/06New-Version-of-iOS-Includes-Notification-Center-iMessage-Newsstand-Twitter-Integration-Among-200-New-Features/.

a 1992 survey found: Robert Hopper. 1992. *Telephone Conversation*. Indiana University Press.

I tried replicating the survey: Gretchen McCulloch. December 22, 2017. twitter.com/GretchenAMcC/status/944395370188234753.

Even if nothing particular: Gretchen McCulloch. December 22, 2017. twitter.com/GretchenAMcC/status/944400462861783041.

caller ID became widely available: Anthony Ramirez. April 4, 1992. "Caller ID: Consumer's Friend or Foe?" *The New York Times*. www.nytimes.com/1992/04/04/news/caller-id-consumer-s-friend-or-foe.html.

In the 1970s, 80s, and 90s: Paul F. Finnigan.

1983. "Voice Mail." *AFIPS '83 Proceedings of the May 16–19, 1983, National Computer Conference.* American Federation of Information Processing Societies. pp. 373–377. Linda R. Garceau and Jayne Fuglister. 1991. "Making Voicemail a Success." *The CPA Journal* 61(3). p. 40.

"butler lies": Jeff Hancock, Jeremy Birnholtz, Natalya Bazarova, Jamie Guillory, Josh Perlin, and Barrett Amos. 2009. "Butler Lies: Awareness, Deception and Design." *Proceedings of the SIGCHI Conference on Human Factors in Computing Systems.* pp 517–526.

Op-ed articles: Ian Shapira. August 8, 2010. "Texting Generation Doesn't Share Boomers' Taste for Talk." *The Washington Post.* www.washingtonpost.com/wp-dyn/content/article/2010/08/07/AR2010080702848.html. Sally Parker. October 23, 2015. "Dear Old People: Why Should I Turn Off My Phone?" *The Telegraph.* www.telegraph.co.uk/technology/social-media/11951918/Dear-old-people-why-should-I-turn-off-my-phone.html.

younger people find: Stephen DiDomenico and Jeffrey Boase. 2013. "Bringing Mobiles into the Conversation: Applying a Conversation Analytic Approach to the Study of Mobiles in Co-Present

Interaction." In Deborah Tannen and Anna Marie Trester, eds., *Discourse 2.0: Language and New Media.* Georgetown University Press. pp. 119–132.

idea of a third place: Matthew Dollinger. June 11, 2008. "Starbucks, 'The Third Place,' and Creating the Ultimate Customer Experience." *Fast Company.* www. fastcompany.com/887990/starbucks-third -place-and-creating-ultimate-customer -experience.

What Ray Oldenburg: Ray Oldenburg. 1989. *The Great Good Place: Cafes, Coffee Shops, Community Centers, Beauty Parlors, General Stores, Bars, Hangouts, and How They Get You Through the Day.* Paragon House.

Examples include pubs: Leo W. Jeffres, Cheryl C. Bracken, Guowei Jian, and Mary F. Casey. 2009. "The Impact of Third Places on Community Quality of Life." *Applied Research in the Quality of Life* 4(4). pp. 333–345.

When Facebook and Twitter: Clive Thompson. September 5, 2008. "Brave New World of Digital Intimacy." *The New York Times.* www.nytimes.com/2008/09/07 /magazine/07awareness-t.html.

While early tweets: 2006 tweets are via the bot @VeryOldTweets, twitter.com/

515

veryoldtweets, which retweets tweets from 2006. Tweets: Ray McClure. March 30, 2006. twitter.com/rayreadyray/status/696. Biz Stone. April 13, 2006. twitter.com/biz/status/2033. Sharon. May 9, 2006. twitter.com/sharon/status/3913. Telene. June 18, 2006. twitter.com/telene/status/7030. (The last is a quote of @jack's first status.) Jason_G. June 8, 2006. twitter.com/jason_g/status/6335. Sara M. Williams. April 7, 2006. twitter.com/sara/status/1483. Note the lack of @mentions: Jack. May 3, 2006. twitter.com/jack/status/3431. Jeremy. May 16, 2006. twitter.com/jeremy/status/4532. Dom Sagolla. April 8, 2006. twitter.com/dom/status/1607.

an average of fifty minutes: James B. Stewart. May 5, 2016. "Facebook Has 50 Minutes of Your Time Each Day. It Wants More." *The New York Times.* www.nytimes.com/2016/05/06/business/facebook-bends-the-rules-of-audience-engagement-to-its-advantage.html.

Yet social media posts: J. J. Colao. November 27, 2012. "Snapchat: The Biggest No-Revenue Mobile App Since Instagram." *Forbes.* www.forbes.com/sites/jjcolao/2012/11/27/snapchat-the-biggest-no-revenue-mobile-app-since-instagram/#1499ff0e7200.

like Instagram and Snapchat: Somini Sengupta, Nicole Perlroth, and Jenna Wortham. April 13, 2012. "Behind Instagram's Success, Networking the Old Way." *The New York Times.* www.nytimes .com/2012/04/14/technology/instagram -founders-were-helped-by-bay-area -connections.html.

a new format for posts: Robinson Meyer. August 3, 2016. "Why Instagram 'Borrowed' Stories from Snapchat." *The Atlantic.* www.theatlantic.com /technology/archive/2016/08/cameras -with-constraints/494291/. Ian Bogost. May 3, 2018. "Why 'Stories' Took Over Your Smartphone." *The Atlantic.* www.theatlantic .com/technology/archive/2018/05 /smartphone-stories-snapchat-instagram -facebook/559517/.

"Third place conversation": Ray Oldenburg. 1989. *The Great Good Place: Cafes, Coffee Shops, Community Centers, Beauty Parlors, General Stores, Bars, Hangouts, and How They Get You Through the Day.* Paragon House.

Popular email lists: (No author cited.) January 7, 2000. "Mailing List History." *Living Internet.* www.livinginternet.com/l /li.htm.

later technology such as: Lori Kendall.

2002. *Hanging Out in the Virtual Pub: Masculinities and Relationships Online.* University of California Press. Eric Thomas and L-Soft International, Inc. 1996. Early History of LISTSERV®. *L-Soft International.* www.lsoft.com/products/listserv-history .asp. David Barr. 1995. "So You Want to Create an Alt Newsgroup." FAQs.org. www.faqs.org/faqs/alt-creation-guide/.

Multiplayer online games: Constance A. Steinkuehler and Dimitri Williams. 2006. "Where Everybody Knows Your (Screen) Name: Online Games as 'Third Places.'" *Journal of Computer-Mediated Communication* 11. pp. 885–909.

import your friends: Valentina Rao. 2008. "Facebook Applications and Playful Mood: The Construction of Facebook as a 'Third Place.'" In Artur Lugmayr, Frans Mäyrä, Heljä Franssila, and Katri Lietsala, eds., *Proceedings of the 12th International Conference on Entertainment and Media in the Ubiquitous Era.* ACM. pp. 8–12.

most popular general-interest forum: Alexa Internet, Inc. Visited May 2018. "The Top 500 Sites on the Web." Alexa. www.alexa.com/topsites.

has subdivisions for everything: r/ShowerThoughts and r/IAmA, respectively.

Estimates are low: Amanda Lenhart and

Susannah Fox. July 19, 2006. "Bloggers." Pew Research Center. www.pewinternet .org/2006/07/19/bloggers/.

regularly participate in forums: Jakob Nielsen. October 9, 2006. "The 90-9-1 Rule for Participation Inequality in Social Media and Online Communities." Nielsen Norman Group. www.nngroup .com/articles/participation-inequality/.

technologist Jess Kimball Leslie: Jess Kimball Leslie. 2017. *I Love My Computer Because My Friends Live in It.* Running Press.

These IM status messages: Georgia Webster. May 26, 2012. "Sparkly Unicorn Punctuation Is Invading the Internet." *Superlinguo.* www.superlinguo .com/post/23773752322/sparkly-unicorn -punctuation-is-invading-the. Eric S. Raymond, ed. December 29, 2003. "studlycaps." The on-line hacker Jargon File, version 4.4.7. www.catb.org/jargon/html/S /studlycaps.html.

"~* iT's ThE eNd Of An ErA *~": *The New York Times.* December 14, 2017. twitter.com /nytimes/status/941337112598675458, linking to: Daniel Victor. October 6, 2017. "A Going-Away Message: AOL Instant Messenger Is Shutting Down." *The New York Times.* www.nytimes.com/2017/10

519

/06/technology/aol-aim-shut-down.html. Emma Gray. September 18, 2012. "'Your Away Message' Twitter Makes Us Nostalgic for Our AIM Days (BRB! LOL! A/S/L?)." *The Huffington Post.* www.huffingtonpost .ca/entry/your-away-message-twitter -millenials-nostalgia_n_1893749.

Studies note that post-internet teens: Jean W. Twenge. December 27, 2017. "Why Teens Aren't Partying Anymore." *Wired.* www.wired.com/story/why -teens-arent-partying-anymore/. (No author cited.) January 11, 2018. "Cutting Adolescents' Use of Social Media Will Not Solve Their Problems." *The Economist.* www.economist.com/news /leaders/21734463-better-give-them-more -homework-and-let-them-hang-out-more -friends-unsupervised-cutting.

Moreover, third places: Robert Kraut, Carmen Egido, and Jolene Galegher. 1988. "Patterns of Contact and Communication in Scientific Research Collaboration." In *Proceedings of the 1988 ACM Conference on Computer-Supported Cooperative Work.* ACM. pp. 1–12.

privacy of political or religious: Philipp K. Masur and Michael Scharkow. 2016. "Disclosure Management on Social Network Sites: Individual Privacy Perceptions and User-Directed Privacy Strategies." *Social Media + Society* 2(1). Natalya N. Bazarova. 2012. "Public Intimacy: Disclosure Interpretation and Social Judgments on Facebook." *Journal of Communication* 62(5). pp. 815–832. Natalya N. Bazarova and Yoon Hyung Choi. 2014. "Self-Disclosure in Social Media: Extending the Functional Approach to Disclosure Motivations and Characteristics on Social Network Sites." *Journal of Communication* 64(4). pp. 635–657.

A law paper by Woodrow Hartzog: Woodrow Hartzog and Frederic D. Stutzman. 2013. "Obscurity by Design." *Washington Law Review* 88. University of Washington School of Law. pp. 385–418.

A study of Estonian teens: Egle Oolo and Andra Siibak. 2013. "Performing for One's Imagined Audience: Social Steganography and Other Privacy Strategies of Estonian Teens on Networked Publics." *Cyberpsychology: Journal of Psychosocial Research on Cyberspace* 7(1).

A study of queer youth: Stefanie Duguay. 2014. "'He Has a Way Gayer Facebook Than I Do': Investigating Sexual Identity Disclosure and Context Collapse on a Social Networking Site." *New Media & Society* 18(6). pp. 891–907.

521

Technologist danah boyd: danah boyd and Alice Marwik. 2011. "Social Steganography: Privacy in Networked Publics." Presented at International Communication Association conference, May 28, 2011, Boston. www.danah.org/papers/2011 /Steganography-ICAVersion.pdf. danah boyd. August 23, 2010. "Social Steganography: Learning to Hide in Plain Sight." Originally posted to *Digital Media & Learning*. Archived at www.zephoria .org/thoughts/archives/2010/08/23/social -steganography-learning-to-hide-in-plain -sight.html.

"Thanks @RyanS": Autumn Edwards and Christina J. Harris. 2016. "To Tweet or 'Subtweet'? Impacts of Social Networking post Directness and Valence on Interpersonal Impressions." *Computers in Human Behavior* 63. pp. 304–310.

they might write: An Xiao Mina. 2014. "Batman, Pandaman and the Blind Man: A Case Study in Social Change Memes and Internet Censorship in China." *Journal of Visual Culture* 13(3).

"Harmony" itself: Jason Q. Ng. 2013. *Blocked on Weibo: What Gets Suppressed on China's Version of Twitter (and Why).* New Press. Victor Mair. August 23, 2013. "Blocked on Weibo." *Language Log.*

languagelog.ldc.upenn.edu/nll/?p=6163.
Other accounts simply became inactive: Eshwar Chandrasekharan, Umashanthi Pavalanathan, Anirudh Srinivasan, Adam Glynn, Jacob Eisenstein, and Eric Gilbert. 2017. "You Can't Stay Here: The Efficacy of Reddit's 2015 Ban Examined Through Hate Speech." *Proceedings of the ACM on Human-Computer Interaction* 1(2). pp. 31–53.

Researchers asked soccer fans: Leonie Rösner and Nicole C. Krämer. 2016. "Verbal Venting in the Social Web: Effects of Anonymity and Group Norms on Aggressive Language Use in Online Comments." *Social Media + Society* 2(3). Anil Dash. July 20, 2011. "If Your Website's Full of Assholes, It's Your Fault." *Anil Dash: A blog about making culture. Since 1999.* anildash. com/2011/07/20/if_your_websites_full_of _assholes_its_your_fault-2/.

Chapter 7. Memes and Internet Culture

A lot of people will declare: Bert Vaux and Scott Golder. 2003. The Harvard Dialect Survey. Harvard University Linguistics Department. www4.uwm.edu/FLL /linguistics/dialect/staticmaps/q_95.html.
A smaller number of people: Gretchen McCulloch. June 20, 2017.

twitter.com/GretchenAMcC/status /877250919053885440.

So clear was it to residents: Marek Stachowski and Robert Woodhouse. 2015. "The Etymology of Istanbul: Making Optimal Use of the Evidence." *Studia Etymologica Cracoviensia* 20(4). pp. 221–245.

When Richard Dawkins introduced: Richard Dawkins. 1976. *The Selfish Gene.* Oxford University Press.

"Someone made an extension": Modeled after the real-life example cited here with simply a minor pop-cultural update. The original extension hid the name "Justin Bieber," but the millennials > snake people extension does exist. Philip Hensher. October 12, 2012. "Invoke the Nazis and You've Lost the Argument." *The Independent.* www.independent.co.uk /voices/comment/invoke-the-nazis-and -you-ve-lost-the-argument-8209712.html.

in an article for *Wired*: Mike Godwin. October 1, 1994. "Meme, Counter-Meme." *Wired.* www.wired.com/1994/10 /godwin-if-2/.

Existing netizens: Eric S. Raymond, ed. December 29, 2003. "September that never ended." The on-line hacker Jargon File, version 4.4.7. www.catb.org/jargon/html/S

/September-that-never-ended.html.

Weird cultural artifacts: Limor Shifman. 2014. *Memes in Digital Culture.* MIT Press.

Rather than re-uploading: Bill Lefurgy. May 28, 2012. "What Is the Best Term to Categorize a Lolcat Image and Text?" *English Language & Usage Stack Exchange.* english.stackexchange.com /questions/69210/what-is-the-best-term -to-categorize-a-lolcat-image-and-text. Hugo. September 11, 2008. "Antedatings of 'image macro.'" LINGUIST List. listserv.linguistlist.org/pipermail/ads -l/2013-September/128420.html, via Ben Zimmer. 2011. "Among the New Words." *American Speech* 86(4). pp. 454–479.

People started sharing pictures: Lev Grossman. July 16, 2007. "Lolcats Addendum: Where I Got the Story Wrong." Techland, *Time.* techland.time.com/2007 /07/16/lolcats_addendum_where_i_got_t/.

the lolcat phenomenon: Lev Grossman. July 12, 2007. "Creating a Cute Cat Frenzy." *Time.* content.time.com/time /magazine/article/0,9171,1642897,00.html.

had their text added manually: Jerry Langton. September 22, 2007. "Funny How 'Stupid' Site Is Addictive." *Toronto Star.* www.thestar.com/life/2007/09/22 /funny_how_stupid_site_is_addictive.html.

These meme generator sites: Kate Brideau and Charles Berret. 2014. "A Brief Introduction to Impact: 'The Meme Font.'" *Journal of Visual Culture* 13(3). pp. 307–313.

Technologist Kate Miltner: Kate Miltner. 2014. "There's No Place For Lulz on LOLCats: The Role of Genre, Gender, and Group Identity in the Interpretation and Enjoyment of an Internet Meme." *First Monday* 19(8). www.ojphi.org/ojs/index .php/fm/article/view/5391/4103.

Rather than dive: Lauren Gawne and Jill Vaughn. 2012. "I Can Haz Language Play: The Construction of Language and Identity in LOLspeak." *Proceedings of the 42nd Australian Linguistic Society Conference.* pp. 97–122. digitalcollections.anu.edu. au/bitstream/1885/9398/5/Gawne_ICan Haz2012.pdf. Jordan Lefler. 2011. "I Can Has Thesis?" Master's thesis, Louisiana State University and Agricultural and Mechanical College. assets.documentcloud .org/documents/282753/lefler-thesis.pdf. Aliza Rosen. 2010. "Iz in Ur Meme / Aminalizin Teh Langwich: A Linguistic Study of LOLcats." *Verge 7.* mdsoar.org /bitstream/handle/11603/2606/Verge_7 _Rosen.pdf?sequence=1&isAllowed=y.

pondered the quotes: triscodeca. June 26, 2000. *Quoteland* forums. forum.quoteland

.com/eve/forums/a/tpc/f/487195441/m
/840191541. The Philosoraptor image
wasn't created until 2008.

Its organizers ultimately decided: Tim
Hwang and Christina Xu. 2014. "'Lurk
More': An Interview with the Founders
of ROFLCon." *Journal of Visual Culture*
13(3). pp. 376–387.

Japanese teacher Atsuko Sato: Kyle
Chayka. December 31, 2013. "Wow
this is doge." *The Verge.* www.theverge
.com/2013/12/31/5248762/doge-meme
-rescue-dog-wow.

wrote a linguistic analysis: Gretchen
McCulloch. February 6, 2014. "A Linguist Explains the Grammar of Doge.
Wow." *The Toast.* the-toast.net/2014/02/06
/linguist-explains-grammar-doge-wow/.

"My moment of reckoning": Ryan M.
Milner. 2016. *The World Made Meme: Pub-
lic Conversations and Participatory Media.*
MIT Press.

"Know Your Meme was written": Whitney Phillips. 2015. *This Is Why We Can't
Have Nice Things.* MIT Press.

This phenomenon spawned: Dawn
Chmielewski. September 30, 2016. "Internet Memes Emerge as 2016 Election's
Political Dog Whistle." *USA Today.* www
.usatoday.com/story/tech/news/2016/09/30

/internet-memes-white-house-election
-president/91272490/. Douglas Haddow.
November 4, 2016. "Meme Warfare:
How the Power of Mass Replication Has
Poisoned the US Election." *The Guardian.* www.theguardian.com/us-news/2016
/nov/04/political-memes-2016-election
-hillary-clinton-donald-trump. Gabriella
Lewis. March 20, 2016. "We Asked an Expert If Memes Could Determine the Out-
come of the Presidential Election." *Vice.* www
.vice.com/en_us/article/kwxdqa/we-asked
-an-expert-if-memes-could-determine
-the-outcome-of-the-presidential-election.

a Know Your Meme entry: Mom Rivers.
February 22, 2016. "2016 United States
Presidential Election." *Know Your Meme.*
knowyourmeme.com/memes/events/2016
-united-states-presidential-election.

official HillaryClinton.com meme: Elizabeth Chan. September 12, 2016. "Donald
Trump, Pepe the Frog, and White Suprem-
acists: An Explainer." The Office of Hill-
ary Rodham Clinton. www.hillaryclinton
.com/feed/donald-trump-pepe-the-frog
-and-white-supremacists-an-explainer/.

"By all means, compare": Mike Godwin.
August 13, 2017. twitter.com/sfmnemonic
/status/896884949634232320.

cute doggos and puppers: Brian Feldman.

August 10, 2016. "The Next Frontier in Internet Culture Is Wholesome Memes About Loving Your Friends." *New York.* nymag.com/selectall/2016/08/the-next -frontier-in-internet-culture-is-wholesome -memes.html knowyourmeme.com/memes /wholesome-memes.

"We're the ones": Taylor Lorenz. April 27, 2017. "Inside the Elite Meme Wars of America's Most Exclusive Colleges." *Mic.* mic.com/articles/175420/ivy -league-college-meme-wars.

the newer memes: Aja Romano. May 15, 2018. " 'Is This a Meme?' The Confused Anime Guy and His Butterfly, Explained." *Vox.* www.vox.com/2018/5/15/17351806 /is-this-a-pigeon-anime-butterfly-meme -explained.

Harold Godwinson: Martin Foys. 2009. *Pulling the Arrow Out: The Legend of Harold's Death and the Bayeux Tapestry.* Boydell and Brewer. pp. 158–175.

members of the Leek Embroidery Society: Reading Borough Council. 2014. "Britain's Bayeux Tapestry at Reading Museum." www.bayeuxtapestry.org.uk /bayeuxinfo.htm.

***Game of Thrones* Bayeux Tapestry:** www. ireland.com/game-of-thrones-tapestry/ . Felicity Campbell. July 25, 2017. "Northern

Ireland Unveils Giant Game of Thrones Tapestry." *The National.* www.thenational.ae /arts-culture/television/northern-ireland -unveils-giant-game-of-thrones-tapestry -1.614078.

I later learned that Susan Kare: Alex Soojung-Kim Pang. September 8, 2000. "Interview with Susan Kare." *Making the Macintosh: Technology and Culture in Silicon Valley.* web.stanford.edu/dept/SUL /library/mac/primary/interviews/kare/ trans.html. Alexandra Lange. April 19, 2018. "The Woman Who Gave the Macintosh a Smile." *The New Yorker.* www .newyorker.com/culture/cultural-comment /the-woman-who-gave-the-macintosh-a -smile.

a 1902 dictionary: William Dwight Whitney. 1902. *The Century Dictionary and Cyclopedia.* Century.

Physically mailed chain letters: Daniel W. VanArsdale. 1998. "Chain Letter Evolution." www.silcom.com/~barnowl /chain-letter/evolution.html. Daniel W. VanArsdale. June 21, 2014. "The Origin of Money Chain Letters." www.silcom .com/~barnowl/chain-letter/TOOMCL -Final.html.

"faxlore" or "Xeroxlore": Michael J. Preston. 1974. "Xerox-lore." *Keystone*

Folklore 19(1). babel.hathitrust.org/cgi/pt?i d=inu.30000108623293;view=1up;seq=19.

mock-German warning: Eric S. Raymond, ed. December 29, 2003. "blinkenlights." The on-line hacker Jargon File, version 4.4.7. www.catb.org/jargon/html/B /blinkenlights.html.

Public figures and archetypes: Jimmy Stamp. October 23, 2012. "Political Animals: Republican Elephants and Democratic Donkeys." *Smithsonian.* www.smithsonianmag.com/arts-culture /political-animals-republican-elephants -and-democratic-donkeys-89241754/.

Martin Luther, in a pamphlet: Dan Backer. 1996. "A Brief History of Political Cartoons." xroads.virginia.edu/~ma96 /puck/part1.html.

Personifications of places: David M. Robinson. 1917. "Caricature in Ancient Art." *The Bulletin of the College Art Association of America* 1(3). pp. 65–68.

Laughing at a racist: Ronald de Souza. 1987. "When Is It Wrong to Laugh?" In J. Morreall, ed. *The Philosophy of Laughter and Humor.* State University of New York Press. pp. 226–249.

far-right discussion forums: Alice Marwick and Rebecca Lewis. May 15, 2017. "Media Manipulation and Disinformation

Online." Data & Society. datasociety.net /output/media-manipulation-and-disinfo -online/.

Erin McKean tweeted: Erin McKean. June 21, 2017. twitter.com/emckean /status/877711672684584960.

It's never been easier: An Xiao Mina. January 26, 2017. "How Pink Pussyhats and Red MAGA Caps Went Viral." *Civicist.* civichall.org/civicist/how-pink-pussyhats -and-red-maga-caps-went-viral/.

The Library of Congress archives: Erin Blakemore. June 15, 2017. "Why the Library of Congress Thinks Your Favorite Meme Is Worth Preserving." *Smithsonian.* www .smithsonianmag.com/smart-news/library -of-congress-meme-preserve-180963705/. (No author cited.) (No date cited.) Web Cultures Web Archive. Library of Congress. www.loc.gov/collections/web -cultures-web-archive/.

full-time jobs in advanced memology: Justin Caffier. May 19, 2017. "Meme Historians Are an Inevitability." *Vice.* www .vice.com/en_us/article/meme-historians -are-an-inevitability.

Our meme dissertators from 2014: Whitney Phillips and Ryan M. Milner. 2017. *The Ambivalent Internet.* John Wiley & Sons.

"The ostensibly unfinished": Limor

Shifman. 2014. *Memes in Digital Culture.* MIT Press.

sixty times larger: 5.5 million English Wikipedia articles. Wikimedia Foundation. February 25, 2018. "Wikipedia: Size comparisons." Wikipedia. en.wikipedia.org /wiki/Wikipedia:Size_comparisons.

Though fanfiction existed: Anne Jamison. 2013. *Fic: Why Fanfiction Is Taking Over the World.* Smart Pop.

They've gathered on blogs: Estimates as of February 2018: 3.6 million works on Archive of Our Own. archiveofourown .org/. 8.1 million works on Fanfiction .net extrapolated from: Charles Sendlor. July 18, 2010. "FanFiction.Net Member Statistics." *Fan Fiction Statistics - FFN Research.* ffnresearch.blogspot.ca/2010/07 /fanfictionnet-users.html. fffinnagain. November 23, 2017. "Lost Works and Posting Rates on fanfiction.net and Archive of Our Own." *Sound Interest.* fffinnagain.tumblr .com/post/167805956488/lost-works-and -posting-rates-on-fanfictionnet-and. destinationtoast. January 2, 2016. "2015 a (statistical) year in fandom." *Archive of Our Own.* archiveofourown.org/works/5615386. Thanks to fffinnagain and destinationtoast for personal communication on calculating fanfic stats. Wattpad representatives did not respond to several requests for clarification about what their reported numbers meant, so stats from Wattpad are not reported here. Gavia Baker-Whitelaw. January 21, 2015. "Tumblr Launches Tool to Measure the Most Popular Fandoms." *The Daily Dot.* www.dailydot.com/parsec /tumblr-fandometrics-trends/.

Chapter 8. A New Metaphor

I searched for "English language": Getty Images, Shutterstock, iStock, Adobe Stock, Pixabay, Bigstock, Fotolia, Stock-Snap.io, Fotosearch, ImageZoo, Solid Stock Art, Pexels, Crestock, Alamy, SuperStock, Stock Photo Secrets, Depositphotos, Thinkstock, Stock Free Images, Unsplash. Compiled by cross-referencing several lists of top stock photo sites and removing sites that didn't return at least ten results for "English language."

neuroscientists invoke computers: Gary Marcus. June 27, 2015. "Face It, Your Brain Is a Computer." *The New York Times.* www .nytimes.com/2015/06/28/opinion/sunday /face-it-your-brain-is-a-computer.html.

Wikipedia only has articles: Wikipedia Foundation. As of March 2019. "List of Wikipedias." Wikimedia. meta.wikimedia .org/wiki/List_of_Wikipedias.

Google Translate supports: Google Translate: Languages. translate.google.com/intl /en/about/languages/. As of March 1, 2018.

Major social networks: (No author cited.) (No date cited.) "Localization." *Facebook for Developers.* developers.facebook. com/docs/internationalization. (No author cited.) (No date cited.) "About the Twitter Translation Center." Twitter Help Center. support.twitter.com/articles/434816.

Even relatively substantial national languages: Jon Henley. February 26, 2018. "Icelandic Language Battles Threat of 'Digital Extinction.'" *The Guardian.* www.theguardian.com/world/2018/feb/26 /icelandic-language-battles-threat-of -digital-extinction.

versions of these statistics: Google Translate listed 103 languages in both August 2016 and March 2019; Wikipedia listed 283 active languages in August 2016 and 293 in March 2019.

Nonetheless, users are still figuring out ways: https://www.theringer.com /tech/2018/11/5/18056776/voice-texting -whatsapp-apple-2018.

Popular culture and internet culture: Molly Sauter. July 31, 2017. "When WWW Trumps IRL: Why It's Now Impossible to Pretend the Internet Is Somehow Less

Real." *National Post.* nationalpost.com /entertainment/books/book-reviews/when -www-trumps-irl-why-its-now-impossible -to-pretend-the-internet-is-somehow-less -real.

ABOUT THE AUTHOR

Gretchen McCulloch writes about linguistics for a general audience, especially internet language. She writes the Resident Linguist column at *Wired* (and formerly at *The Toast*). McCulloch has a master's in linguistics from McGill University, runs the blog *All Things Linguistic,* and cohosts *Lingthusiasm,* a podcast that's enthusiastic about linguistics. She lives in Montreal, but also on the internet.

The employees of Thorndike Press hope you have enjoyed this Large Print book. All our Thorndike, Wheeler, and Kennebec Large Print titles are designed for easy reading, and all our books are made to last. Other Thorndike Press Large Print books are available at your library, through selected bookstores, or directly from us.

For information about titles, please call:

(800) 223-1244

or visit our Web site at:

http://gale.cengage.com/thorndike

To share your comments, please write:

Publisher
Thorndike Press
10 Water St., Suite 310
Waterville, ME 04901